GOD AND
INSCRUTABLE EVIL

God and Inscrutable Evil

In Defense of Theism and Atheism

David O'Connor

ROWMAN & LITTLEFIELD PUBLISHERS, INC.
Lanham • Boulder • New York • Oxford

BT
102
.029
1998

ROWMAN & LITTLEFIELD PUBLISHERS, INC.

Published in the United States of America
by Rowman & Littlefield Publishers, Inc.
4720 Boston Way, Lanham, Maryland 20706

3 Henrietta Street
London WC2E 8LU, England

Copyright © 1998 by Rowman & Littlefield Publishers, Inc.

British Cataloging in Publication Information Available

Library of Congress Cataloging-in-Publication Data

O'Connor, David, 1949–
    God and inscrutable evil : in defense of theism and atheism /
David O'Connor.
        p.   cm.
    Includes bibliographical references and index.
    ISBN 0-8476-8763-5 (hardcover : alk. paper). — ISBN 0-8476-8764-3
(pbk. : alk. paper)
    1. God—Proof.   2. Good and evil.   3. Atheism.   4. Theism.
I. Title.
BT102.029   1997
231—dc21   97-34277
                                                                        CIP

ISBN 0-8476-8763-5 (cloth : alk. paper)
ISBN 0-8476-8764-3 (pbk. : alk. paper)

Printed in the United States of America

∞ ™ The paper used in this publication meets the minimum requirements of
American National Stardard for Information Sciences—Permanence of Paper for
Printed Library Materials, ANSI Z39.48–1984.

To my father, David O'Connor

Contents

PREFACE

A couple of years ago I realized that several papers I had written on various topics in the philosophy of religion, papers conceived and written as free-standing pieces, were related to one another in substantive but unintended ways. It occurred to me that it might be interesting to work out the ways in which they were related. This book is the result.

First impressions to the contrary notwithstanding, the book's subtitle is not an oxymoron. However, first impressions being what they are, a word of explanation is in order. As the subtitle says, I argue in defense of theism and atheism. That is the denouement of this book. But, given that those two theories have mutually exclusive truth-values and that one of them is true, my argument in part 2 is not for the impossible, namely, that both are true. Instead, the position I defend there is that, relative to certain facts and capacities, theism can be justified for certain persons in certain circumstances, atheism for others in other circumstances. (Or, if both theories are justified for the *same* persons, necessarily the different circumstances include different times.) I describe my final position as a detente between "friendly" atheism and "friendly" theism: the adjective is William L. Rowe's. The facts and capacities to which this detente is relative are certain known facts of evil and certain capacities (and in particular, incapacities) of ours as human beings in estimating what a God-made world and a non-God-made world, respectively, would be like.

This detente is not agnosticism. For, as I understand it, agnosticism is essentially the following conjunction: first, one alone of theism and atheism is true, but, with the information available to us, no-one is in a position to know which; and second, given that information, no-one can be justified in believing that theism is true and atheism is false, and vice versa. But the second conjunct is false, and fundamentally at odds with the position I defend in part 2 of this book. The essential difference between that position and agnosticism is that between upholding the justifiability of each of two rival theories, in circumstances where neither can be known to be true (or false), on the one hand, and, on the other, declining to uphold the justifiability of either one in those same circumstances. (As expressed, the latter point is not strong enough to do justice to the views of all agnostics, for some *deny* the justifiability of each of theism and atheism in the circumstances mentioned. But we need not dwell on differences between weak and strong versions of agnosticism, as the detente for which I argue reduces to neither.) To sum up the point: like both kinds of agnostic, I maintain there is important epistemic parity between theism and atheism. However, the parity for which I argue is not the same as that offered in agnosticism of either strength, thus, it does not warrant agnosticism as a preferred third position—the suspension of both theistic and atheistic belief, coupled with official neutrality between them.

It is an essential feature of my case for detente that what I call the standard model of debate on the problem of God and evil suffers from a disabling fault. But if it does not, then, as I maintain in part 1, the atheistic side has the better of the argument over God and evil, and there is no detente between the two theories.

Among contemporary philosophers of religion whose work I discuss here, I have learned a great deal from the writings of William P. Alston, Richard M. Gale, J. C. A. Gaskin, William Hasker, Daniel Howard-Snyder, J. L. Mackie, Michael Martin, Alvin Plantinga, William L. Rowe, George N. Schlesinger, Richard Swinburne, Peter van Inwagen, and Stephen J. Wykstra. And, although I am critical of positions defended by some of these philosophers, I wish to emphasize that, without exception, my criticism is rooted in high regard. I am twice indebted to Daniel Howard-Snyder. First for the reason mentioned, and second because I have had the enormous benefit of his criticism of the penultimate draft of this book. His criticism was deep, painstaking, and illuminating, and it has saved me from mistakes and infelicities. I express my gratitude to George Mavrodes who, as a reader for the publisher, made helpful comments on, and suggestions for improvements to, a portion of an early draft. I am indebted to the colleagues and friends whose help I acknowledge in the papers from which this book is descended, Gerard J. Dalcourt in particular. I thank Louis DeBello for commentary on a early draft of the first two chapters. I am grateful to Adrian O'Connor and to Jeremy O'Connor for checking portions of the original draft for readability and for commentary on this preface, and to Sarah O'Connor both for computer know-how and for three printings of the manuscript. I owe thanks to Deirdre Mullervy at Rowman & Littlefield for help on production-related matters. Last, but certainly not least, I thank Margaret Chiang for uncomplaining secretarial assistance, no matter how many times I asked her to print a draft of a chapter.

The papers I mentioned in the beginning, those to which the book's ancestry traces, are the following, and I acknowledge in each case editorial permission to use material from them. The chapters on Plantinga, Schlesinger, and Swinburne originated, respectively, in: "A Reformed Problem of Evil and the Free-Will Defense," *International Journal for Philosophy of Religion* 39, no. 1 (February 1996); "Schlesinger and the Morally Perfect Man," *The Journal of Value Inquiry* 20, no. 3 (1986); and, in Swinburne's case, both "Swinburne on Natural Evil," *Religious Studies* 19, no. 1 (March 1983), and "Swinburne on Natural Evil from Natural Processes," *International Journal for Philosophy of Religion* 30, no. 2 (October 1991). Chapter 3 grew out of "Hasker on Gratuitous Natural Evil," *Faith and Philosophy* 12, no. 3 (July 1995); while chapters 9, 10, and 11 trace, in conception, although not much in their specific arguments, to the following papers: "On the Problem of Evil's Not Being What It Seems," *The Philosophical Quarterly* 37, no. 149 (October 1987); "On the Problem of Evil's Still Not Being What It Seems," *The Philosophical Quarterly* 40, no. 158 (January 1990); "On Failing to Resolve Theism-versus-Atheism Empirically," *Religious Studies* 26, no. 1 (March 1990); and "A Skeptical Defense of Theism," *Proceedings of the American Catholic Philosophical Association* 44 (1990).

1

INTRODUCTION: THEISM'S
PROBLEM OF EVIL

There is a great deal of evil in the world, much of it seemingly pointless. Intuitively, then, there seems to be a discordance between certain facts of inscrutable evil and the theistic conception of the world as God-made. That conception is of a world designed and created for a good purpose by an omnipotent, omniscient, perfectly good, personal being, lovingly interested in the welfare of all creatures. This apparent discordance raises some obvious questions: for instance, could evil for which we can discern neither point nor justification ever exist in a God-made world? Even if it could, does not such evil make it improbable that the world was made by God? Why would a God-made world contain evils for which we can discover no point or justification? And, even if there is a reason that a world made by God contains evils of that sort, why so much and so many varieties?

Such questions pose theism's philosophical problem of evil. Some preliminary ground clearing and distinction making will help to frame what I propose doing with this problem here, and how I will do it. I devote this chapter to that task, underlabor, as Locke described it.

Some Basic Concepts and Distinctions

Defense and Theodicy

The four questions just asked are different, and a division of labor within theistic apologetics will equip us to classify the different kinds

1

of theistic responses to them. The division in question is the one between defense and theodicy.

Of its nature, a defense tries to ensure that the defendant survives the charge or attack against which he or she, or, in this case, it, is being defended. That being so, a successful defense does not have to prove theism true and atheism false. Nor does it have to establish that the evils cited in a given antitheistic argument are logically consistent with God, or that their occurrence is probable if God exists. Furthermore, it does not have to explain the existence of any or all evil in a supposedly God-made world. To do any of these things would constitute a substantive, and, in the first case, a maximal defense of theism, whereas a nonsubstantive and considerably more minimal defense, if successful, is sufficient. Thus, against a prosecuting argument whose aim is to show that certain facts of evil are inconsistent with God, a defense succeeds if it shows that the prosecuting argument fails to establish its conclusion. And likewise for a defense against an argument aiming to show that some fact or facts of evil are improbable on theism. And a defense could succeed in doing those things on a technicality; for instance, by exposing a weakness in the prosecuting argument that might block its access to its conclusion. In order to be successful, a "technicality" defense would not have to deny any fact of evil cited in the prosecuting argument, and neither would it have to address the conclusion drawn from those facts. I examine a range of theistic defenses here, the least minimal and most substantive of which is Richard Swinburne's version of the greater-good defense, while the most minimal and least substantive is the skeptical defense offered by Stephen J. Wykstra, William P. Alston, and others. And we will see that in this matter, substantiveness and success are not commensurate.

A defense, understood in any of the ways just specified, is an appropriate response to the first two of the four questions posed above, but not to the third or the fourth. To answer those questions would require a theodicy, a theodicy being an attempt to answer, in a systematic and comprehensive way, the question, "what is the source of the evil we find, and why does God permit it?"[1] So understood, a theodicy tries to explain the ways of God to human beings, whereas a defense need not.

Consistent with these descriptions, my interest here is defense, not theodicy. In particular, I am interested in testing how theism's best and most prominent self-defenses fare against certain arguments from evil, and then in the implications for the entire philosophical debate on the problem of evil of certain things learned in the course of testing those defenses. For this reason, I do not discuss theodical questions at all.

While a theodicy's task is wider than a defense's, it is neither the more basic nor the more important, at least in one way of comparing defense and theodicy. This is because theism's need to be adequately defended against arguments based upon manifest evils, and in particular manifest evils for which we can discern no point or justification, has logical priority over the development of a theodicy in the following important sense: if the theistic defenses are not up to their job, then the theory stares defeat in the face.[2] And if theism is defeated, then the theodical project will be redundant. But if the defenses hold, then while the need to solve the theodical problems remains, their solution could plausibly be understood as a work in progress and its completion not urgent, or, at least, less urgent than the need for a defense. In this sense, then, defense has priority over theodicy.

Specified and Unspecified Arguments from Evil

Philosophical problems of evil may be formulated in either a broad or a narrow way. The problems of evil discussed here are versions of the latter. As I use the term, a formulation of the problem is broad if its operating assumption is that evil as such is either inconsistent with theism or improbable on theism. With a focus on inconsistency and not improbability, J. L. Mackie provides a succinct description of the problem, so understood: "in its simplest form the problem is this: God is omnipotent; God is wholly good; and yet evil exists. There seems to be some contradiction between these three propositions."[3]

By contrast, an argument reflecting what I call a narrow version of the problem restricts itself to citing certain facts of inscrutable evil as ones that we have good reason to think are gratuitous, and so incompatible with the world's being God-made. Because, narrowly formulated, the argument is specific to some facts of quantity, intensity, distribution, or duration of evil, let us think of it as a specified version of the argument. But, as when formulated broadly, an argument from evil is not specific in those ways, we may think of such formulations as unspecified formulations. I agree with Richard Swinburne that the specified version of the problem of evil is the more vexing and challenging of the two possible types of formulation,[4] hence it is specified arguments that I discuss here. But, while a specified argument is specific to certain facts of quantity, duration, or distribution of evil, it need not be specific to certain *instances* of evil. Thus, for example, an argument citing the overall quantity of evil in the world, or the overall quantity of a certain kind of evil, natural evil resulting just from natural processes, say, would be a specified argument, under the meaning of the term, but it would not be an argument whose evidential base was certain instances of evil. Nor would its evidential base be certain types of evil, as such. My argument here will draw upon the amount of natural evil resulting from the operations of natural processes alone.

Logical and Empirical Arguments from Evil

The foregoing distinction between specified and unspecified formulations of the argument from evil cuts across another distinction, namely, that between logical and empirical arguments from evil respectively. In *Dialogues Concerning Natural Religion*, Hume distinguishes between, on the one hand, the question whether God and certain facts of evil are mutually compatible, in the purely logical sense of compatibility, and, on the other, whether and to what extent certain facts of evil are counterevidence either to certain theistic supporting arguments or to religious belief itself. He grants without ado that God and evil are not inconsistent with one another in the logical sense, but devotes considerable attention to whether certain facts of evil in a supposedly God-made world either disconfirm or tend to disconfirm the proposition that God exists,[5] that is, he devotes considerable attention to the empirical problem of evil.

Although the distinction between logical and empirical problems of evil has been a staple in philosophical debates over God and evil since then, it has not always been drawn in precisely the same manner by all makers and users of the distinction. Since I discuss in this book both logical and empirical forms of the argument—concentrating on the former through chapter 7, then on the latter—I should say something about where I draw the line between them.

Since Hume's *Dialogues*, it has been standard practice to make the distinction as follows. The gist of the logical arguments is that certain facts of evil—perhaps the fact that there is any evil at all in the world, or that there is too much, or, more narrowly, perhaps the existence of some specific types or tokens of evil—are inconsistent, in the strictly logical sense of consistency, with some essential proposition of theism. By contrast, the gist of the empirical arguments is typically that certain facts of evil are inconsistent with theism in the sense that they disconfirm, or, in a weaker version, tend to disconfirm, that theory. Inconsistency in the latter sense does not preclude the possibility that, on the facts of evil cited in a given empirical argument, theism could be true, while inconsistency in the logical sense *does* rule out that possibility. For, the sense of consistency in question in logical arguments is that if two things are inconsistent with one another, then there is no possible world in which they coexist, and they are mutually consistent if there is such a possible world. In sum, then, a logical argument from evil typically aims to demonstrate that theism could not possibly be true, given certain facts of evil, while an empirical argument from evil typically aims to show that, given certain facts of evil, there is good, but not necessarily compelling, reason to think theism is either false or unjustified. Let us think of this as the traditional understanding of the difference between logical and empirical arguments from evil.

In a recent departure from tradition, Daniel Howard-Snyder redraws the difference between logical and empirical arguments from evil. He derives his account of the difference from examination of paradigm cases of both types. In Howard-Snyder's description, a logical argument will have a premise stating that God is inconsistent, in the logical sense of inconsistency just described, with some known fact of evil, whereas an empirical argument will lack such a premise.[6]

This account of the difference between logical and empirical forms of the argument from evil is arguably an improvement upon tradition. However, notwithstanding the merits of Howard-Snyder's formulation, I shall operate here with the more traditional version. I do so for three reasons:

1. In chapters 4 through 7, much of my interest is in certain prominent theistic defenses deployed against the logical argument as traditionally understood; for, in those chapters, the principal issue in dispute between my version of the logical argument and the theistic defenses in question is whether any of those defenses is able to establish that certain facts of inscrutable evil are either not logically inconsistent with certain core credenda of orthodox theism or that those facts of evil are not shown to be logically inconsistent with those credenda; the principal issue in dispute is not whether we know those facts of evil.

2. While it is true that in my formulation of the logical argument I do not claim that the relevant facts of evil are known, as opposed to being reasonably or justifiably believed, to be facts of evil, thus making my argument not a logical argument in Howard-Snyder's sense, yet, given the prevalence of the traditional understanding of the logical and empirical forms of the argument from evil, and given my emphasis through the first seven chapters upon the logic of theism and evil, for me to refer to my argument in those chapters as an empirical argument runs an unnecessary risk of misunderstanding.

3. I do not think that in the present context much turns on the distinction per se, for, agreeing with Howard-Snyder, it is the arguments themselves, not their classifications, that matter. Thus, staying with the traditional terms of reference, I refer to the argument I develop and deploy through chapter 7 as a version of the logical argument. However, as we will see presently, it is a *reformed* version of the logical argument.

Nowadays the logical form of the problem of evil seems to be going out of fashion. In Paul Draper's words, "logical arguments from evil are a dying . . . breed."[7] And Draper is not alone in assessing so dimly the fortunes of the logical arguments, thus of the logical problem. Other influential philosophers of religion, theists and atheists alike, agree. From the latter group, William L. Rowe, for instance, describes the current state of play as follows: "the theist need not be unduly troubled by the logical form of the problem of evil, for, as we've seen, no one has established that [God exists and is omnipotent, omniscient, and perfectly good] and [Evil exists] are inconsistent."[8]

From the context it is clear that Rowe intends consistency and inconsistency to be understood in the logical sense. From the theistic side of the debate, Peter van Inwagen agrees with Rowe's assessment: "It used to be widely held that evil . . . was incompatible with the existence of God: that no possible world contained both God and evil. So far as I am able to tell, this thesis is no longer defended."[9] Though possibly nowadays well on its way to becoming a consensus, the view is not unanimous: Richard Gale and Michael Martin, for instance, dissent for cause.[10]

A First Look at the Reformed Logical Argument against Orthodox Theism

While I think these recent death notices for the logical form of the problem of evil are at least premature, I shall not directly argue the point against its obituarists. This is because the logical argument under discussion is a *reformed* logical argument, whereas, by contrast, the logical argument as nowadays widely written off is unreformed. And the reformation matters. For, although the reformed argument moves in the direction of the traditional goal of logical arguments, I do not claim to actually reach that goal (nor, for that matter, do I try), namely, a definitive proof that a certain fact of evil is logically incompatible with the existence of God. Instead I show that against the reformed argument and within the framework of what I describe in chapter 2 as the standard philosophical debate on the problem of evil, theism's best and most prominent self-defenses against logical forms of the argument from evil fail to defend a central, arguably *the* central, version of theism. I refer to this formulation of theism as orthodox theism, OT for short. Arguably, OT is the version of theistic theory that best represents the mainstream of the Abrahamic tradition, which comprises the Christian, Islamic, and Jewish traditions within monotheism.[11]

In essence, OT is a philosophical theory whose ontological commitments are not restricted to the proposition that God exists, although, clearly, that proposition is an essential credendum of the theory. The following are among orthodox theism's essential posits: God, understood as the omnipotent, omniscient, perfectly good

7

designer, creator, and sustainer of the universe; a divine plan for human beings and their world; a network of reciprocal relations between God and God's human creatures, such that, in the final analysis, we are or are not granted an eternity in the presence of God; divine culpability for no evil. I give a full description of OT in chapter 4.

The reformed logical argument against OT is developed in two stages that, together, comprise part 1 of this book: first, the presentation of the argument within the framework of the Hume-inspired, standard philosophical debate on the problem of evil (chapters 1 through 4); second, the argument in competition with the best theistic defenses that, within the framework of the standard debate, are deployed against logical forms of the argument from evil (chapters 5 through 7). The distinction between these stages is porous and a bit arbitrary. For in chapter 3, thus within the first stage, I examine two theistic defenses. I examine them there and not later, for they challenge (albeit not to the same extent) a key point in the mainstream understanding of theism, and if the more radical and extensive of the two challenges—the one made by William Hasker—is successful, then the reformed logical argument will be stillborn and the remainder of this book undercut. By contrast, the reformed argument can, and does, accommodate the less radical challenge (by Peter van Inwagen) to the mainstream understanding of theism. At any rate, staying with this two-stage description of my enterprise in part 1, the upshot of the two stages is that none of the defenses discussed in part 1 successfully defends orthodox theism against the reformed argument.

The difference between my formulation of the logical argument and the versions of the argument common in the literature comes from the two following points. First, as Nelson Pike points out, God and evil could be mutually consistent even if we can never think of a God-justifying reason for a given evil or type of evil, or indeed for any evil at all, to exist.[12] Pike seems to be supposing here that a defense will only be successful if it provides a substantive rebuttal—a God-justifying reason for a given fact of evil, for instance—but that would be setting the mark of defensive success too high. So, let us take the liberty of reading his point more liberally than he may have intended. That is, let us agree that God and evil could still be mutually consistent if neither a successful substantive nor even a minimal technical defense is available. In effect, the atheologian might *always* have the better of the argument, yet all the while, unknown to us, God and whatever facts of evil are in question are mutually consistent: for the ontological fact of the matter is not a function of what we can figure out. Second, even if the defenses mentioned fail to provide necessary support to OT, it is still always possible that other defenses, or other formulations of the same defenses, will fare better against that argument. This second point, reflecting less pessimism about future defenses, even if no past or present defenses succeed, than the point taken from Pike, traces to Sextus Empiricus. In his words,

> whenever someone propounds an argument we are not able to dispose of, we make this reply: "Before the birth of the founder of the school to which you belong, this argument of your school was not yet seen to be a sound argument. From the point of view of nature, however, it existed all the while as such. In like manner it is possible, as far as nature is concerned, that an argument antithetical to the one now set forth by you is in existence, though as yet unknown to us. This being so, the fact that an argument seems solid to us now is not yet a sufficient reason why we must assent to it."[13]

This quotation indicates open possibilities, even for a theory whose defenses fail to block or defeat an argument against one or more of its essential propositions. But the quotation does not mean, nor do I suggest, that radical skepticism (whether Pyrrhonian or another kind) is necessary in order for theism to stave off refutation by the reformed logical argument. Rather, the point is that the reformed argument *itself* writes in an escape clause for OT. Right from the start, then, it is agreed that the reformed logical argument's success against the defenses of OT that are examined does not mean orthodox theism could not be true or justified. (In part 2 I examine another form of skeptical response to arguments from evil, and find it sufficient for a minimal defense of OT. Furthermore, and assuming that the cost in skepticism of a Pyrrhonian defense is too high for orthodox theism to be able to pay, I believe that a skeptical

9

defense of a non-Pyrrhonian sort is necessary for a successful defense, although I do not argue for this point.)

But from the inclusion in the reformed logical argument of an escape clause for OT theists should take only cold comfort. For the failure of a theory's presumptively best defenses to defend it against an argument attacking essential propositions of the theory is a fact that, although falling short of refuting the theory in the sense of showing it to be false, yet significantly undermines its epistemic standing. It is a fact that gives us good, although not compelling, reason to regard the theory as either unjustified or false, and as such to reject it.[14] And that is the essence of my argument in chapter 8, an indirect empirical argument developed out of the reformed logical argument. That argument is the second stage of my two-stage argument in part 1 of this book.

Here now is the gist of the reformed argument that I construct within the framework of the standard debate on the problem of evil:

1. Any God-made world containing human persons will be a world in which it is possible for those persons to develop into mature moral and spiritual agents able to responsibly choose their own individual destinies.
2. Such development is part of the divine plan for a world containing human persons, and such development is possible in the actual world.
3. No world containing gratuitous evil could be a world made by God.[15]
4. The actual world contains a class of evils, natural evils that come about through natural processes (henceforth NENP), as well as both moral evil and other sorts of natural evils.[16]
5. There are two subclasses of NENP—natural evils whose original cause is natural processes and which result solely from the operations of such processes, and natural evils whose original cause is not blind processes in nature itself, that is to say, natural evils that do not result solely from the operations of natural processes. Let us refer to the former subclass as NERNP, natural evils resulting solely from processes in brute nature, and to the latter subclass as NE˜RNP, natural evils not resulting solely from natural processes. An example of the former would be a

genetic mutation resulting in disease, when no human person is morally responsible for the mutation or its resulting disease, while an example of the latter would be your accidentally cutting your finger. Both NERNP and NE~RNP exist in great abundance in the actual world, as does moral evil.[17]

6. In addition to the actual world, there is another world, a possible world W^P. In W^P, the moral and spiritual development called for in the divine plan is just as possible as in the actual world. W^P and the actual world are mutually exclusive, but, prior to the actualization of the actual world, W^P was a world actualizable by God. There is far less natural evil in W^P than in the actual world, for in W^P there is no natural evil resulting solely from natural processes (NERNP), or, if there is, there is much less than in the actual world.[18] W^P contains no NENP (of either sort) inconsistent with God (henceforth the class of NENP that is inconsistent with God will be identified as $NENP^i$).

7. The class of $NENP^i$ is either coextensive with NERNP or, if $NENP^i$, it is a subclass of it. It is natural evil solely from natural processes in excess of a certain level (whatever that level is) consistent with God.[19]

8. Given the availability for actualization of W^P, it appears that either all or some of the great abundance of NERNP in the actual world is $NENP^i$, thus that the actual world is not a God-made world.

9. Within the standard-debate framework, Richard Swinburne's greater-good defense, Alvin Plantinga's free-will defense, and George N. Schlesinger's no-best-possible-world defense, arguably both the best of their respective kinds as well as the best-known defenses of theism against logical arguments from evil,[20] are available to defend OT. But the reformed argument overcomes those defenses. Overcoming them completes the reformed argument and also the first stage in the two-stage argument from prima facie $NENP^i$ that is central to part 1 of the book. But overcoming those defenses is further reason to believe that some or all NENP in the actual world is $NENP^i$, and that point is the substance of the second stage of my two-stage argument in part 1—an indirect empirical argument

from evil that, in chapter 8, I develop atop the reformed logical argument's success against Swinburne's, Plantinga's, and Schlesinger's defenses.

The upshot is that, on the standard model of debate on the problem of evil, there is good reason to think the actual world contains NENP[i], thus that atheism is true. But an additional promissory note should be issued at this point, namely, that in part 2, I constrict the scope of the indirect argument's conclusion in such a way that, while my answer to the question of whether we have good reason to think some evil in the actual world is NENP[i] is still yes, it is a "yes" weaker and narrower in scope than before. Furthermore, it is a "yes" that theism can, and (I venture to say) should, accept.

But these things are in the future. Our focus at present belongs on the reformed version of the logical argument. And in that regard, here now are five ways in which my formulation of the logical argument differs from the version that, since its emergence into prominence in the 1950s through the work of J. L. Mackie, A. G. N. Flew, H. J. McCloskey, and H. D. Aiken, has been standard.[21]

First of all, I do not claim to prove definitively that God and any facts of evil are logically inconsistent with one another. And neither is it my goal to prove that any *other* essential proposition of orthodox theism is logically inconsistent with any fact of evil. The conjunction of my Pyrrhonian disclaimer and my agreement with Pike on the point cited sees to it that, on the question of whether there is NENP[i] in the actual world, my position is agnostic. But this agnosticism is not equidistant between both ends of its spectrum, for an essential part of my thesis is that for some of us at least there is good reason to think some facts of natural evil are inconsistent with the world's being God-made.

Second, the reformed logical argument expressly addresses an expanded, as opposed to restricted, formulation of theism, namely, orthodox theism.[22]

Third, the reformed argument is a specified logical argument, under the stipulated meanings of the terms "specified" and "logical." Its emphasis is upon a specific fact of evil, namely, the amount of natural evil that we have good reason to think is NENP[i], and not upon evil, or natural evil, or even natural evil resulting solely from natural processes, as such. Many diseases, much pain and suffering, as well as many other things, belong to the category of natural evil under discussion.

Fourth, in examination of the reformed version of the logical argument, it is the fortunes of the major theistic defenses deployed against it that principally interest me, not the logic of God and evil itself, and so the main focus of the reformed logical argument is on the arguments that are used in defense of OT, not on OT itself.[23] In keeping with this, the main thrust of the reformed argument is that, on the standard model of debate on the problem of evil, none of the best theistic defenses against logical arguments from evil, or at least none of the best defenses against logical arguments that we know of, is successful in defending orthodox theism against the reformed logical argument from prima facie $NENP^i$. The result is that, insofar as those defenses are concerned, we have good reason to think there is $NENP^i$, thus that OT is false.

Fifth, following examination of Swinburne's, Plantinga's, and Schlesinger's respective defenses, I migrate from a logical to an empirical form of the argument from evil and draw an empirical conclusion from OT's being undefended (by those defenses) against the reformed argument, namely, that within the framework of the standard philosophical debate on the problem of evil, the defensive failure in question seriously weakens the epistemic credentials of OT. This is to say that those defenses' failure is strong, albeit indirect, empirical evidence against OT and for atheism. In this migration I switch from citing as evidence certain facts of natural evil to citing as evidence facts about certain theistic defensive arguments, namely, Swinburne's, Plantinga's, and Schlesinger's. Considering the nature of the evidence I use in this empirical argument, it is an *indirect* empirical argument. As such, it grows on the same family tree as Michael Martin's indirect empirical arguments.[24]

Defensive Strategies

As noted, theistic defenses against arguments from evil have one or both of two basic objectives, and a particular defense against a particular argument will typically be a variation on one or the other of these. The two basic defensive objectives in question are: first, to show that the conclusion of a given argument from evil is not established—this being the defensive strategy of disputing the prosecution's case or of arguing against the admissibility as evidence of certain propositions, or both; second, to show that the evils in question in a given argument are not in fact incompatible with the version of theism under attack—this being the defensive strategy of providing an alibi. The former is the less ambitious of the two approaches, but if successful, it is sufficient to defend theism. The latter approach, although closer than the former to theodicy, does not amount to a theodicy, in that it does not, or at any rate does not have to, pretend to go beyond postulating a *possible* God-justifying reason for God's permitting or not preventing whatever fact of evil is in question to postulating an *actual* reason that God might have for permitting or not preventing that particular fact. And the offer of a purportedly actual reason is the price of admission to the game of theodicy: in Richard Gale's words, "a theodicy . . . is a defense plus an empirical argument for the actual existence of the possible world articulated in the defense."[25]

The second of these defensive strategies is itself further divisible, as compatibility may be read either logically or empirically. So, for example, in the case of a logical argument from prima facie NENP[i], a sufficient alibi is provided by establishing the logical possibility of God's having a morally sufficient reason for actualizing or permitting a world containing the evils in question. For, to establish the mere logical possibility that something, e, is compatible with something else, t, is sufficient to defeat an argument whose conclusion is either that e and t are logically inconsistent with one another or that e and t are shown to be logically inconsistent with one another, whereas, establishing such a mere logical possibility is not sufficient to defeat, or even to block or deflect, an empirical form of the argument from evil. This is because empirical forms of the argument do not dispute logical consistency. So, against them, the theistic defender whose defensive goal is to provide an alibi must establish the possibility in question as a *live*, and not just a bare logical, possibility.[26]

In all, six brand-name defenses of theism will be examined here, the three previously mentioned defenses against the reformed logical argument, a non-Pyrrhonian skeptical defense against a direct form of the empirical argument, and two defenses —one apiece by William Hasker and Peter van Inwagen—that seek to establish a version of the radical point that gratuitous evil is not inconsistent with God in the first place. The non-Pyrrhonian line of skeptical defense falls into the category of defenses that concentrate on attacking some aspect or assumption of the prosecution's case, as do the defenses offered by Hasker and van Inwagen, while the others offer alibis. Schlesinger's defense is difficult to classify: arguably it belongs in both categories. The non-Pyrrhonian form of skeptical defense also repudiates the basic model of the standard debate, and in fact its repudiation of it is the essence of that defense. By contrast, the defenses offered by Plantinga, Schlesinger, and Swinburne are committed to the standard model. This difference vis-a-vis the standard debate has an important bearing on the relationship between the conclusions I draw in chapters 8 and 11, respectively.

A final thought on kinds of defenses. In his books *The Coherence of Theism, The Existence of God*, and *Faith and Reason* combined, Richard Swinburne makes a positive case for the existence of God—in his recent *Is There A God?* he gives us a "short version" of that case[27]— and arguably this amounts to an attempt at maximal defense. Be that as it may, however, my focus here on theism's defenses (including Swinburne's greater-good defense) takes "defense" in the minimal sense specified and only in that sense. Thus I will be asking less of Swinburne's defense than he does.

Kinds of Evils

My development of an argument based on an amount of evil in the world that we have good reason to think is incompatible with OT, reflects two distinctions that are standard in the philosophical literature on the problem of evil: first, the distinction between moral evils and natural evils, and second, the distinction between gratuitous and nongratuitous evils. Let us look at these in turn.

By moral evil is meant evils for which human persons are responsible in the moral sense of responsibility. It is the concept theologians denote by the term "sin." Moral evils, then, would include, but would not be restricted to, cruelty, malice, theft, neglecting to help a victim when, without harm or loss, we could have done so, lying, planning a crime, murder, and so on. In sum, moral evils are the morally culpable intentions, actions, or omissions of sufficiently mature, free, moral agents.

In contrast to moral evil there is natural evil. Natural evil is evil for which human persons are not responsible in the moral sense of responsibility. Included among such evils would be the following: the painfulness of pain—its raw feel (in Herbert Feigl's term), which is to say its phenomenological quality—diseases for which no human being is culpable, birth defects for which no human being is culpable, Heideggerian Angst, if I understand the concept aright, natural disasters, and so on.

Before going further, a brief digression may be useful to explain why it is that among philosophers of religion the term "natural evil" is commonly used to refer to pain, suffering, and so on for which no human person is responsible in a moral way, for it may seem an odd use of "evil" to extend it to such cases.

The apparent oddity may be brought out in the following way. Suppose there is no God, nor supernatural beings of any sort. On that supposition, there is no source or explanation beyond nature (including human nature) of any occurrence, thing, or state of a thing. In those circumstances there is, in the last analysis, no ulterior explanation of why something exists rather than nothing at all, of why there are *these* laws of nature rather than others, no explanation beyond or behind the brute-fact explanation of saying that there has to be *some* state, even if it is a state of nothingness. If there is neither God nor powerful supernatural beings of any kind, then birth defects, cancers, and so on, not due to culpable human action or omission, but instead resulting just from genetic bad luck, are defects only relative to a statistical norm. And there is a plausible sense in which the word "evil" has a false ring to it when applied to such occurrences, namely, the sense in which "evil" connotes responsibility and culpability. However, the appearance of oddity is dissipated by the fact that the philosophical problem of evil, and especially the philosophical problem of natural evil, exists only given the theistic hypothesis of a supreme, personal, creator being or another hypothesis very like it. And so with antitheistic arguments from evil predicated on the idea, granted for the sake of argument, that God exists, the reference to such phenomena as birth defects for which there is no human culpability whatever as *evils* of a certain kind is not misleading after all. For it seems intuitively right to think that, if there is no balancing, outweighing, or otherwise God-justifying, reason for them, such occurrences could, should, and would have been avoided in any world designed and made by God, and that if they are not, then they are evils to be laid at God's door.[28]

Gratuitous and Nongratuitous Evils

Let us turn now to the distinction between gratuitous and nongratuitous evils. For the present, pending fuller discussion in chapter 3, let us identify gratuitous evils as evils for which there is no morally sufficient reason. In the case of natural evils, gratuitous evil would be natural evil for which there is no morally sufficient reason, in the sense that there is no God-justifying reason for such evil to exist. By contrast, nongratuitous natural evils are evils for which there *is* a morally sufficient reason. In examining the question of whether there is good reason to believe that some natural evil is NENP[i], I sometimes discuss specific instances of prima facie NENP[i]. But, as emphasized before, the reformed logical argument is an argument from the quantity of such evil in a supposedly God-made world. That being so, I cite those instances as "typical members of [one of] the main classes of observable [natural] evils in the world," to borrow Swinburne's phrase.[29]

Theism as Theory and Practice

I refer to theism as a philosophical theory and propose to examine a version of it. But perhaps theism is not a theory at all, and if it is not, then the long-established philosophical practice of treating it as one has involved a pernicious reductionism whereby, in Robert Audi's terms, belief in God is cut back to the belief that God exists.[30] And if theism is a theory, in what sense is it a theory?

Nelson Pike lends weight to the idea that theism is misrepresented when cast (and discussed) as a theory. Talking about Hume's *Dialogues,* he makes the following point:

It ought not to go unnoticed that Philo's closing attack on Cleanthes' position has extremely limited application. Evil in

17

CHAPTER 1

the world has central negative importance for theology only when theology is approached as a quasi-scientific subject, as by Cleanthes. That it is seldom approached in this way will be evident to anyone who has studied the history of theology. Within most theological positions, the existence of God is taken as an item of faith or embraced on the basis of an a priori argument. Under these circumstances, where there is nothing to qualify as a "hypothesis" capable of having either positive or negative "evidence," the fact of evil in the world presents no special problem for theology.[31]

Now, Pike may or may not be right about theology, but if "theism" in this context were read as a synonym for either "religious faith" or "religious belief," then he would certainly be right that religious belief is not a theory. For clearly, belief in God as we discover it in the lives of the faithful is not held as either a theory or an hypothesis. In Pike's term, belief in God is first and foremost an article of faith. While not disputing that, my point here is that religious belief also has propositional content. And it is that feature of it that interests me. It is what I mean by theism. Thus I use the word "theism" to mean a *dimension* of religious belief, its propositional, cognitive, or theoretical dimension: as I use it here, then, the word "theism" is a technical, or at least a quasi-technical, term. It refers to the cognitive or theoretical content of religious belief in the Abrahamic tradition. Likewise, "orthodox theism" and its shorthand "OT" are technical terms, standing for a particular specification of theism.

Furthermore, we saw that theism comes in different sizes, restricted and expanded. Accordingly, it is the cognitive dimension of a version of the latter that I examine here. Now to my reasons for thinking that belief in God has discussable cognitive content. They are essentially as follows.

Let us start with an obvious fact. It is that, for many believers in God, their faith shapes and guides their lives. Faith is first and foremost existential and engaged, not intellectual and detached; it is personal, but within a community of faith. It is a felt personal relationship with God, involving, among other things, trust in God, being in love with God, engagement with one's fellow human beings

18

in ways that seek and promote goodness, justice, truth, charity, compassion, forgiveness, and so on, all the while doing so on the understanding that it is God's will. A person's religion is often a source of strength, confidence, comfort, hope, and inspiration. It belongs to the very fabric of the believer's life, giving a certain kind and dimension of meaning to that life.

But while shaping the life of the believer, belief in God is not exhausted therein, nor is it a free-floating set of attitudes or actions. Belief in God in the life-guiding sense also incorporates a certain set of credenda, among them the propositions that God exists, that human beings are creatures of God, that God cares about and perhaps for God's creatures, that death may not be the end of an individual person's life, that there is value and meaning in each human being's life independent of his or her own choosing, that no significant amount of evil lacks a God-justifying reason, and so on.

Now, even if the believer is wholly uninterested in these propositions and never adverts to them as such, understanding his or her belief in God to be life guiding only, the cognitive dimension is yet latent in the life guiding. For, while the believer may not *believe* the foregoing credenda, in the sense of belief that Audi calls unqualified, yet he or she, in day-to-day life, presupposes their truth, and his or her life in faith reflects them. Robert Audi makes the point as follows:

> A true attribution of faith *in* God in some sense *presupposes* God's existence, in that—apart from inverted commas uses of the term—we cannot have faith in a non-existent being. But this ontological presupposition permits a person of faith to have associated cognitive attitudes as modest as presuming, rather than unqualifiedly believing, the relevant truths . . . Presuming the truth of a proposition does not require holding it in the way characteristic of belief.[32] [italics original].

Finally and importantly, consistent with his or her faith, such a person does not, indeed cannot, *disbelieve* those credenda: that is, he or she cannot be disposed to think them false.[33] The upshot is that belief in God entails belief that God exists, or something very close to it. Furthermore, these credenda are either true or false, thus their conjunction too has a truth value.

19

CHAPTER 1

In addition to the logical relationship between the two senses of belief discussed, in Audi's terms attitudinal and propositional, respectively, the centrality to religious belief of its propositional or cognitive dimension has traditionally been acknowledged in the mainstream theistic religions. Those religions maintain that they teach important lessons, that their teachings are not just beneficial but true, and that the lessons taught are rooted in a right understanding of the world, in effect, in a certain ontological story. Parenthetically, the revised, cognitionally weakened descriptions of the ontological commitments of religious belief offered by such deflationary theologians of recent times as Rudolf Bultmann, Don Cupitt, and Paul Tillich, serve here as exceptions proving the rule.

It might be thought that assenting to the proposition "God exists" would entail an existential commitment as well, but there is no entailment here, as the following story illustrates. As told in the Old Testament, Satan and Satan's cohorts believe that God exists. Presumably they have the best of reasons for this, for they have seen God. (Given this, to say that Satan believes that God exists is an understatement, although it is not false. For, in the circumstances, Satan *knows* that God exists.) But Satan and Satan's cohorts do not believe *in* God, under the meaning of the term specified above. They believe *that*, without believing *in*. However, to get back to my main line of argument in this section, while "belief that" does not entail "belief in," the latter does entail the former, or at least something very close to it, and my position in this book is predicated on this being so.

In sum, granting the fact that belief in God does not reduce to belief that God exists, my point that theism is a theory and my treating it as such is essentially a simple, straightforward, and modest one: it is that the Abrahamic religions are committed to certain credenda, to a certain conception of how the world is —for instance, made by God to be a place in which it is possible for human persons to know and love God, as well as being a place in which it is possible for them to develop into morally and spiritually mature beings able to responsibly choose their own individual destinies—and that this conception is either true or false. Furthermore, the theistic story of supernatural design and creation is discussable in light of our experience of the world, for instance, the world's being seen to contain a large quantity, variety, and distribution of evils, some of which are inscrutable to us. My characterization of theism as a theory, then, is a characterization of it as having discussable propositional content and cognitive commitments. Since the life-guiding sense of religion presupposes the propositional, whether as belief or presupposition, a philosophical examination of the merits and credentials of belief (or presupposition) that God exists is more than just legitimate: it is important and relevant to belief in God, and necessary for an adequate philosophical appraisal of it.

A revision of a metaphor often used to represent the relation between reason and faith may provide us another way of looking at the link between the two senses of religious belief under examination here, as well as at the importance of "belief that" to "belief in." Let us approach with a focus on the task of theistic apologetics.

The primary job of theistic apologetics is to support religious belief, under both descriptions of the concept of belief. But a natural and obvious interpretation of support is foundationalist. So it is natural to think of theistic apologetics—which is to say, certain philosophical arguments, individually and together—as standing under religious belief and holding it up. This metaphor of support, while not entailing the view that religious belief, in either sense, derives from argument, may be seen by some to lend weight to that view. And, to the extent that it *does* lend weight to that view, the fact that religious belief is not usually (or, very probably, ever) acquired as a conclusion may perhaps be assumed by some to be strong evidence for the view that philosophical supporting arguments are not important at all for such belief. But the fact that religious belief does not stand atop an argument does not mean that the epistemic standing of that belief, its reasonableness or its warrant, for instance, is unconnected to the success or failure of supporting arguments.

There is another and better way of viewing the relationship between reason and faith, argument and religious belief, than as first floor to second floor, and this other way of looking at that relationship enables us to see clearly—that is, without clouding our view with the true but irrelevant point that faith typically does not issue from premises—that religious belief is not impervious to arguments. I propose a revised metaphor for reason's support of faith, and, in particular, for how theism's philosophical self-defenses stand in relation to belief in God.

Theism's philosophical defenses are analogous to a country's defenses of itself against actual or potential attack. A country has borders or coastlines, and if its government has good reason to think either might be attacked, it deploys armies or navies or other defensive systems in readiness to defend them. With that image in mind, the focus of the proposed metaphor is this: philosophical defenses of theism do not stand beneath it as part of a foundation holding it up, and certainly not as the source from which belief in God, or even belief that God exists, comes. Their role, rather, may be likened to how a country's defensive ring protects the everyday life of the community within the borders or between the coasts. Such defensive systems are often remote from the concerns or interests of the citizenry, and may even seem, if and when noticed by the citizens, to be either distasteful or wasteful in various ways. Yet, if overrun by external enemies, or even if only seriously threatened by them, both the need for, and role of, adequate defenses are as clearly evident as the perceived threat to everyday life in the hinterland. In parallel fashion, in the everyday life of faith, the abstract, seemingly arcane, issues of academic philosophy of religion are of minimal interest at best, and so go virtually universally unnoticed and unremarked in that everyday life. Yet, just as in times of peace the military systems arrayed along borders or coasts or in the air contribute in ways mostly unnoticed and unappreciated, save by the cognoscenti, to the security and quality of life in the hinterland, so too with the philosophical defenses of theism. Viewed spatially, this military metaphor shows the relationship between faith and the philosophical defenses of its cognitive content—OT in the present context—to be horizontal, not vertical as the foundationalist image has it. A variation on this metaphor could easily be devised to cover a country's (thus, by analogy, theism's) defenses against internal threats, actual or perceived, but there is no good reason to do so here.

Whose Burden of Proof?

There is an assumption implicit in my bringing (in part 1) a form of the logical argument from evil against orthodox theism and then drawing an empirical conclusion about the epistemic status of that theory from its best defenses' failure, within the framework of the standard debate on the problem of evil, to defend it successfully against that argument. It is the assumption that casting OT in the role of defendant is legitimate from the start. But why should OT play the defendant's role and be made to answer the antitheistic challenge? Why shouldn't the antitheistic challenger first establish the credentials of his or her own position, thereby earning it the right to challenge a central version of such a long-standing (not to mention long-suffering) theory as theism?

In his 1982 book *Religious Belief and Religious Skepticism*, Gary Gutting argues convincingly that atheism, no less than theism, is inseparable from a set of ontological and other theoretical commitments, not all of which are obviously more plausible than their theistic counterparts.[34] It might initially be supposed that Gutting's point supports the aforementioned protest against the assumption, both mine here and widespread in the literature on theism and evil, that, on the standard model of debate, theism's rightful place is in the dock. But it does not support that protest at all. For, although well taken in its context, Gutting's point is not relevant here. That is because, in the philosophical debate over the problem of evil, we are not, at bottom, comparing philosophical theories or their respective ontologies, whether implicit or explicit, and neither are we choosing among rival theories, whether on the strength of such a comparison or for other reasons. (The detente for which I argue in part 2 is a good illustration of this point.) Instead, the fundamental thing we do is to take a long-standing theory on its own terms, with a view to examining its ability to cope with an indigenous problem. True, this problem is often pressed upon theism by atheists or agnostics whose intent, relevant to certain data, is to show theism to be inferior to atheism or agnosticism or to show it to be false, but that is incidental. Examination of theism's ability to cope with the problem of evil does not require us to be either atheistic or agnostic. The theist himself or herself can just as naturally pursue the question as his or her atheistic counterpart. Theism can be just as threatened from inside as from outside — that is, by an argument from evil put forth by a theist even if the theist's intent is not to threaten or defeat theism—as by the same argument put forth by an atheist whose interest may be less benign.

OT is not compatible with all possible states of affairs. In particular, given the goodness, knowledge, and power clauses in the definition of "God," it is incompatible with evil for which there is no God-justifying reason.[35] Thus we have a clear conception of something, NENP[i] say, that, if found to exist, would falsify the theory. Furthermore, there is prima facie good reason to suppose that such falsifying facts do indeed obtain and are available to us.[36] In this regard, consider John Hick's concession that, on theism, there is a baffling problem of excessive and widespread suffering.[37] Furthermore, in the words of the theistic Demea from Hume's *Dialogues Concerning Natural Religion,*

> Why should man . . . pretend to an exemption from the lot of all other animals? The whole earth . . . is cursed and polluted. A perpetual war is kindled amongst all living creatures. Necessity, hunger, want stimulate the strong and courageous; fear, anxiety, terror agitate the weak and infirm. The first entrance into life gives anguish to the new-born infant and to its wretched parent; weakness, impotence, distress attend each stage of that life, and it is, at last, finished in agony and horror.[38]

Thus, it is both proper and interesting to examine OT's defensive resources against arguments that draw upon such ubiquitous facts, particularly the amount, distribution, and duration of inscrutable natural evil resulting solely from natural processes.

Notwithstanding all of this, there *is* a sense in which the theistic protest at being so quickly put in the dock has merit. A distinction between the respective evidentiary obligations of prosecution and defense in regard to the indictment of OT will help to clarify the key point, namely, that the challenger to theism carries a significant burden of proof.

Evidence is needed to justify placing under indictment a long-standing theory that enjoys support from several arguments that, intuitively, have some appeal—arguments from the fact of order in the world, from the fact (if it is a fact) that nothing exists uncaused, and from the fact of certain persons' experience (religious or even mystical), to mention three. In the case of our investigation here, I interpret this need to supply evidence justifying the indictment of theism, first, as my obligation to uphold in the face of attack a proposition usually just taken for granted on all sides, namely, that gratuitous evil, understood a certain way and in excess of a certain (unspecified) level, is indeed incompatible with some essential propositions of orthodox theism, and then, second, as my obligation to provide good reason for thinking that there is evil in the world that is gratuitous in the sense and amount in question. If this two-part burden of proof at indictment is met, then a strong presumptive case will have been made out against the version of theistic theory in question, and so the cognitive credentials of OT may fairly be judged on its ability to answer that case. I will discharge the first part of this obligation in chapter 3 and the second in chapters 5 through 8. In those chapters, as well as throughout the book, I take orthodox theism and its principal defenses on their own terms, as is fitting when examining a theory's capacity to deal with an indigenous problem.

But, in proposing as I do here to treat the philosophical problem of evil as uniquely *theism*'s problem of evil, am I not merely bringing an ad hominem argument against OT? And isn't the theist within his or her epistemic rights in declining to answer such an argument, inasmuch as ad hominem "evidence" is only evidence manqué?[39]

There is a weak sense in which the point is correct, but it amounts to a misleading way of characterizing the problem of evil. To describe an argument from evil as ad hominem suggests that, because the argument is directed specifically against some formulation of theism, attention is thereby being deflected from a matter of substance to some merely local features of a given theist's, or class of theists', formulation of theism. But that is misleading, inasmuch as the philosophical problem of evil only arises in the first place on the supposition that God, as standardly understood within the Abrahamic tradition, exists, made the world, and stands in various other important relationships to it. In essence then, given orthodox theism's acknowledgment of the facts of evil, the problem of evil is that theory's problem of apparent self-incrimination. Hence, construing evil (of a certain kind and above a certain level) as evidence, there is no way of formulating the problem that does not call either the truth of orthodox theism or the reasonableness of believing it true into question. Thus, the argument from evil's being weakly ad hominem in the way described does not serve to justify theism's not having to defend itself against it, nor does it immunize theism from the effects of a failure to do so successfully.

PART 1

2

IN THE SPIRIT OF HUME

Positive and Negative Evidentialism

In a transformation that began with Locke in the late 1600s, theism's supporting arguments were maneuvered into a forced migration from natural theology, as that had been understood since the Middle Ages, to what Nicholas Wolterstorff calls evidentialist apologetics,[1] a journey that was completed almost a century later under the influence of Hume's posthumously published *Dialogues Concerning Natural Religion*. The current mainstream in the philosophy of religion—analytical philosophy of religion—reflects this evidentialist turn. In the evidentialist point of view, theism is required to maintain itself by argument or, in the event of failure, to see its cognitive credentials curtailed or even revoked. The effect is that, among philosophers, theism is more or less permanently on trial for its life, the niceties of double jeopardy not being observed here or, for that matter, anywhere in academic philosophy.

It had not been so in the Middle Ages. In the philosophical world of a medieval natural theologian, a proof for the existence of God could be attempted, or an effort made to explain certain phenomena—for instance, evils in a world taken to be God-made—without, in the event of failure, putting any proposition of theism itself at risk. Accordingly, if it happened that the best arguments of the natural theologians failed in their given tasks, neither the truth nor the rationality of religious belief thereby fell into doubt. In the modern period, though, under the primary influence of Locke's *Essay Concerning Human Understanding*, rationality came to be understood as proportionate to evidence, thus too the rationality of religious belief. Accordingly, failure to make out, or at least to have available, a sufficient case for such belief meant that the believer's epistemic right to believe was called proportionately into question. Locke's seminal statement of this position is the following:

> There is another use of the word reason, wherein it is opposed to faith, which, though it be in itself a very improper way of speaking, yet common use has so authorized it that it would be folly either to oppose or hope to remedy it; only I think it may not be amiss to take notice that, however faith be opposed to reason, faith is nothing but a firm assent of the mind; *which, if it be regulated, as is our duty, cannot be afforded to anything but upon good reason,* and so cannot be opposite to it. He that believes without having any reason for believing may be in love with his own fancies; but neither seeks truth as he ought, nor pays the obedience due to his Maker, who would have him use those discerning faculties he has given him, to keep him out of mistake and error. He that does not this to the best of his power, however he sometimes lights on truth, is in the right but by chance; and I know not whether the luckiness of the accident will excuse the irregularity of his proceeding. This at least is certain, that he must be accountable for whatever mistakes he runs into; whereas he that makes use of the light and faculties God has given him, and seeks sincerely to discover truth by those helps and abilities he has, may have this satisfaction in doing his duty as a rational creature: that, though he should miss truth, he will not miss the reward of it. *For he governs his assent right and places it as he should who, in any case or matter whatsoever, believes or disbelieves according as reason directs him.*[2] [italics added]

As was Locke before him, Hume was committed to these evidentialist principles. However, in Hume although not in Locke, we find this line of thought pushed to an embryonic form of the idea, primarily associated in the present century with the work of Karl Popper, that a theory's epistemic status depends less upon how much the theory is confirmed by evidence than upon how well the theory is able to handle potentially deadly counterevidence.[3]

The potentially deadly evidence put forward as such by Hume is certain facts of evil in a world that, according to the theistic account, was designed and actualized for a good purpose by a perfect spiritual being, a nonhuman person whose power, knowledge, and good intentions are supreme. As presented by Hume, the philosophical problem of evil is intended to do two things: one, to curb the natural theologian's inference from certain prominent and commonplace features of the world—regularity in nature, for instance—to some transcendent cause—a supernatural designer, for instance—and therefrom to the God of the Abrahamic religions; and two, by presenting certain facts of evil as a threat, not just to theism's supporting arguments (the design argument in particular), but to theism itself, to put theism at risk. On the latter point, then, theism's epistemic credentials and fate are made to turn upon its ability to defend itself against arguments based on those facts of evil.

Hume's development of this aspect of the relationship between the rationality of theism and the relevant evidence beyond where Locke had left it represented an important shift in the center of gravity within the movement to evidentialism in the philosophy of religion. Let us mark it here as the shift from positive to negative evidentialism. By the former I mean a view that sees the rationality of theism as proportionate to the strength of the arguments that support the theory in the sense that they constitute its base, and by the latter I mean a view that sees the rationality of theism as proportionate to the strength of the arguments that defend and sustain it against potentially deadly attacks upon some of its core propositions. The two are not mutually exclusive, of course. A negative evidentialist is not a positive evidentialist by virtue of emphasizing the latter proportionality over the former, but such emphasis requires no repudiation of the former in its own right. Discussion of the problem of evil within contemporary analytical philosophy of religion tends to reflect negative, not positive, evidentialism, with the earlier-noted result that theism seems to be perpetually in the dock on capital charges.

In parts X and XI of Hume's *Dialogues*, a wellspring of negative evidentialism within analytic philosophy of religion, the question under discussion is whether God and evil are mutually compatible. Hume pursued this as an empirical question, conceding that, in regard to bare logical possibility, God and evil are not inconsistent

with one another: "I will allow that . . . [evil] . . . is compatible with
. . . the Deity."[4] He tells us to read him here as meaning "mere
possible compatibility."

Granting logical consistency, then, Hume frames the empirical
question of God and evil as follows: "is the world, considered in
general and as it appears to us in this life, different from what a
man or such a limited being would, *beforehand*, expect from a very
powerful, wise, and benevolent Deity?"[5] It is clear from the neigh-
boring text that he believes the correct answer is no. To suppose
otherwise, he thinks, would be "strange prejudice" indeed. Within
the epistemic framework that he is here presupposing, surely Hume
is right. To a disinterested observer, "a stranger [who drops] on a
sudden into this world," the world is not at all "what we expect from
infinite power, infinite wisdom, infinite goodness," for it is a world
in which there is a great abundance and variety of inscrutable evil.[6]
To such an observer it will seem obvious that the world is subject to
improvement in a large number of important ways, and that God,
no less than we (and arguably much more so), could contribute
enormously to the improvement: the fact of medical research into
the nature of the many diseases that kill and cause misery for so
many people and animals testifies to the existence, plausibility, and
spread of belief in the world's improvability.

Several related strands of argument are suggested in the question
and answer just quoted from Hume, and, briefly, it will be useful to
distinguish between two of them. The first pertains directly to theistic apologetics (or natural theology as the case may be) and the
second to theism itself. Let us address them in sequence.

The Design Argument

Arguably the strongest of the positive evidentialist (and natural
theological) arguments is the design argument for the existence of
God. It is also the positive evidentialist argument principally examined by Hume in the *Inquiry Concerning Human Understanding*
(henceforth, the first *Inquiry*) and the *Dialogues*. The design argument is an inductive argument, analogical in nature, whose principal claims are two: first, in the last analysis, the existence of certain
features of the world cannot plausibly be accounted for except as

products of design, that is, as products of intention and intelligence; and second, given the nature and commonality of those features, their postulated designer cannot plausibly be thought of other than as vastly more intelligent, knowledgeable, powerful, and benevolent than we are, perhaps supremely so.

This line of thinking has a certain initial attractiveness to the reflective mind.[7] Hume himself accepted a modest form of it, described by J. C. A. Gaskin as "attenuated deism."[8] However, there is also a counterpoint urged by Hume in both the first *Inquiry* and the *Dialogues*, and suggested in the passage quoted just above, namely, that there are *other* features of the world that, when interpreted without prejudice, make serious, and perhaps insuperable difficulty for any version of the design argument whose conclusion is that the God of traditional monotheism is the postulated designer. Thus, the question that Hume puts into the mouth of Philo—whether the world as we find it is a world we would expect of the God of traditional theism—serves at least to counteract and, within the framework of the standard philosophical debate on the problem of evil, perhaps greatly to erode the initial intuitive appeal of the hypothesis of design. For, by drawing attention to the manifest evils in the world, Philo's question suggests a point of view on the debate that seems at least as intuitively appealing as the one reflected in the design argument, and, in addition, it suggests a way of testing the design intuition (and hypothesis) itself. Because of this promise of a test, what Hume via Philo is suggesting is, within the framework of the standard debate, arguably *more* intuitively appealing than any robustly theistic (as opposed to attenuatedly deistic) form of the design intuition.

If Hume is right in the answer that, as Philo, he gives to Philo's question—that is, if there are indeed prominent and widespread features of the world that are strongly disanalogous to the products of the choices and deliberate actions of intelligent, benevolent, moral human beings—then the design argument's analogical inference to the theistic God is proportionately compromised. Given the design argument's status as perhaps the most compelling of the positive evidentialist's arguments, a consequence of its becoming compromised would be a significant diminishment of the central project of positive evidentialism, namely, that of establishing by fair, open, unprejudiced, inductive, argument that the God of the Abrahamic religions exists.

It might be objected that the last point is overstated, that the fate of positive evidentialism (or of natural theology) as a whole is not set back by the failure of any one of its arguments alone, inasmuch as positive evidentialists' other arguments would still be available for use in the philosophical effort to prove that God exists. But that objection miscarries. For the god in question is a being whose goodness, fairness, and benevolence are perfect by definition. So if Hume is correct in citing various widespread features of the world—certain ubiquitous natural evils—as strongly disanalogous to products of benevolent design, and if it is true both that gratuitous evil of a certain kind is logically inconsistent with God and that, prima facie, some of the natural evils thus cited are gratuitous in the relevant sense, then, prima facie, no inference to a *perfectly good, fair, benevolent* creator-sustainer of the world is epistemically justified until further notice; in particular, until the relevant argument or arguments from evil have been blocked or refuted. True, inferences to an *all-powerful* or *all-knowing* designer-creator would not be closed off by the disanalogies in question, but, without perfect goodness, fairness, benevolence, and the like, no such inferred creator could be *God.* Thus, unless the argument or arguments from evil in question are either blocked or defeated, the positive evidentialist project cannot go through to completion.

Such a curtailment of positive evidentialism (or its predecessor, natural theology) would be no minor thing, for it would leave theism unsupported in ways that, since Locke, have often been deemed essential. However, such a failure of positive evidentialism would not entail the falsity of theism, inasmuch as, from the failure of a theory's supporting arguments to establish it as true it does not follow that the theory is false. Seen in context of the apparent blockage of an inference to the alleged moral attributes of the deity, Hume was arguably a moral atheist, to use Gaskin's illuminating term, although not a total atheist.[9]

On Theism's Need for Self-defense

As they pertain directly to positive evidentialism (or to natural theology), the issues discussed represent one strand of thought in the question and answer quoted from Hume. But, more than blocking, whether temporarily or permanently, the design argument in particular or positive evidentialism in general, and more important than blocking or even defeating them, there is also the suggestion in the lines quoted from Philo that those features of the world Hume describes as evils tend to show much more than that theism is unsupported by adequate argument, namely, that theism is false. That is a second strand in Philo's question and answer. In this way of reading them, the quoted lines obviously represent a bigger and more important challenge to theism—and by extension to the Abrahamic religions—than any danger posed by a threat just to positive evidentialism. For, in the lines quoted, Hume is inviting us to indict theism, to put it on trial for its life and, in so doing, to demand that it make a defense of itself. So taken, theism, and in our present context OT specifically, cannot remain in good epistemic standing as a philosophical theory if it fails to defend itself. In the next section we will see why.

Theories and Arguments

The foregoing discussion of Hume's thinking reflects a certain conception of the logical and epistemological relations among theories, their supporting arguments, and prima facie damaging data. That conception will repay development.

The positive evidentialist, seeing beliefs and systems of belief as rational only if supported by argument, and seeing them to be only as rational as those supporting arguments, and, furthermore, seeing religious belief as a belief or belief system like any other in that regard, demands that religious belief make out (or be able to make out) a case for itself. The positive evidentialist, circa 1700, arguably did not see religious belief as any more urgently in need of supporting argumentation than any given set of widely accepted secular beliefs, indeed perhaps less so. Thus his demand for support would likely not have cast any aspersion of epistemic weakness upon religious belief, or would have been intended to.[10] Indeed, Locke tended to see himself as *strengthening* religion by making its rationality manifest in strong supporting arguments.

In the case of orthodox theism, the first level of such supporting arguments' work is to establish an explanatory need for a supernaturalist account of certain occurrences in the natural world. That established, the second level of those arguments' work is to meet that need with a cogent, plausible theory that both offers an appropriate supernaturalist ontology and connects, as adequate transcendent explanans, the entities posited therein to the mundane explananda. Implicitly, this enterprise puts the supernaturalism of OT into competition with various naturalistic theories purporting to account in a deep way for the same natural occurrences. This was as true at the end of the seventeenth century as it is now, but there are two important, interrelated differences nonetheless. They are, one, that the naturalistic rivals available then were weak compared to what is currently available, and, in large part as a consequence of this development; two, OT is no longer the presumptive explanatory champion.

Meeting opposition, and especially when its own core propositions come under attack, a theory needs defenses. As an historical matter, the most important of OT's defensive arguments have been deployed in defense of the theory against arguments from evil, although it is not on grounds of evil alone that the theory comes under attack and needs to be defended. Since the Enlightenment, in the main, theistic arguments have been adapted or developed to meet the negative evidentialist demand that theism defend itself against the various evil-based cases brought against it. By contrast, arguments offered in response to the positive evidentialist demand for support are arguments that advance the theory in the sense that they take orthodox theism's case for itself into the free market of ideas in the first place. In actual practice, of course, the distinction between these two kinds of theistic supporting arguments— arguments that advance OT's case and arguments that defend the theory when it comes under attack, respectively—is neither as neat or clean as the foregoing sketch might make it seem. This is because the relationship between a theory, on the one hand, and its various supporting arguments, on the other, is dynamic and multidimensional. Yet, although rough, the distinction between two kinds of theistic supporting arguments is adequate for present purposes.

In addition to the two sorts of roles—to advance a theory and to defend a theory—that supporting arguments can play, this taxonomical sketch of relations between a philosophical theory and its supporting arguments has two further dimensions worth noting. G. E. Moore, in a different context, provides us with useful language for representing the first of them.

A theory is a unified system of principles, assumptions, laws, stipulations, conjectures, data, analyses, and arguments whose principal goals are to prove or disprove a proposition or to explain certain puzzling phenomena. From among these various components of a theory, our focus here is on the arguments that support it in either of the ways described. Both arguments that advance a theory and arguments that defend it are arguments that support the theory, but there is a distinction worth making between two kinds of support that a theory's supporting arguments may give. Some arguments provide necessary support to a theory, while the support provided by others is not necessary. Arguments of the former kind will be indispensable to a theory, whereas arguments of the latter kind will not.

A theory's relationship to arguments that provide it necessary support is, for the theory, an internal or essential relation.[11] As Moore describes it, an internal relation is a relation that, if lost, entails that its former owner is no longer numerically identical to its former self. The contrast is with external relations. An external relation is a relation that may be lost without entailing any loss of numerical self-identity. A theory's relationship to those among its supporting arguments whose support is not necessary support is an external relation. Clearly, some of a theory's supporting arguments are optional: they lend support to the theory, but the theory will not collapse if their support is withdrawn. But the same is not true of all of a theory's supporting arguments, at least not of all of them simultaneously, and that is the point I wish to emphasize. For if the arguments whose support is necessary to the theory are lost, then, in the absence of alternative arguments filling the gap, so may be the theory itself. It is to describe this indispensability to a theory of some among its supporting arguments that I am borrowing from Moore the term "internal relation."

Switching now from the point of view of the theory supported by arguments to that of the arguments that provide the support, we note that, typically, a theory's supporting arguments, even those providing necessary support to the theory, stand in an external relation to the theory. Thus, while a theory has an internal relation to its necessary supporting arguments, the relation is typically not reciprocated. For the arguments, without loss to themselves, can usually be examined in their own right. By contrast, if the theory is separated from all its necessary supporting arguments and examined in isolation from them, it is no longer a theory at all: it is thereby reduced to just a set of claims and analyses.

Applying this to the point made at the close of the previous section, we get the following: if OT is not able to defend itself against the reformed logical argument, it is at serious risk. Since the counter-arguments we are discussing in part 1 include those arguments that, arguably, are the best and most influential contemporary defenses against logical forms of the argument from evil, namely, Plantinga's, Schlesinger's, and Swinburne's, and as those defenses are by and large stronger, as well as more sophisticated and nuanced than their predecessors—a development due to the fact that they combat contemporary formulations of the logical argument that, by and large, are stronger, more sophisticated, and more nuanced than *their* predecessors—it is plausible to think one of those defenses is necessary for support of OT against the reformed logical argument. But it must be acknowledged that we do not know that one of them is necessary in this way, whether in its own right or representing a type of theistic defense. However, going on the plausibility of supposing one of them *is* necessary, if all three of Plantinga's, Schlesinger's, and Swinburne's defenses are shown to fail in defense of OT against the reformed logical argument, and if we have reason to think the reasons for their respective failures would apply to other known formulations of the same types of arguments, then, in the absence of either successful repair of those defenses or their replacement by successful alternatives, OT is at serious risk. In this context, I refer to Plantinga's, Schlesinger's, and Swinburne's defenses, specifically, for they are substantive defenses of OT. But Hasker's defense could also be included.

Second, a distinction can be made between two sorts of successful outcomes of a theory's supporting arguments. On the one hand, an argument or set of arguments may, in principle, settle a disputed issue in favor of one theory, thus against its rivals. But, on the other hand, an argument or a set of arguments may sustain a theory, while not settling the disputed issue one way or the other. For instance, if a defensive argument really established that certain facts of prima facie gratuitous evil are not incompatible with God, it would, insofar as those facts are concerned, have *settled* the issue in the theist's favor. If a defensive argument showed (only) a disabling fault in a prosecuting argument, it would have *sustained* the theistic position while leaving the substantive issue of the cited evil itself unsettled one way or the other. In the latter case a further distinction will be useful: the fault established in the prosecuting argument might be generic or it might be specific to only the particular argument offered. If the former, then, pending repair, OT would be sustained against all arguments of that type, but if the latter, it would be sustained only against the particular argument. But either way further arguments based on the same facts of evil as those cited in the faulty arguments could be expected: in the former case, arguments of a different type; in the latter, either other (better) arguments of the same type or arguments of another type, or both. For the raw materials of the argument would be unaffected by the fault in the argument. Those raw materials are certain facts of inscrutable evil and certain deep and plausible intuitions about inscrutable evil in a world made by God.

I will retrieve both the distinction between kinds of support and the foregoing taxonomy in chapter 8, and then use them throughout part 2.

In the Spirit of Hume

In more than one place in this book, a Humean note will be heard. That being so, a short description of the Humean notes sounded may be useful. To a certain extent this will involve my issuing promissory notes concerning things to be explained or argued later, but I shall try to minimize getting ahead of myself in this way.

Within analytic philosophy of religion the debate on the problem of evil is by and large characterized by adherence to two assumptions. I refer to the debate so characterized as the standard debate on the problem of evil or, alternatively, as the standard model of philosophical debate on that problem. The two assumptions are:

39

1. In thought experiments, the condition of the actual world of our experience can be compared, to a sufficient degree to make a judgment possible, to how the world would be if God existed and to how the world would be if God did not exist.

2. On the basis of such thought-experimental comparisons, a reasoned, justified verdict can in principle be reached as to which of the two sides, the theistic or the antitheistic, has the stronger evidence and so the better of the argument about theism and evil.[12]

Let us think of these two assumptions of the standard model as the comparison assumption and the judgment assumption, respectively. Together they provide the groundwork not only for the proposed test of the design hypothesis that I referred to earlier but also for virtually the entire, standard-model, evidentialist debate over theism and evil.[13] I extract these two assumptions from the question already quoted from Hume, namely, "is the world, considered in general and as it appears to us in this life, different from what a man or such a limited being would, *beforehand*, expect from a very powerful, wise and benevolent Deity?" together with its answer, "it must be strange prejudice to assert the contrary." Expanded, the answer is this:

It must, I think, be allowed that, if a very limited intelligence whom we shall suppose utterly unacquainted with the universe were assured that it was the production of a very good, wise, and powerful being, however finite, he would, from his conjectures, form *beforehand* a different notion of it from what we find it to be by experience; nor would he ever imagine, merely from these attributes of the cause of which he is informed, that the effect could be so full of vice and misery and disorder, as it appears in this life.[14]

The idea of a comparison of possible worlds embodied in the first assumption is crucial to the standard debate. It is only to the degree that we are able to compare, in terms of evil, the actual world with what it seems plausible to suppose a God-made world would be like, or to compare the actual world with what it seems plausible to suppose a Godless world would be like, that certain facts of evil in the actual world can be interpreted as evidence against theism in the first place.

Inasmuch as it concerns these very grounding assumptions of the standard debate, we may think of this level of Hume's influence on that debate as the Ur-level. As such, it is not just contemporary atheistic or agnostic philosophers of religion—Flew, Gale, Mackie, Rowe, for instance—who work on the Humean model, but also some of the most prominent of their theistic opponents, at least in their counterarguments to the evil-based challenges to theism, for instance, Hick, Plantinga,[15] Swinburne. For, on both theistic and atheistic sides of the standard debate, it is either assumed or argued that a God-made world containing human beings would or would not have certain features found in the actual world—free will, order, natural evil, and so on—while not having others—gratuitous evil of a certain kind or quantity, for instance—that may or may not be found in the actual world.

Let us now bring together the two senses of evidentiary support of a theory discussed in the previous section with the two assumptions of the standard debate. In doing so let us focus on the second of those assumptions, inasmuch as it speaks of evidence supporting a conclusion. When we focus on that assumption in the context specified, we see that the assumption is open to two kinds of readings that, relative to one another, we may think of as strong and weak respectively. A strong reading is one on which the comparison of worlds spoken of in the first assumption is understood to provide, in principle even if not in practice, a basis for a *settlement* of the issue of God and evil one way or the other. By contrast, a weak reading will be one on which a more limited comparison of worlds is understood to provide a basis only for *sustaining* one side or the other, not for settling the disputed issue in favor of either one. And let it be understood that various degrees of strong and weak readings are possible.

These things being said, my two-stage argument in part 1, comprising the reformed logical argument and the indirect empirical argument issuing from it, is developed in context of a strong reading of the second assumption, although in neither argument do I claim actually to settle the question at issue. By contrast, my position in part 2 is tied to a weak reading of that same assumption. But that position is developed within a context where I take seriously the skeptical view that both assumptions of the standard debate must be repudiated. That being so, the following question naturally arises: in what ways, then, are *all* of my arguments in the spirit of Hume? The question is open to a broader interpretation as well, namely, as a question about how to characterize Hume's legacy to contemporary analytical philosophy of religion at large. On the one hand, the standard debate represents part, indeed a very important part, of Hume's legacy to the philosophy of religion. However, on the other hand, the recent repudiation of that debate within an influential segment of theism represents another part of his legacy. This latter point is the key to the answer to the question. Let us address the broader version of the question first—how to characterize Hume's legacy to contemporary analytical philosophy of religion.

Essentially the answer to it is that Hume is of two minds about epistemic relations between evil and theism, an ambivalence reflected in contemporary analytic philosophy of religion.[16] On the one hand, within the framework of the standard debate, Hume, as Philo, makes out a powerful case against the orthodox theistic attribution of moral qualities to God—"his justice, benevolence, mercy, and rectitude, [said] to be of the same nature with these virtues in human creatures"[17]—thus against the concept of God essential to OT. Among the lasting effects of this is the ascendency of negative evidentialism within analytic philosophy of religion. But, on the other hand, Hume, also as Philo, tempers that effect but without retracting any of the points made in favor of moral atheism, inasmuch as "such a limited intelligence [i.e., a human being] must be sensible of his own blindness and ignorance, and must allow that there may be many solutions of those phenomena which will forever escape his comprehension."[18]

Furthermore, in a related vein, and in his own voice, Hume maintains that "it seems evident that the dispute between the skeptics and dogmatists is entirely verbal, or, at least, regards only the degrees of doubt and assurance which we ought to indulge with regard to all reasoning; and such disputes are commonly, at the bottom, verbal and admit not of any precise determination."[19] The latter points contextualize Philo's successes by reminding us of their location within a framework that is not self-evident and is open to doubt. And it is that doubt about the capacities and limits of human understanding that is the wellspring of the current skeptical defenses of theism against arguments from inscrutable evil. In effect, then, Hume's two-mindedness reflects two levels of discourse—the first level reflects the assumptions of the standard debate, while the second level reflects a skepticism about the first level—and both are represented within contemporary analytical philosophy of religion. On the first level we engage directly with the problem of God and evil, but on the second level serious questions are raised about our ability in principle to make the kind of progress that, on the first level, we think we can make. And in the current debate, those second-level misgivings work to theism's advantage.

Now taking the question more narrowly, as a question about the Humean pedigree of this book, the answer is that not all of my arguments draw from the same part of Hume's thinking on the problem of evil. Most of those arguments are committed, strongly or weakly, to the Hume-inspired standard debate. But what makes the portion of my argument in part 2 that countenances outright rejection of the standard model Humean? This: it draws on the skeptical defense of theism set forth in recent years by Stephen J. Wykstra, William P. Alston, Peter van Inwagen, and others, and the skepticism in that line of defense traces to Hume, in particular, to his skepticism about the reach of human understanding. In different ways and to varying degrees, then, all my arguments in this book are Humean in spirit.

The denouement of the book is bilevel in that, first, if we operate strictly on the basis of the standard model, the two-stage argument in part 1 calls the epistemic credentials of OT into serious question, but second, if a Wykstralike skeptical defense is accepted, then OT is immunized against defeat by arguments from evil. But this immunization does not win for theism a victory over atheism, for that position too is undefeated. Like Hume, then, I am of two minds in this book: on the strong interpretation of the standard debate's operating assumptions, the antitheistic side has the better of the argument and gives us good reason to think theism is false; but on both the weak interpretation of those assumptions and the (non-Pyrrhonian) skeptical theist's repudiation of them, no such reason is forthcoming. But as my second thoughts are the dominant ones, my final position is that claims of victory and defeat must be tempered, such that, as Nicholas Rescher, in a different context, puts it, "[it is] altogether rational that we should endorse and rest content with the implications of the experiential perspective that is in fact ours," while simultaneously acknowledging in principle that others may rest content as well, even though the implications of *their* experiential perspectives are both different from ours and incompatible with them.[20]

Appendix: Who Speaks for Hume?

This appendix takes me a bit off track, insofar as the main line of argument in this book is concerned. The question I address here is (obviously) germane to my reading of Hume, thus to my casting the book's thesis in the spirit of Hume, but it is not germane to whether my thesis is true or false, adequately or inadequately supported. Thus, by those measurements, it could be skipped without loss to either my case or a reader's judgment on that case.

I claim to sound certain Humean notes in this book. And I draw principally from *Dialogues Concerning Natural Religion*. But, seeing that, when we exclude from consideration both of the *Dialogues'* minor characters, as well as Hume himself in the footnote quoted above, there are three voices in the *Dialogues*, and seeing that those voices are not in harmony with one another—certain agreements, or seeming agreements, between Demea and Philo, for instance, or between Cleanthes and Philo, to the contrary notwithstanding— how can I be justified in saying that I sound *Humean* notes, for who is to say for sure which notes are Humean?

It is obvious that in acknowledging as I do a certain indebtedness and fealty to Hume, I presuppose a certain interpretation of his thinking on religious belief, and especially his thinking on philosophical arguments that are used, whether as natural theology or defense, to support it. But, as this book is intended as neither a treatise on nor an examination of Hume's philosophy of religion, our digression in this appendix can be brief. Perhaps the best and most efficient way to reveal my interpretation of Hume's thinking on matters pertaining to the philosophy of religion is to answer the two following questions: who, in the *Dialogues*, speaks for Hume and what is that character's thinking?

But first a clarification of the question, "who speaks for Hume?" A natural interpretation of the question would be, "who *alone* speaks for Hume?" So taken, it would be equally natural to expect we should be able to put some main character or characters in the *Dialogues* to one side as not representing the author's views at all. In this vein, think of Hylas in Berkeley's *Three Dialogues between Hylas and Philonous* and of Euthyphro in Plato's dialogue that is named for him. But, in the present instance, I do not take the question of spokesmanship that way. Instead, I ask and answer it as the question, "who *principally* speaks for Hume?" In answering this version of the question, I follow Kemp Smith and more recently Gaskin, to a large extent, in maintaining that Philo principally speaks for Hume, but that other characters in the *Dialogues*, to the extent their thoughts are not inconsistent with Philo's, also speak in their master's voice. I shall include among those other voices Hume's own in the footnote to the text of the *Dialogues* quoted above.

In our present context, it seems inappropriate and unnecessary to enter into the long-standing dispute among Hume scholars over which character in the *Dialogues* is Hume, or closest to Hume. Thus, I do not argue here for the aforementioned relative preferment of Philo's as the main voice of the author. For I believe that, in several places, Gaskin has done so convincingly.[21]

If it were not for two things, both Philo's thinking on arguments for and against the existence of God and the acknowledgment of him as principal spokesman for the author would be clear. The first thing complicating this interpretation of Philo's thinking is that, while throughout most of the *Dialogues* he brings powerful skeptical arguments against theism—arguments that are consistent with Hume's skepticism in both *A Treatise of Human Nature* and the first *Inquiry*—he agrees with Demea that it is not the existence, but only the nature, of the deity that is in question, inasmuch as the *existence* of God is not open to serious question: "surely, where reasonable men treat these subjects, the question can never be concerning the *being* but only the *nature* of the Deity. The former truth, as you well observe, is unquestionable and self-evident."[22]

The second complication comes in part XII of the *Dialogues* with Philo's concession to the natural theologian, Cleanthes, against the run of play, so to speak, that, "notwithstanding the freedom of my conversation and my love of singular arguments, no one has a deeper sense of religion impressed on his mind, or pays more profound adoration to the Divine Being, as he discovers himself to reason in the inexplicable contrivance and artifice of nature," and, more important in the present context, "the existence of a Deity is plainly ascertained by reason."[23]

However, there is less to these complications than meets the eye. In addressing them it is useful to keep in mind, first, that "God" is an equivocal term and second, that the concepts "nature" and "existence," in the relevant sense of each, are importantly linked at a deep level. This is because, whenever we posit or deny the existence of something, we are positing or denying it as something with a certain nature and so as falling under a certain description. Thus, for instance, one person's theism may be atheism to another— Spinoza's unfortunate treatment at the hands of the Jewish authorities in Amsterdam in 1656 being a good illustration of how a version of the former could be taken for a version of the latter. So, if by "God" is meant the omnipotent, omniscient, perfectly good, infinite creator and sustainer of the universe, and even if the terms of debate do not reach beyond the nature of the deity to its existence, then it is clear from his skeptical arguments throughout the *Dialogues* that Philo, in the lines quoted above, is not committing himself to the existence of a god as defined just now, the God of Abrahamic religion. Indeed, as we saw, insofar as *that* concept of God is concerned, Hume, like Philo, is a moral atheist. But, while not admitting, in the lines quoted, the existence of God so understood, neither is Philo's position unequivocal atheism, where that means outright, unqualified denial of any kind of designer-creator of the world, nor is it complete agnosticism.

Arguably Gaskin guides us best here in portraying Hume's position as an attenuated deism. So construed, Philo's remark to Cleanthes in part XII of the *Dialogues* may be read frugally to mean that, while reason leads us to posit *some sort* of nonnatural designer-creator of the world, the evidence does not warrant positing the God of the Abrahamic religions. For, on Philo's interpretation of the available evidence, the attributes of this being are unknown to us. The furthest we are entitled to go is to say that, with regard to intelligence, there may be some remote similarity between us and the attenuated deistic creator. But Philo's, thus Hume's, skepticism about our ability to know the attributes of any nonnatural designer-creator only goes so far. Its most important limit becomes apparent in the case of the moral properties traditionally ascribed by theists to God. For, with respect to those, such skepticism is not appropriate. There we have good reason to deny that any being answers to the full theistic description of the God of Abraham, the God of orthodox theism.

Finally, the ambiguity in the term "God" suits Philo's purpose in certain places in the *Dialogues*, as, presumably, it suited Hume's in a place and time when explicit denial of the God of orthodox theism could reasonably be expected to bring on unpleasant consequences at best, and dangerous at worst.[24]

3

THEISM AND
GRATUITOUS EVIL

A basic assumption in the philosophical debate over God and evil, perhaps the most basic assumption, is that evil that seems to be gratuitous in the sense that we can discover no God-justifying point or reason for it represents a serious problem for theism.[1] But does it really? This is rarely asked as a serious question, perhaps because its answer is assumed to be too obvious to require justification. But certain contemporary attacks on the assumption establish that the question *is* serious, and even if the standard answer turns out to be right, as, with an amendment, I think it does, it is no longer permissible to believe that answer is self-evident and in need of no justification.

There are two main parts to the basic assumption, each of which is currently embattled. The first part is that, on virtually every formulation of theism, gratuitous evil is logically inconsistent with the existence of God, given the respective meanings of the terms "gratuitous evil" and "God." Let us think of this as the logical component in the assumption. The assumption's second part is epistemological. It is that evils for which we can discern no God-justifying reason are evils that we have good reason to think *have* no such reason and so, given the logical component, are evils that we have good reason to think are logically inconsistent with the existence of God. And if both of these points are true, evils for which we can discover no God-justifying reason *do* pose a potentially deadly threat to theism. But maybe neither point is true. In this chapter we will

49

examine challenges to the logical point, and in part 2, a challenge to the epistemological.

The prominent contemporary challenges to the logical component come from William Hasker, George N. Schlesinger, and Peter van Inwagen.[2] I discuss Hasker's and van Inwagen's arguments here, and Schlesinger's in chapter 7. My reason to postpone discussion of Schlesinger's argument is that it is an essential part of his overall defense of orthodox theism against arguments from evil, and in chapter 7 I discuss that defense as a whole. Thus, postponement saves repetition. Schlesinger's position aside, then, in this chapter I show, first, that the proposition "God and gratuitous natural evil are logically inconsistent with one another" does not succumb to Hasker's attack upon it, and second, that while van Inwagen arguably gives us good reason to restrict the scope of that proposition, he does not give us good reason to judge it false simpliciter.

Back to Basics

It is implicit in the concept of a good person that he or she, as much as possible, avoids permitting or doing evil and permits or does good instead. Insofar as human persons are concerned, even good persons sometimes do or permit, or have to do or permit, harmful or hurtful things: for instance, causing pain to a child while setting a cast on his broken leg. Furthermore, we recognize that sometimes even the good intentions of a good human being fail, and that, for instance, he or she does not work as carefully or behave as conscientiously as he or she could. We acknowledge such things, and others like them, as part of our human condition, and we temper our understanding of what constitutes a good human person accordingly. In the concept of a good human person, then, there is provision for our natural frailties and limitations.

Our concept of God, as that concept is reflected in the Abrahamic religions and focused here in OT, is drawn in large part from an analogy to our concept of a human person. God, then, is understood to be a person, although not suffering from the shortcomings implicit in being a human person. Consistent with this, all of the divine attributes that are relevant in the philosophical debate over theism and evil—power, knowledge, benevolence, freedom, and so on—are to be understood analogically. So, for instance, the theistic belief about divine goodness is that, while hugely exceeding ours, it is not so different from ours that the word "goodness," as we use it of some of our own intentions, actions, and omissions, simply has no application at all to the goodness of God. On the analogy at the core of theism, the difference in degree is never so great as to be tantamount to a difference in kind, thereby making attribution of goodness to God wholly unintelligible to us. To take a single illustration: if our conception of human goodness is broadly utilitarian, then we will tend to see God as the supreme maximizer of utility; if our concept of human goodness is other than utilitarian, so will be our conception of the goodness of God.

The strength of the analogy between divine and human attributes is important, for, if the analogy is either weak or admitted to be weak, then orthodox theism's credentials as a theory able to contend in a serious way with rival naturalistic theories will be proportionately weak or admitted to be so. If the analogy is vague, imprecise, or tangential, then theistic descriptions of God in terms of power, knowledge, goodness, and so on will suffer accordingly. And if that is so, then the theory cannot rightly claim to deserve serious and respectful consideration, inasmuch as the concept of God is central to it. Thus, if, under attack, the philosophical proponent of theism seeks safety in obscurantism by insisting on the frailty and tenuousness of the analogies giving meaning to the key attributes predicated of the deity, then the theory's cognitive credentials will suffer proportionately.

As we find the concept of God in the Abrahamic religions, God's goodness or benevolence never fail God. They could not, for, in the Abrahamic mainstream of the monotheistic tradition, God is understood to be *essentially* good and *essentially* benevolent. In addition, God is understood to be essentially omnipotent and essentially omniscient. Essential omnipotence is consistent with God's being unable to do certain things, even a large number of things—determining the free choice of a free being, for instance—and likewise, essential omniscience may be compatible with God's being ignorant of certain things, the future perhaps. In short, the concept of God articulated in OT is not the concept of a being who is absolutely unrestricted. Thus, there might be evils that God could not, consistent with some aspect of God's nature, prevent. But, in any such case, God would have a morally sufficient reason for either permitting or not preventing the evil in question. So, while the concept of God we are considering may not be incompatible with the existence of evil per se, it is a virtual orthodoxy among philosophers of religion that the concept of God is incompatible with avoidable evil, divinely avoidable evil in particular. By avoidable or preventable evil I mean evil that could be avoided or prevented without thereby forfeiting any greater or outweighing good. Let us refer to such evil as gratuitous evil. In a word, then, the consensus is that gratuitous evil is incompatible with God, as God is standardly understood within the mainstream of the monotheistic tradition. This opinion enjoys virtual unanimity among philosophers of religion, as I expect it does both among theologians as well as laypeople who might think on the matter. It is the established position, the status quo. It is the position that, subject to a restriction discussed in the fourth section below, I defend in this chapter.

Typically, the theistic response to arguments from evil is that, despite its seeming to be so, the evil cited as evidence in a particular antitheistic argument is not gratuitous at all. Or, more weakly, but still sufficient to defend theism, the response is that the seemingly gratuitous evil cited as evidence is not shown to be gratuitous. But William Hasker takes a quite different approach. His position is that the two concepts, "gratuitous evil," on the one hand, and "God," as the concept is used in orthodox theism, on the other, are simply not logically inconsistent with one another at all. That being so, his position is that the standard philosophical debate on the problem of evil is seriously misguided on a fundamental issue.

If Hasker is right, three consequences are clear: OT will have to reformulate some key aspects of its thinking on God's relations with the world, the negative evidentialist cast of the philosophical problem of evil will be effectively undermined, and this book's thesis will be blocked. The theodical problem of explaining why certain evils exist in a God-made world would still remain a live problem if no gratuitous evil is logically inconsistent with God, but the relatively more fundamental problem of *defending* theism against arguments from prima facie gratuitous evil would be nullified. Clearly, then, apart from the other features of Hasker's position that make it interesting, it puts a lot at stake insofar as the evidentialist, and especially the negative evidentialist, cast of the problem of evil is concerned.

A parenthetical point as we begin examination of Hasker's argument: at several points in this book I have expressed my position on God and gratuitous evil with a qualification, namely, that God and gratuitous evil *of a certain kind* are not mutually consistent. Implicit in this is a concession that perhaps not all kinds or instances of gratuitous evil are inconsistent with God. I make that concession explicit in the fourth section below. But neither the concession nor the differentiation among types or tokens of gratuitous evils that is the basis of it is necessary for discussion of Hasker's arguments. For his position is that the proposition "God and gratuitous evil are mutually inconsistent" is false for *any* type or token of gratuitous evil.

Hasker's Arguments

Hasker begins his challenge to the established position as follows: "it seems to many to be almost self-evident that a good God would not allow gratuitous evil. But arguments for this contention are not easy to come by, and I think it may well be possible to show that theism requires nothing of the sort."[3]

Specifically, his argument is that belief in the mutual inconsistency of God and gratuitous evil is not just not self-evident, but false. For much of his argument he concentrates on whether gratuitous moral evil is logically inconsistent with God. Here, however, as the focus of my interest is those evils resulting from the operations of natural processes themselves alone, I shall discuss only his arguments for the proposition that God and gratuitous natural evil are not logically inconsistent with one another.

The concept of God in Hasker's argument is the orthodox theistic one, while the concept of gratuitous evil that he uses is evil "such that an omnipotent being could have prevented it without thereby having prevented the occurrence of some greater good."[4] While discussing certain views of William L. Rowe's, Hasker describes such evil as *genuinely* gratuitous evil, which he then distinguishes from ostensibly gratuitous evil. In his words, let us designate as genuinely gratuitous evils those . . . evils which could have been prevented by an omnipotent being without losing any greater good. And let us use the term "ostensibly gratuitous evils" to designate evils which could be prevented by God without thereby preventing the existence of any greater good, *apart from the benefit God's permission of such evils may have in preventing the undermining of morality.*[5]

The difference between genuinely and ostensibly gratuitous natural evil, then, is that the former is natural evil whose permission by God is not necessary to the occurrence of any greater goods *whatever*, while the latter is natural evil whose permission by God is necessary to prevent the undermining of morality but is not necessary to the occurrence of any *other* greater good.[6] (Two parenthetical points: first, in the wider literature on the problem of God and evil, gratuitous evil is standardly understood as what, after Hasker, in this chapter we will now call genuinely gratuitous evil; second, I spoke earlier of prima facie gratuitous evils, that is, evils that seem to us to be gratuitous inasmuch as they are evils for which we are not able to discern any point or justification which would justify God in permitting or not preventing them. That is not the same concept as Hasker's concept of ostensibly gratuitous evil. For the former is evil that seems to be *genuinely* gratuitous, and in some cases arguably is.) In the case of natural evil, then, Hasker is undertaking to show that God and genuinely gratuitous natural evil are not mutually inconsistent.

For brevity and conciseness, let us refer to genuinely gratuitous natural evil as GGNE and to ostensibly gratuitous natural evil as OGNE, and for the same reasons let us cast Hasker's thinking in terms of possible worlds. So cast, Hasker's route to his conclusion is through arguments to establish that there is no possible world in which God, consistent with God's nature or with God's objectives in world making, could prevent the occurrence of all GGNE. Hasker approaches this task in "what if?" fashion. Specifically, what if God *did* prevent all GGNE? Hasker's point is that, in any possible world PW, if God prevented all GGNE, an outcome inconsistent with God's nature or goals in world making and world governance would result, thus that God could not prevent all GGNE. And if it is logically impossible for God to prevent all GGNE, then God has a morally sufficient reason to not prevent all GGNE.

Hasker's arguments to that conclusion are divisible into two groups, the first consisting of two arguments that examine implications of our not knowing that God prevents all GGNE in PW, while the second consists of a single argument examining implications of our *knowing* that God prevents all GGNE in PW. The object of the three arguments is the same: to establish that God and GGNE are not mutually exclusive. I shall begin with the third of these arguments, namely, an argument to show that God and GGNE are not mutually exclusive in a world where both God prevents all GGNE and we know it.

Knowing that God Prevents All Genuinely Gratuitous Natural Evil

To the question, what would be the consequences if God were known to prevent all GGNE?, Hasker answers:

> it is evident that the consequences with regard to the list of goods noted above—knowledge, prudence, courage, foresight, cooperation, and compassion—would be rather drastic. Surely the motivation to acquire and/or respond in accordance with any or all of these goods would be greatly reduced, if not eliminated entirely, if we *really believed* that God would prevent any natural evils which were not essential to the realization of still greater goods. To be sure, we might still have some inclination to avoid outcomes that seemed especially distasteful to us personally—but such an inclination would be of questionable rationality, inasmuch as by preventing those outcomes we would also be preventing the occurrence of goods which are at least equal and possibly greater.[7]

This is to say that, if God both prevents all GGNE in PW and we know it, morality is undermined in PW. Thus, if the occurrence of morality is a divine desideratum in designing and creating a world with free human beings in it, and according to OT it is, then it could not be true in PW that God both prevents all GGNE and we know it. In essence, that is Hasker's argument.

To facilitate discussion of this argument, let us distinguish between:

(i)   God is known to prevent all GGNE in PW, inasmuch as God is known to prevent all natural evil in PW

and

(ii) God is known to prevent all GGNE in PW, but there is still natural evil in PW, thus what is known is that all the natural evil in PW is necessary to the occurrence of greater goods, specifically, in the present context, necessary to the maintenance of significant morality (or, more weakly, necessary to the maintenance of the possibility of significant morality). Here, then, it is known that all the natural evil in PW is OGNE, as that is defined by Hasker.[8]

It is clear from his text that it is (ii), not (i), that reflects Hasker's understanding of what we know, if we know that God prevents all GGNE in PW. So, I examine his argument on the basis of (ii) and not (i). Furthermore, let us concentrate on the greater goods at issue in Hasker's argument, namely, moral goods such as courage, prudence, compassion, and tolerance.

When (ii) is true in PW, Hasker thinks that in combatting and counteracting the natural evil that exists in that world (namely, the OGNE remaining once GGNE has been prevented)—for instance, by combatting and curing disease, by alleviating pain and suffering, and so on—we would be preventing the occurrence of those possibly greater moral goods for which (or for the possibility of which) that natural evil is necessary. As he put it in the passage quoted just above, "by preventing those outcomes [i.e., instances of OGNE in PW] we would also be preventing the occurrence of goods which are at least equal and possibly greater."

In a purely logical sense, Hasker is right. We can see this plainly in the following example having nothing whatever to do with morality: with the presence here of oxygen being a necessary condition for the occurrence here of fire, if I prevent oxygen from being present here, I prevent the occurrence here of fire. By parity of reasoning, then, it would seem that, by preventing OGNE in PW, we are preventing those greater goods—courage, compassion, tolerance,

and so on—for whose occurrence OGNE is necessary. But, with regard to the connection between the existence of OGNE and the
occurrence of such goods, things are not what they seem, as the
following illustration shows.

Let Socrates be a person now suffering great pain from a conta-
gious disease for which neither he nor anybody else is responsible
in the moral sense. In short, to avoid confusing our discussion with
issues peripheral to it, both Socrates' disease and pain are natural
evils issuing just from the operations of natural processes themselves
alone. Given that Socrates is suffering in PW, where there is known
to be no GGNE, we, knowing that, know that Socrates' pain is a
natural evil that is ostensibly (but not genuinely) gratuitous. We are
moved by Socrates' pain and treat it. Our intention in treating his
pain is to alleviate it. Our intention and action, in short, are moral.
Suppose we succeed, and Socrates' pain is alleviated. Being an instance of OGNE, Socrates' pain is a necessary condition of the occurrence of certain instances of such goods as courage, compassion,
and so on, and so, by alleviating his pain—in Hasker's term, by preventing it (in the present context, the prevention is of the pain's
continuation)—we prevent certain future instances of those goods.
For instance, we prevent my courageously, compassionately, prudently, heroically treating his pain tomorrow. But there is something
very queer in describing our being moved by, and our treatment
and alleviation of, Socrates' pain as, in Hasker's earlier-quoted
words, only "an inclination to avoid outcomes that seemed especially distasteful to us personally . . . an inclination . . . of questionable rationality, inasmuch as by preventing those outcomes we
would also be preventing the occurrence of goods which are at least
equal and possibly greater."

Where does the queerness lie? Here: by being moved by, treating,
and alleviating (preventing) Socrates' pain as we did, and with the
motivation we had, *we are instantiating precisely those greater moral goods*
for which, in this case, Socrates' pain, as OGNE, is necessary—
courage (given the known risk of contagion), compassion, prudence, and so on. The point is open to generalization: preventing
OGNE in cases such as the present is precisely the occurrence of
the greater moral goods for which OGNE is necessary. Thus, it is
false to believe, simpliciter, that prevention of OGNE entails the

prevention of those greater goods. Of course, as already observed, if we today alleviate (prevent) Socrates' suffering, and noncontroversially assuming that this alleviation has a lasting effect, we *do* prevent my alleviation of it tomorrow when it might be even worse and, accordingly, more difficult to alleviate. So, in that sense, we *do* prevent the occurrence of a greater good. But it is perverse to characterize this as, in Hasker's words, only avoiding "outcomes that seemed especially distasteful to us personally . . . [and] . . . of questionable rationality."

The perversity is twofold: first, if we avoid alleviating Socrates' pain today so that you or I can do it with greater expenditure of moral effort tomorrow, we are condemning Socrates to extra suffering in the meantime. Second, *every* time anybody alleviates another's suffering, potentially the occurrence of greater moral good tomorrow is prevented.

My argument turns on, and may be expressed in terms of, a distinction between two kinds of prevention. For lack of better terms, I shall refer to these as pre-emptive prevention and responsive prevention. If, in PW, all OGNE is pre-emptively prevented, then there never is any OGNE in PW. Thus, there could be no such moral goods in that world as courage, compassion, fortitude, and so on. And, given God's values and desiderata in world making, such a world could never be actualized by God. But now consider responsive prevention. Pain and suffering occur in PW and we respond by trying to alleviate them, that is, by trying to prevent their continuation and future occurrence. But, as we saw just above, this response (and, if we are successful, prevention of their continuation) is precisely the realization of the greater moral goods at issue. Thus it is the realization of an important divine desideratum in world making, namely, significant morality. Furthermore, as pain and suffering are not diminishing resources, our alleviation (responsive prevention) of any specific instance is not the pre-emptive prevention of all future pain and suffering (which, in PW as presently described, is future OGNE). Thus, ample opportunity is provided by our responsive prevention of OGNE for future instances of courage, compassion, and so on. Thus Hasker's argument fails.

At this point, we may anticipate the following objection. Although it is true that Socrates will suffer more if we do not help him than if we do, his extra suffering, while a gratuitous natural evil, will not be a *genuinely* gratuitous natural evil, for, ex hypothesi, no natural evil in PW is GGNE. And we, knowing that no natural evil in PW is genuinely gratuitous, know that Socrates' extra suffering is not genuinely gratuitous. Thus, and this is the point of the objection, we are not morally obliged to help him.[9] Nor, for the same reason, are we morally obliged to ever help anybody in PW who is suffering. And so, the objection concludes, Hasker is right, in the passage quoted earlier, when he says

> surely the motivation to acquire and/or to respond in accordance with any or all of these goods [knowledge, prudence, courage, foresight, cooperation, compassion, and so on] would be greatly reduced, if not eliminated entirely, if we *really believed* that God would prevent any natural evils which were not essential to the realization of still greater goods.

Let us examine this objection. In the situation as described, our choice is between helping and not helping Socrates who is suffering. As described, the situation is one in which we must choose and in which, whatever we do, we either help him or not. The options before us bring two possible successor-worlds to PW into prospect, PW1 and PW2, one alone of which will be set in process by our choice and action, inasmuch as PW1 and PW2 are mutually exclusive. PW becomes PW1 when we help Socrates, and PW becomes PW2 when we do not. The subsequent histories of these two possible worlds will diverge, but, notwithstanding any and all differences, PW1 and PW2 share an interesting ontological feature, namely, neither one contains any GGNE. The thinking reflected in the objection is that our knowing they are alike in that ontological respect means there is no significant moral difference between our options as we confront the suffering Socrates. But that is false. Let us see why.

In choosing, all we know for sure is that, whether we help Socrates or not, there will be no GGNE. This knowledge is the pivot of the objection that is before us. Now, if this piece of knowledge were the sole, or overwhelmingly the most important, factor relevant to the choice we must make, there would be something to the objection. But in fact this piece of knowledge is neither. Indeed, it is arguably the case that our knowledge that there will be no GGNE, whichever option we choose, is neutral between the two options. The reason for thinking this is the following. On the one hand, there is the Hasker-derived idea that, because we know no GGNE will result from our not helping Socrates, we are not obligated to help him, and that, furthermore, we may, in good conscience, ignore his plight, even though we know he will have to endure extra suffering that we could have prevented. But, on the other hand, there is the idea that, because we know that, if we help him, we run no risk of inadvertently causing him (or anybody else) gratuitous harm, a possible inhibitor of our helping him is removed, namely, the fear that we might unintentionally cause him (or another) needless suffering. In my view, the latter idea—a variation on the medical maxim, "first, do no harm"—is at least as plausible as the former, arguably more so. If I am right about this, there is at a minimum rough equality between, on the one hand, the tendency of our knowing there will be no GGNE to discourage our helping Socrates and, on the other, the tendency of that knowledge to encourage our helping him. If I am right about this, that knowledge is not a decisive factor. The question then is what factors, if any, *are* decisive. The following items are, and they establish that, in the situation as described, our moral obligation is to help Socrates.

Notwithstanding the fact that there is no GGNE in either PW1 or PW2, and notwithstanding the fact that, in PW2, Socrates' suffering is not gratuitous, Socrates (as well as everybody else) can still be harmed in both successor worlds, and harmed more in one world than in the other. There being no GGNE in either world does not entail that Socrates' (or anybody's) lot will be equally happy in both. Furthermore, from the fact that there is no GGNE in either successor-world, it does not follow that there is not more natural evil overall in one than the other. In PW2 we do not help Socrates, despite his suffering and our ability to help through prevention of his extra suffering. Suppose now that our failure to help Socrates is not just an ad hoc omission but instead that it reflects a maxim we live by: never help anybody in pain, for no pain is genuinely gratuitous natural evil. In PW2, then, we do not exercise or develop the moral goods in question. Suppose also that we are orthodox theists committed to a life of trust in God and of doing God's will as we understand it. On the subject of what, in world making, God wants to achieve, Hasker tells us that "the maintenance of significant morality is *an overriding concern* in the divine governance of the world."[10] But surely a world with significant morality is a world in which human beings *do* give preference to acting compassionately, prudently, charitably, courageously, and so on over not acting in those ways. In short, with the maintenance of significant morality being an overriding concern of God's in world making and world governance, God would want any world containing human beings to be a world with the best possible ratio of prudence, tolerance, compassion, courage, selflessness, and so on to imprudence, intolerance, un-compassion, cowardice, selfishness, and so on.

In now drawing together the factors I set forth above—knowledge that, despite the nonexistence of GGNE, there can be, and prima facie is, more natural evil in one possible world than another; knowledge that Socrates, like any sentient being, can be harmed more in one possible world than another; knowledge that, prima facie he *is* harmed more in PW2 than in PW1; knowledge that, if we are theists, God's will is that we practice and develop those moral virtues mentioned; knowledge that, if we practice some of those virtues in this case, Socrates will be harmed less than he would otherwise have been—we find them converging to show that our moral duty is to help Socrates and to not ignore his suffering.

In both drawing and buttressing this conclusion about what is the right thing to do in the Socrates situation, as described, it is worth noting Hasker's quotation of the following lines from William Frankena's *Ethics*: "moral reasons consist of facts about what actions, dispositions, and persons do to the lives of sentient beings, including beings other than the agent in question, and the moral point of view is one which is concerned with such facts."[11] Hasker then continues in his own voice:

> this claim of Frankena's is not uncontroversial, but it seems to me that it enjoys strong intuitive support. Frankena's principle . . . say[s] that morally relevant reasons must *in some way* have to do with the tendency of the action in question, or the class of actions of that kind, to do good or harm to sentient beings. And it seems to me that this is correct—that if we become

convinced that certain ostensibly moral requirements or prohibitions have *no connection whatever* with the weal or woe of any rational or sentient being, then we soon cease to regard such commands or prohibitions as morally serious. . . . If this principle of Frankena's is correct, it establishes a very close connection between the notion of a *morally wrong action* and the idea of *harm* to some person or other sentient being. And this, in turn, suggests two requirements which must be met in the lives of persons who have significant obligations towards others. First of all, it must be *possible* for these persons to act in ways that are significantly harmful to themselves and others. . . . Furthermore, they must be able to *know* that it is possible for them to act harmfully.[12]

I agree with Hasker about Frankena's principle, and I emphasize that, in the Socrates test case before us, both of Hasker's requirements for a morally wrong action are met, namely, the possibility of harming others and knowledge of that possibility. Thus, knowing all that we know in the situation as described, if we fail to help Socrates, we are harming him, notwithstanding our knowledge of the fact that there is still no GGNE in PW2. Thus, in ignoring his extra suffering, we are committing a morally wrong action. Thus, the objection to my argument fails. The objection defeated, let us return to our discussion of Hasker's argument that God and GGNE are not mutually exclusive in a world where both God prevents all GGNE and we know it.

Hasker's case for that conclusion is open to a different counterargument as well. For the sake of argument, let us agree with him that, in world making and world governance, God's overriding concern is the maintenance of significant morality. (This agreement is just for the sake of argument, for the position I would advocate as being OT's is weaker, namely, that in world making and world governance, God's overriding concern is the maintenance of the possibility of significant morality.) In PW, then, that is God's overriding concern. In PW, as hypothesized, we know that no natural evil is genuinely gratuitous, that all natural evil is necessary to the occurrence of greater moral goods. Thus, in PW, unless we respond morally to OGNE, God's goal in actualizing PW—the maintenance in it of significant morality—cannot be met. For, while OGNE is necessary for the occurrence of those greater goods in question here, it is not sufficient for their occurrence. Furthermore, knowing what we know, we know that, without our responding to OGNE in a certain way, God's goal could not be met. Thus, we know that in PW our responding to OGNE in a certain way *really matters*, that it has important consequences. Would not that knowledge enhance our motivation to respond to OGNE in that way? It seems to me clear that the answer is yes, inasmuch as we would not believe that, in the big scheme of things, our responding compassionately, courageously, prudently, tolerantly, gently, and so on amounts to nothing. Now it is a clear fact of our experience that a belief in the pointlessness or futility or inevitable failure of a contemplated action is a serious inhibitor of motivation to act. But in PW, knowing what we would know, our motivation would not be inhibited in that way at all. Thus, contrary to Hasker, our moral motivation would not be sapped: arguably it would be strengthened.

Before switching to his two other arguments, a final thought on our knowing that, in PW, there is no genuinely gratuitous natural evil. Is not such a world significantly akin to the actual world, as the actual world is understood within orthodox theism? That is, is it not a central precept of OT that in the actual world, notwithstanding its seeming to be genuinely gratuitous, all natural evil is really only ostensibly gratuitous, and so justified in a God-made world: for instance by its being necessary to the occurrence of some balancing or greater good?[13] Hasker seems to agree that this is a standard theistic belief, albeit one he thinks both unnecessary and unhelpful to theism, but, up till now, standard nonetheless. In his words, "it seems to many [presumably theists included] to be almost self-evident that a good God would not allow gratuitous evil."[14]

But the orthodox theist, believing that, in the final analysis, all natural evil is OGNE, is not robbed of motivation to acquire or respond in accordance with moral goods. Nor, as my arguments have shown, should he or she be. The obvious question to put to Hasker, though, is whether it is an intended consequence of his position that theists' moral motivation rests on a mistake.

Not Knowing that God Prevents All Genuinely Gratuitous Natural Evil

Let us now take up Hasker's two other arguments on the subject of God and gratuitous natural evil. Unlike the argument discussed in the section above, the presumption in each of these arguments is that we do *not* know that all natural evil is really only OGNE, although in fact it is. According to Hasker, this ignorance preserves our motivation to acquire moral goods, thus, in the possible world under consideration, this ignorance is of great importance to God. However, Hasker argues, our being and remaining ignorant of the fact that all natural evil is really OGNE in PW would necessitate a certain strategy on God's part, a strategy whose principal component would be a disinformation campaign.[15] But, Hasker continues, it would be impossible for God to engage in such a campaign, as it would be simultaneously "morally dubious in itself" and at cross-purposes with one of God's chief aims in creating free rational beings.[16] Thus Hasker concludes that God, consistent with God's nature or with God's goals in world making, could not engage in such a campaign. Thus, we would not remain ignorant of the fact that God (pre-emptively) prevents all GGNE in PW. Thus, in the argument of Hasker's we considered in the section above, morality would be undermined. Thus, again, God could not prevent all genuinely gratuitous natural evil in PW, leaving only ostensibly gratuitous natural evil. Thus, God and GGNE are not mutually inconsistent.

As noted, the two arguments of Hasker's we are now considering end up depending on his first argument. But as that first argument was shown to fail, the two other arguments fail as well. Notwithstanding that, however, let us examine each of those other arguments on its own terms. In doing so, we will find that they fail for other reasons too.

The key to both of these arguments—the first leading to the conclusion of moral dubiousness, the second leading to the cross-purposes conclusion—is Hasker's assumption that, to assure our ignorance of his prevention of GGNE in PW, God would have to pursue a strategy involving a disinformation campaign. Let us, then, examine that assumption. The assumption turns on the idea that, if God prevents GGNE in PW, we would, in the normal course of events, know it. That is, it would be unnatural for us to not know it.

As Hasker sees it, then, a possible world in which God prevents all GGNE will be, in its essentials, the possible world I shall call PW3.

PW3 is a possible world in which the development and maintenance of significant morality is an overriding concern of God's. In PW3 there is the same amount, variety, and distribution of moral evil as in the actual world, and likewise the same amount, variety, and distribution of both OGNE and GGNE as in the actual world, assuming that the actual world does in fact contain GGNE. That is, to begin with, PW3 is the actual world in respect of evil. Then God removes all the GGNE from PW3 and prevents its recurrence. In removing GGNE from PW3, God would be removing a large and significant amount of natural evil, and so, naturally, if events ran their normal course, we, the human inhabitants of PW3, would notice the absence of GGNE—how could we not?—and so would come to know that all natural evil is only OGNE.[17] However, events do not run their normal course in PW3, for God intervenes to prevent our knowing about his removal of GGNE. The intervention is the disinformation campaign that Hasker has in mind.

The focus of my challenge to the foregoing argument of Hasker's is its central idea, namely, that, unless God prevents us by means of disinformation, we will know that God has prevented all GGNE in PW3. Here is a counterexample of a possible world, containing all the relevant divine desiderata that apply to both PW3 and the actual world, but necessitating no disinformation campaign to conceal the fact that God has prevented all GGNE. Let us refer to this possible world as PW4.

PW4 is a possible world in which the development and maintenance of significant morality is an overriding concern of God's, and in it there is no, and never was any, GGNE, inasmuch as, from the start, or at least before human beings appeared on the scene, God pre-emptively prevented GGNE in PW4. However, PW4 does contain the same amount, variety, and distribution of both moral evil and OGNE as both PW3 and the actual world. We, the human inhabitants of PW4, never know that there is no GGNE in PW4, nor is there any good reason to think that, in the normal run of things, we would ever discover it, for, in PW4, things being the way they are would be perfectly natural to us. In PW4, God does not inform us that, right from the start, he has prevented GGNE, just as, for instance, in the actual world God keeps us in the dark about the origin and ultimate fate of the actual world, and there is nothing morally shady about God's silence on any of these matters. PW4, then, is a possible world in which all GGNE is prevented by God and in which we, without benefit of disinformation or any other kind of deceit, do not know it. In PW4, we would be as morally motivated as we are in the actual world, which is to say that morality in PW4 would be no more undermined than it is in the actual world.[18]

With PW3 and PW4 in mind, let us go back to Hasker's argument. Hasker is right that God could not actualize PW3, for God, consistent with God's nature, could not engage in deception. But from the fact that God could not actualize PW3, it does not follow that God could not, without deception, actualize a world without GGNE but with full provision for significant morality, for God could actualize PW4 (or the actual world, if the actual world contains no GGNE by virtue of God's having pre-emptively prevented the occurrence of any GGNE in the actual world). Thus, in a world where all GGNE had been prevented, the dilemma Hasker foresees and on which his argument is predicated, namely, divine deception or no significant morality, is a false dilemma. Thus, Hasker's argument fails.

The second of Hasker's two arguments predicated on our not knowing that God prevents all GGNE is that, in actualizing a world in which we do not know God prevents all GGNE, God would be undermining one of his own chief purposes in creating free rational beings, namely, that those beings should freely come to knowledge of God, or at least have full opportunity of doing so, including knowledge that, "it is just *because* God is an omnipotent, omniscient, wholly good being that there cannot be [GGNE]."[19]

Hasker thinks this because of his assumption that it is only by deceit that we could be kept from knowing that God had prevented all GGNE. The conjunction of these two points is that God would be in the impossible position of simultaneously wanting us both to know and not know that he prevents GGNE. So, as acting at cross-purposes is an outcome of the disinformation campaign, God could not engage in such a campaign, for acting at cross-purposes is inconsistent with God's essential nature. But then we would know both that there was no GGNE and that all natural evil was OGNE, and, knowing this, we would be robbed of moral motivation (or so the argument of Hasker's that we first considered in the section above tells it).

In response I shall make two points. First, if God does prevent us knowing he has prevented GGNE, and granting that it is among God's purposes in creating free rational beings such as we that we come to know him in the way specified by Hasker, then of course Hasker is right: God would be acting at cross-purposes. But, in being predicated on the idea that God would have to prevent our coming to know he had prevented all GGNE, Hasker's present argument is committed to a conception such as PW3. But, as we saw, with PW4 and the actual world (assuming they are different) available as better alternatives, PW3 is not a possible world that God could actualize. Hence, this argument of Hasker's is undermined. And second, as we have already seen, given the availability of a possible world such as PW4, all that would be required of God to guarantee our not knowing that he had pre-emptively prevented the occurrence of GGNE would be an *uninformation* campaign, not a disinformation campaign, and there is nothing morally dubious in that. So, consistent with God's perfect goodness, having actualized PW4, God could remain silent about it without moral shadiness. The relevance of this point to the present argument is now this: with God remaining silent about God's prevention of GGNE, we, the human inhabitants of PW4, would be in precisely the same position with respect to God's desire that we should come to know God, including our coming to know the fact that, from God's nature, God prevents GGNE, as are we, the human inhabitants of the actual world. Thus, in actualizing either PW4 or the actual world, God would not be acting at cross-purposes, and so Hasker's third argument fails.

It might be thought that, as follows, Hasker's position can be saved after all. With all natural evil in PW being ostensibly gratuitous natural evil, no natural evil in PW is inconsistent with God or with PW's being a God-made world. For, with all the natural evil in PW being necessary to the occurrence of greater goods, there is a morally sufficient reason for God to permit all the natural evil that there is in PW. With that being so, might not the following defense of Hasker's position be made? That, in granting OGNE in PW to be consistent with God, I grant Hasker his case, namely, that God and gratuitous natural evil are not mutually inconsistent. But that defense, if made, would fail: for that conclusion, if drawn, would be unjustified. For OGNE is *ostensibly* gratuitous natural evil, that is, natural evil that seems to be gratuitous but that, in fact, is not, for it is evil that is necessary for the occurrence of some greater good. Thus, it is not gratuitous, really or genuinely gratuitous, at all. It is only gratuitous natural evil manque. And so Hasker's position cannot be saved in this way.

Hasker has another strategy, too. He maintains, assuming for the sake of argument that he is successful in showing that genuinely gratuitous *moral* evil is not inconsistent with God, that he is not obliged to succeed with regard to genuinely gratuitous *natural* evil.[20] But, even if he is successful with regard to genuinely gratuitous moral evil, he must still succeed with GGNE. The reason is this.

While the problem of evil comes in many versions, each of those versions, broadly speaking, is articulated in either a specified or an unspecified form, as I used those terms in the first chapter. The argument is put in unspecified form when what is maintained is that evil as such is incompatible with God, and it is in specified form when the claim is that some particular facts of evil are incompatible with God. Success in defense is measured in proportion to the argument (or attack) being defended against. That is a truism, but it is an important truism. Thus, in the former case, a defense is successful when it is able to show either that some evil or other—that is to say, any evil at all—is not incompatible with God, or that, for internal reasons, the particular antitheistic argument in question fails to deliver its conclusion, while in the latter case a defense is successful when it is able to show either that whatever particular fact of evil is at issue is not incompatible with God, or again that, for internal reasons, the particular antitheistic argument in question fails to establish its conclusion. Apart from that "internal reasons" line of defense, a theistic defense could establish either directly or indirectly that a specified argument fails: directly, by establishing that the particular fact or facts of evil cited are not inconsistent with God, and indirectly, by establishing that no facts of evil are inconsistent with God. Hasker and Schlesinger offer an extreme form of the indirect strategy, inasmuch as, for both of them, no actual or possible fact of evil is inconsistent with God.

Equipped with these distinctions, let us now go back to Hasker's idea that success in showing that genuinely gratuitous moral evil is not inconsistent with God would win him success with regard to GGNE, too. The following point made by Swinburne will help us to see why it would not:

> it follows that if theodicy [or a defense] is to show that God is justified in allowing each of the actual evils of this world *e* which occur, it needs to show that (1) in allowing *e* (or an evil equally bad) to occur, God would bring about a logically necessary condition of some good state of affairs *g* which could not be achieved in any other morally permissible way; (2) if *e* occurs, *g* is realised, (3) it is morally permissible that God allow *e* to occur, (4) the comparative condition is satisfied. Now theodicy [or a defense] cannot be required to show this in respect of every actual evil in the world if it is to show that the appearance that evil counts against God's existence is mistaken. It is surely enough to show that these conditions are satisfied in respect of typical members of the main classes of observable evils in the world; that would be grounds enough for supposing that these conditions are satisfied generally. By analogy, no scientist needs to show that every observable mechanical datum is as Newton's theory predicts, if he is to be justified in believing Newton's theory. He needs only to show that typical members of the main classes of observable mechanical data are as Newton's theory predicts. And as for the scientist, so for the theodicist [and defender], "show" means only "demonstrate that it is probable."[21]

Swinburne's point is well taken. To use his term, moral evil is certainly one of "the main classes of observable evils in the world." But natural evil is another main class. Hence, success with the former—assuming, for the sake of the point, that Hasker does in fact succeed in showing that gratuitous moral evil is not inconsistent with God—does not entail success with the latter.

An Unintended Consequence of Hasker's Position

Hasker's distinction between genuinely gratuitous and ostensibly gratuitous natural evil unintendedly provides antitheism with a somewhat new, prima facie vexing, formulation of the argument from evil, as follows. We have seen that PW3 is not a world that God, consistent either with God's nature or God's objectives in world making, could actualize. That leaves PW4 and the actual world, still assuming they are different. The possibility of significant morality is equally viable in each, as is our ability to come to knowledge of God. If PW4 and the actual world are different, then, in our present context, the only significant difference between them is the absence from the former, and the presence in the latter, of genuinely gratuitous natural evil. But, if these two worlds are only different in this way, then, given the availability and attractiveness of PW4, given its full provision for all the relevant divine desiderata in world making, the antitheist can be expected to challenge theism to defend against the point that, in these circumstances, we have good reason to think the existence of God is inconsistent with the existence of the actual world. As, prima facie, the actual world *does* contain genuinely gratuitous natural evil, the challenge would appear to be powerful. With one important qualification stemming from van Inwagen's defense, this challenge, in its essentials, is the reformed logical argument from natural evil. The qualification is that the reformed argument is not predicated on the idea that (genuinely) gratuitous natural evil, as such, is inconsistent with God, for, strong intuitions to the contrary notwithstanding, it may not be: instead, the basic idea in the reformed argument is that a certain class of (genuinely) gratuitous natural evil is inconsistent with God.

So, as Hasker's arguments against the establishment opinion that God and gratuitous natural evil are mutually inconsistent have been shown to fail, we are justified, insofar as Hasker's arguments to the contrary are concerned, in retaining the idea that God and gratuitous natural evil are inconsistent with one another, in the strict logical sense of consistency. Let us turn now to van Inwagen's reasons for thinking that the proposition, "God and (genuinely) gratuitous evil are mutually inconsistent," is false.

van Inwagen on Gratuitousness, Chance, and Drawing Lines

Peter van Inwagen brings two arguments against the proposition that gratuitous evil is inconsistent with God, an argument predicated on the idea that there can be chance occurrences in a world made by God, and an argument about the possibility of gauging certain amounts of evil—in particular, both the supposed minimum amount necessary for the divine plan to be realizable, and amounts that are clearly excessive relative to the divine plan's realizability. van Inwagen means by gratuitous evil genuinely gratuitous evil. However, from now on, I shall drop the qualifier "genuinely," thus restoring "gratuitous evil" to its literal meaning. Let us look at his two arguments in turn.

By a chance event, van Inwagen means that "the event or state of affairs is without purpose or significance; it is not part of anyone's plan; it serves no one's end; and it might very well not have been."[22] If there are chance occurrences in a God-made world, then it is among the consequences of that fact that not everything that happens in a God-made world is part of the divine plan, an idea that, initially, may strike theists as odd. van Inwagen identifies three sources of chance events: free will, causal indeterminism, and the initial state of the universe. Setting the concept of free will aside for later discussion, let us focus in our examination of van Inwagen's first argument on chance events due either to causal indeterminism or the initial state of things. In his words, "it seems very likely that among the events that are due simply to chance or not part of God's plan are certain evils; and perhaps even *all* evils."[23] As before, the evil events or occurrences of particular interest are natural evils resulting just from natural processes (NERNP).

For the sake of argument, let us say that NERNP is due to chance. Under that description, then, NERNP is gratuitous—it is intended for no plan or purpose and it might very well not have been. To agree with van Inwagen that there can be chance evil occurrences in a world made by God, then, is to agree that the proposition "gratuitous evil is logically inconsistent with God" is false.

But this is not the end of the matter. For there are different senses of gratuitousness and we must distinguish between two of them. On the one hand, there is the kind of gratuitousness we have just been talking about, the gratuitousness of chance occurrences. On the other hand, there is the kind of gratuitousness that was in focus in our discussion of Hasker's position. The latter is gratuitousness in the sense of things preventable without loss of something better. For ease of reference let us refer to the first kind just mentioned as gratuitousness^c—the gratuitousness of chance—and to the second kind as gratuitousness^p—the gratuitousness of things that are preventable without loss of any greater good. To agree with van Inwagen that there can be gratuitous^c NERNP in a God-made world, that is, to accept that gratuitous^c NERNP may not be NENP^i, does not entail that there is no gratuitous^p NERNP in a God-made world. In van Inwagen's words, "[the] suggestion . . . that among the events that are due simply to chance and not part of God's plan are certain evils . . . is consistent with the proposition that . . . [God] could have prevented . . . [them]."[24] As it is gratuitous^p NERNP that is under consideration here, the question that is now before us is whether the foregoing argument about the mutual compatibility of God and gratuitous^c evil gives us reason to think that no gratuitous^p evil is logically inconsistent with God. The answer to the question is no.

To see why, let us recall the concept of responsive prevention, prevention of something's continuation—for instance, by alleviation of pain or suffering. Let us suppose, with van Inwagen, that the initial occurrence of NERNP is due to chance. Given that, in order to maintain a tight focus on the question before us now, let us stipulate that God could not actualize a world that did not contain NERNP due to chance, gratuitous^c NERNP. That being granted, some amount of gratuitous^c NERNP is not gratuitous^p. Let us think of this amount, whatever it is, as the first level of NERNP. That first level of NERNP, then, does not belong to the target class of NERNP under discussion here. But from the stipulated fact that first-level gratuitous^c NERNP is not gratuitous^p, it does not follow that additional amounts of gratuitous^c NERNP, second-level gratuitous^c NERNP, are not gratuitous^p. For instance, it is a plain fact that human beings try to responsively prevent sickness, pain, suffering, and so on, falling into the category of second-level gratuitous^c NERNP, and sometimes we succeed. Furthermore, this success is sometimes achieved without loss of a greater good. Thus, van Inwagen's argument about gratuitous^c NERNP gives us no reason to think that no gratuitous^p NERNP is logically inconsistent with God, that is, it gives us no reason to reject the establishment position on God and gratuitous^p evil in its entirety. As we will see below, van Inwagen does not think it does either.

Now to van Inwagen's other argument about gratuitous evil in a God-made world. It is commonplace in the philosophical literature on the problem of evil to focus discussion on certain specific instances of inscrutable evil, and that is the context of van Inwagen's second argument. Strictly speaking, then, van Inwagen is addressing a topic not under discussion in this book, inasmuch as I made it plain at the outset that my interest here is *not* in particular instances of evil as such. van Inwagen's is an argument whose conclusion is that perhaps not every instance of gratuitous^p evil is logically inconsistent with God. At the heart of the argument is his identification of a key assumption in the standard antitheistic position on the problem of evil, namely, that there is an amount of evil that is "the minimum of evil that is required for God's plan to succeed."[25] But van Inwagen goes on,

> this is not a very plausible thesis. It is not very plausible to suppose that there is a way in which evil could be distributed such that (i) that distribution of evil would serve God's purposes as well as any distribution could and (ii) God's purposes would be less well served by *any* distribution involving less evil. (One might as well suppose that if God's purposes require an impressively tall prophet to appear at a certain place and time, there is a minimum height such a prophet could have.) But if there is no minimum of evil that would serve God's purposes, then one cannot argue that God is unjust or cruel for not "getting by with less evil"—any more than one can argue that a law that fines motorists $25.00 for illegal parking is unjust or cruel owing to the fact that a fine of $24.99 would have an identical deterrent effect.[26]

van Inwagen's analogous point, then, is that just as we would (surely) not blame a municipality for levying the $25.00 (as opposed to the $24.99) fine, thereby harming traffic violators to the tune of the difference in amounts, so we ought not to blame God for not preventing certain instances, or intensities, or durations, of gratuitous^p evil.

Like all arguments from analogy, this one stands or falls on the strength of the analogy made. van Inwagen's example of the prophet is well taken, and arguably so, too, is the example of the parking fine, although in the latter case, perhaps marketing surveys would show that there *is* a minimum. Be that as it may, though, how are we to tell if the analogy is a good one? How are we to tell whether there is a minimum of evil necessary for the divine plan to be realizable or not? I do not know how we are to tell. It seems to me quite beyond our ken. At any rate, let us agree that van Inwagen gives us good reason to think there may not be any such minimum, and that is enough to be going on with.

But note that van Inwagen also argues that, while "there may be no minimum appropriate fine for illegal parking . . . (most of us would agree) if a fine of $25.00 would serve whatever purposes a fine for illegal parking is supposed to serve—deterrence, presumably—then it would be wrong to set the fine at five thousand dollars."[27]

And by the same analogy as before, he goes on,

> similarly, if an "age of evil" of twenty years duration, an age during which there were a few dozen broken bones and a score or two of very bad cases of influenza, would have served God's ends as well as the actual evil of human history serves them, then the enormity of His achieving these same ends by allowing the existence of "actual evil" passes all possibility of adequate description.[28]

That is, even if some instances of gratuitous[P] NERNP are not logically inconsistent with God, if there is good reason to believe that a vast amount of NERNP is gratuitous[P], then there is good reason to believe that amount (or a lot of it) is inconsistent with God (i.e., that it is NENP[i]), even though, in the latter case, we cannot specify how much exactly is too much. So, if some instances of gratuitous[P] NERNP are not logically incompatible with God, while some others, if they exist, *are*, then the establishment position on God and gratuitous evil that I am defending stands fast, albeit after having been scaled back a bit: specifically, it must be scaled back from "no gratuitous[P] evil is logically consistent with God" to "some amount of gratuitous[P] evil is not logically consistent with God."

van Inwagen's second argument is about drawing lines of demarcation and about the implausibility of supposing that, on the subject of God and evil, we are in a position to say how much evil is enough for the realizability of the divine plan in world making. But, to grant that we cannot fix with any precision how much evil is enough does not entail we cannot have very good reason to think *some* amount—especially some vast amount for which we can see no God-justifying good—is too much.[29] The upshot of van Inwagen's second argument is that, even allowing both that NERNP comes about by chance and that God may not be culpable in permitting or not preventing some gratuitous[P] NERNP, we are provided with no good reason to suppose that God is not culpable for permitting or not preventing all NERNP. Indeed, even allowing that we are unable to draw exact lines to show how much natural evil is, and is not, too much, van Inwagen's arguments give us no good reason to think that *a very great deal* of NERNP has any God-justifying reason to exist.

As previously noted, van Inwagen does not think his idea about natural evils occurring purely by chance represents a solution to the logical problem of evil. In his words, "this suggestion is in no way supposed to be a 'solution to the problem of evil,' since it is consistent with the proposition that before evil ever was, God knew there would someday be evil and could have prevented it."[30]

This raises an additional question, namely, given the possibility that NERNP could come about purely by chance, how might God actualize a world in which there is no chance NERNP? Two ways come to mind: first, by its just so happening that no chance NERNP occurs in that world, which is to say that, just as a matter of chance, there is no chance NERNP; second, by God's pre-emptive prevention of the occurrence of chance NERNP. I see no impossibility in either one. Furthermore, there is backing for the possibility of a chance-NERNP-free world in a well-known part of Christian mythology, namely, the Garden of Eden story. In the Garden of Eden there was no sickness, pain, death, and so on. In short, there was no NERNP there.

Summary

Broadening our focus now to summarize the conjunction of Hasker's and van Inwagen's arguments about gratuitous natural evil, the position we have arrived at is this: while the proposition "all gratuitous[P] NERNP is logically inconsistent with God" may be false, we have no good reason to think its contrary, "no gratuitous[P] NERNP is logically inconsistent with God," is not false also. So, if there is NERNP that is logically inconsistent with God, it is inconsistent because it is an excessive amount of gratuitous^p evil, even though we cannot be specific either about how much *is* consistent with God or about how much is inconsistent (because it is too much). In light of van Inwagen's argument, let us from now on think of the meaning of the term "NENP^i" as follows: (i) if some amount of gratuitous^p NERNP is compatible with God, then NENP^i is gratuitous^p NERNP in excess of that amount, and so (ii) NENP^i is not compatible with God.

However, neither the points made in this chapter in discussion of Hasker's or van Inwagen's respective positions on the relationship between God and gratuitous evil nor my description of NENP^i establish that there is in fact any natural evil that *is* NENP^i, or any that we have good reason to think is NENP^i. To identify a class of evils (NENP^i) does not entail that the class in question is not empty, or that we are justified in thinking it is not empty. The question of whether it is empty or not, and the question of whether we have good reason to think it is not empty, are yet to be addressed.

4

Orthodox Theism and the Reformed Logical Problem of Natural Evil

T
he focus of the standard debate on the problem of evil is whether certain facts of inscrutable evil are consistent with God's existence, in either the logical or epistemological senses of consistency. That being so, it is a common practice in the standard debate to address the problem as a problem for restricted theism. But, for purposes of discussion, that involves reducing belief in God to the proposition that God exists.[1] In turn, this procedural reductionism has prompted some critics—Louis Dupre being prominent and influential among them—to respond by dismissing restricted theism as unrepresentative of the cognitive side of mainstream religious belief in the Abrahamic tradition, with arguments against restricted theism being proportionately dismissed as attacks on a straw man.[2] But such dismissals are inapposite here, for the version of theism under consideration is a considerably truer-to-life formulation than restricted theism of the essential credenda—implicit and explicit—of religious belief in the tradition in question.

Orthodox Theism

Although belief in God is itself not a theory, it contains a large-scale and ambitious one at its core, namely, orthodox theism. This is a theory whose primary objective is to make sense of the world and our place in it in a radical and comprehensive way. Thus, while a supernaturalist ontology is the explanatory core of OT, in the final analysis the theory is a reasoned response to deep puzzlement about the world of our experience.

Here now are the principal cognitive commitments of OT, thus, by extension, of mainstream religious belief in the Abrahamic tradition:

1. There exists a transcendent personal being, God, who is the creator of the world; God is essentially omnipotent, omniscient, perfectly good, and worthy of worship.
2. The world could not endure without divine support.
3. There is purpose in nature independent of the purposes both of human and other conscious beings.
4. As made by God, both human persons and their world reflect a plan that predates any and all plans that human beings make for their own lives or the lives of others. In essence, this is God's plan to make a world in which it is possible for free, rational agents, largely by dint of their own efforts, to develop into moral, intellectual, and spiritual beings capable of freely choosing their own destinies, and, in particular, into beings who love God and freely choose to serve God.[3] In John Hick's term, the world is made by God to be a place of soul making. Consistent with this capacity of loving and serving God, human persons are disposed to value, seek, and promote truth, justice, knowledge, compassion, and charity, as well as other high-order goods. And within limits appropriate to our human makeup, each one of these goods is in our power to achieve, if we so choose. However, being endowed with significant freedom, and in some cases because of akrasia, it is also an open possibility that we may not so choose or so choose consistently.
5. After his or her life in this world is done, each person is judged by God and appropriately rewarded or punished in a way binding for eternity. On the divine plan as so understood, then, each person's life is, among other things, a test of his or her fitness to enjoy eternity in the presence of God.[4]

6. But while each person who is capable of soul making is judged by God on his or her efforts and achievements in soul making, no person is abandoned to that task. For God values and is lovingly interested in each individual's life and will not rebuff any person who turns to God for comfort, forgiveness, support, or hope; indeed, through gifts of grace, God helps human beings to be worthy of an eternity in God's presence.

7. Human beings either do not die (notwithstanding our seeming to), in the sense that the individual soul—whether understood in Platonic, Cartesian, or Thomistic terms, for instance—does not go out of existence as such at death (which is then understood as the death of the body alone) or, if either we *do* die in that sense[5] or if some nonsoul account of human nature is true, then each one of us is later reconstituted by God as the person he or she was at some point before death.[6]

8. While it is a fact that there is a great deal of evil in the world, including much for which we cannot discern a sufficient reason for God to permit or not prevent, in the last analysis none of it is NENP[i].

9. OT is supportable by reason and argument in either or both of the following senses: first, by arguments to advance its cause and to earn it a place relative to other theories, some of which are its rivals, and second, by arguments to defend it in the face of attack.[7] However, it is not necessary for a given believer either to be interested in the cognitive or theoretical side of religious belief, or to have any of the supporting arguments at his or her fingertips. It is enough to justifiably believe that orthodox theism has the philosophical and other conceptual resources to give a good account of itself.

In contrast to restricted theism, which is proposition 1 alone, this nine-part formulation makes it clear that the actual object of belief in the Abrahamic religions is not just a certain alleged divine being, Kenny's "God of the philosophers," but rather the complex consisting of that being in a network of relationships to human persons and their world. I treat belief in (or acceptance of) that complex as the cognitive heart of religious belief in the tradition in question.

Some Implications of Orthodox Theism

Let us examine some implications of proposition 4, and by extension proposition 5, in the description just given of OT. If it is to be logically possible for human beings to develop in the ways envisioned in the divine plan as described, certain necessary conditions have to be met. Putting the point generally, human beings would have to be a certain way, as would any world in which they lived. For instance, human persons would have to be capable of making moral choices. But that is possible only provided that human persons possess free will, as moral choices are a subset of free choices.

But, while necessary for moral choice to be possible, freedom of choice is neither its sufficient nor sole necessary condition, because, if a person has no beliefs, it will be impossible for him or her to make a moral choice. Thus, a certain epistemic condition must be met. The kinds of beliefs necessary for moral choice to be possible are, on the one hand, normative, specifically moral beliefs and, on the other hand, cause-effect beliefs. As an illustration of the former kind consider, "causing pain without believing oneself to have a prima facie good and sufficient reason is wrong," while "my doing such-and-such in these particular circumstances means that, in all likelihood, so-and-so will result," will illustrate the latter. Let us call beliefs of the former kind moral beliefs and beliefs of the latter kind practical beliefs.[8] Other things being equal, a person having both free will and beliefs of the kinds in question is, in principle, capable of a moral choice.

But the ability to make a moral choice, while necessary for the possibility of human persons' developing into morally mature agents who can responsibly choose their own destinies, is not sufficient for that possibility, and neither is it equivalent to it nor its sole necessary condition. The following logically possible situation both illustrates why not and indicates what must be added.

One day, upon awakening from the coma in which he has lain since birth, a person, Smith, has a moral belief, a practical belief, and free will. He believes, for instance, that it would be wrong for him gratuitously to visit harm upon his neighbor. He also believes that if he switches on his TV set in the next two minutes, his neighbor will suffer agony and then immediately die a horrible death.

80

Without ever wondering about either the truth of these beliefs or about whether he is justified in believing them, Smith *does* believe them, and chooses to switch/not switch on his TV set in the next two minutes, thus making a moral choice. Upon choosing, it so happens that Smith immediately relapses into his coma, and subsequently dies without reawakening. He has made a moral choice, but he has undergone no moral development of any significance. Thus, while having made a moral choice, Smith is not a moral agent in the relevant sense: he has not experienced any significant degree of the kind of growth in consciousness that is inseparable from moral maturity.

As the example indicates, in addition to being able to make a moral choice, human beings must develop a certain quality of consciousness, a nuanced moral outlook, if they are to be morally mature. But the development of such a consciousness is possible only provided further epistemic conditions are met, namely, that human beings are able both to learn various sorts of things for themselves and to be justified in believing the things learned. Furthermore, if human beings are to be able to develop into responsible moral agents who can choose their own destinies, their learning environment must make it possible, and not too difficult, for them to *fail* to so develop. Thus, the possibility of, and opportunity for, actually doing evil must be readily available, as must the temptation to do evil. In addition, human beings must believe that such options are theirs for the choosing and doing, and they must be justified in so believing.

But in order for these epistemic conditions to be met, human beings need to have experience of a certain kind: in particular, experience of occurrences having nonmoral good or ill effects, and of their consistently having those effects under the same or sufficiently similar circumstances. But we can have such experience only provided the world is a certain way: specifically, a world where occurrences of various kinds *do* in fact, under certain circumstances, consistently have nonmoral good or ill effects. So, if morally good and evil deeds are to be possible in a world, and if human beings are to be capable both of learning and of being justified in believing that they are possible, then various sorts of natural evils have to exist

81

in that world and have to be among the things of which human beings have direct or indirect experience.

In our present context, it is not necessary for us to know either how much natural evil, or which specific types or tokens of it, must exist in any world in which it is logically possible for free human persons to become morally mature agents capable of responsibly choosing their own destinies. So let us refer from now on to however much natural evil (of whatever types and tokens) that has to exist in order for those developments to be possible as NEM—natural evil necessary for moral development to be possible. Taking into account the second argument of van Inwagen's that we discussed in the previous chapter, the foregoing point may be better expressed as follows: it is not necessary for us to be able to specify just how much natural evil is too little to be NEM. Let us construe NEM broadly, that is, as any natural evil whatever that is necessary in any way for moral development to be possible. Thus, NEM is not restricted to natural evils that are necessary *in an epistemological way* for moral development to be possible. So NEM is any natural evil that is necessary for the possibility of moral good or evil, say as first-order natural evil for the possibility of second-order moral good or evil, or as second-order natural evil for the possibility of third-order moral good or evil, and so on.

In addition to the requirements already noted, there is a further requirement of a different sort, namely, a world in which the divine plan is realizable has to be one in which order of a certain kind is ubiquitous or virtually ubiquitous, the kind of order presupposed in the sciences, for instance. Finally, God would want the various conditions necessary for God's plan to be realizable to obtain in any world containing human beings. Thus, God would want order, free will, and NEM to exist in a world in which the divine plan, as specified in propositions 4 and 5 of OT, is in effect. Furthermore, seeing that it is of the essence of the divine plan that the natural world is able to be a proving ground for human beings' fitness to be granted an eternity with God, in the last analysis it is God's responsibility to ensure that the appropriate test-conditions obtain. So, in any divinely actualized world to which the divine plan as described applies, those conditions *do* obtain.

Pulling the foregoing points together, then, we may say that any

God-made world containing human beings would have to meet the following criterion:

c1. consistent with the divine plan as that is understood in OT, God could (strongly or weakly) actualize[9] no possible world containing human persons in which it is not possible in principle for human persons to develop into mature, moral, intellectual, and spiritual agents responsible for their own destinies, and in particular in which it is not possible for them to develop into persons who love God and freely choose to serve God.

Given the epistemic and other implications of the divine plan as described, this criterion means that God could actualize no possible world containing human persons in which they did not possess free will and in which NEM did not exist. Drawing further upon OT— proposition 8 especially—a second criterion in divine world making can be stated, namely,

c2. God could (strongly or weakly) actualize no possible world in which there is NENP[i].

Robert M. Adams has argued that, while, in any world created by God, none of its individual creatures would exist in the best of all possible worlds, none of them would have a life so miserable on the whole that it would have been better off not existing at all, and that each creature in that world is, on the whole, at least as happy as it would have been in any other possible world in which it existed.[10] Against this position of Adams's, Philip L. Quinn has argued that it is not happiness so much as moral goodness that would be the principal yardstick in divine world making. In particular, Quinn defends the idea that, "if [God] were to actualize a possible world, he would actualize some actualizable world of unsurpassable moral goodness."[11]

I dispute neither of these sets of criteria, assuming that Adams's criteria are understood as necessary and not sufficient. On that same understanding, then, c1 and c2 are consistent with both Adams's and Quinn's respective sets of criteria.

It should be noted that c1 is both narrower and more basic than either Adams's or Quinn's criteria. It is narrower in that it specifies a minimum criterion in God's actualization of any possible world containing *human* creatures. And it is more basic, inasmuch as it does not require (although it certainly does not preclude) either the actual happiness or moral maturity of any human person. As already observed, my emphasis, in characterizing OT's conception of the divine plan in world making, upon the possibility, and not the actuality, of human development to moral, intellectual, and spiritual maturity reflects John Hick's description of a God-made world containing human persons as a "vale of soul-*making*" (emphasis added). William P. Alston puts the point this way: "God's purpose is to make it *possible* for us to grow into the kind of person that is capable of an eternal life of loving communion with Himself."[12] (italics added)

Proposition c1's principal emphasis being on the *possibility* (of individual development of a certain kind), it is very hard to see how, if OT is right, any God-made world containing human beings could fail to satisfy this criterion, just as hard as it is, given the failure of Hasker's position on gratuitous evil and the limited success of van Inwagen's, to see how any God-made world at all could fail to meet c2.

Orthodox Theism's Reformed Logical Problem of Natural Evil

Human development of the sort provided for in the divine plan requires that human persons experience NEM—the natural evil necessary for moral development to be possible—and so it requires that NEM must exist in a God-made world containing human persons. An obvious question that now arises as a challenge to antitheistic arguments from natural evil (including the reformed logical argument) is whether prima facie $NENP^i$ is or could be NEM. If it is or could be, prima facie $NENP^i$ will not be logically inconsistent with God. The largest class of prima facie $NENP^i$ is NERNP. The focus of the challenge to the reformed argument (as well as to other antitheistic arguments from natural evil) is whether NERNP is or could be NEM, thus, by definition, not inconsistent with God. My response to this question is an argument that (i) NEM is possible in a world with no natural evil resulting just from natural processes, thus that (ii) any such natural evil would be in excess of NEM, thus that (iii) no such natural evil could be (God-)justified that way, namely, as a subset of NEM.[13] Specifically, it is an argument for the availability to God of a possible world, W^P—in effect, the possible world PW4 described in the previous chapter—which contains NEM without needing to contain any natural evil resulting just from natural processes (NERNP).

I develop this argument in three stages: (1) a brief description of the salient features of W^P, (2) further discussion of our distinction (retrieved from chapter 1) between two types of natural evil from natural processes, natural evil that results from natural processes *alone*, NERNP, on the one hand, and natural evil that comes through, but that does not solely result from, natural processes on the other (NE⁻RNP), and (3) a proof that in W^P, no NERNP whatever is necessary for either NEM or the realizability of the divine plan, thus that NERNP that seems to be $NENP^i$ cannot be (God) justified as NEM.

Description of W^P

W^P is a world of regular, orderly occurrences, a world in which the future is predictable on the basis of experience of the present and past with no less accuracy than in the actual world. In W^P there are human beings possessing free will. In W^P there is NEM, and human beings have experience of it, as they do in the actual world. So far, W^P is on a par with the actual world. But there is a crucial and basic difference, and that difference takes one of the two following forms: either (a^i) there is no NERNP in W^P, thus none that could be $NENP^i$; or (a^{ii}) there is some NERNP in W^P, but still no $NENP^i$. Either way there is no $NENP^i$ in W^P. However, in both descriptions, there is natural evil in W^P. There is also moral evil there. Let us look at these alternatives in turn.

Form (a^i)

In this description of W^P, van Inwagen-type considerations about NERNP due to chance as well as about divinely nonculpable gratuitous^P NERNP are set aside. (After all, it is possible that those considerations are false.) But van Inwagen-type considerations will be back in the picture in the second description of W^P, (a^{ii}).

W^P is so regulated—perhaps by a mixture of natural laws such as those in the actual world and the kind of periodic, miraculous, secret, divine intervention that Michael Martin suggests,[14] but not necessarily in that way, for perhaps a modified system of natural laws alone would be the mechanism of regulation—that nobody (or any animal either) ever experiences pain or suffering due only to natural processes. That is, in W^P, there is no NERNP, not even NERNP due to chance. (Recall once again the Garden of Eden analogy.) In W^P, as described, NERNP is pre-emptively prevented by God.

Although this first description of the W^P hypothesis does not stand or fall upon our being able to specify the physics of that possible world, two observations seem in order. First, perhaps God, knowing that due to the initial state of the universe or to chance, the processes of nature, if left to their own devices, would result in NERNP, has built into those processes a kind of circuit breaker such that blind natural processes alone do not in fact result in natural evils. But human beings are also part of nature, so, in the case of human actions, the circuit breaker has an automatic override feature. In this way, we, possessors of free will, can cause harm, pain, suffering, and so on, if we wish. God could either operate both the circuit breaker and override feature on a case-by-case basis—thereby making this aspect of W^P reminiscent in some respects of certain occasionalist theories of the seventeenth century—or, more economically, God, in God's initial (strong) actualization of W^P, could have made a once-for-all-time arrangement of the operations of both the circuit breaker and the override feature. The second observation concerns Alvin Plantinga's extension of the free-will defense from moral to natural evil.

Although I venture to suggest that the central idea in Plantinga's extension—the hypothesis that the evil we regard as natural evil is possibly a class of moral evil due to Satan or Satan's cohorts—is not widely believed to be true, it *is* widely, and rightly, respected as a formidable move in theism's self-defense against logical arguments from evil. Indeed, in a Wordsworthian moment, Richard Gale has described Plantinga's formulation of the free-will defense as "a thing of beauty," and predicts that "[it] will serve as one of the cornerstones in theism's response to evil . . . for many centuries."[15] But what I want to draw attention to now is not Gale's prophecy, but the following transcendental point, namely, that in order for it to be *possible* for Plantinga's Satan hypothesis to be able to work in defense of theism, we must presuppose the possibility that there is no natural evil in the world of nature *itself*. Taking the natural world here in such a way that it excludes the exercise by free creatures of their significant freedom, the foregoing point is specifically the possibility that there is no indigenous NENP, that is, no NERNP. If that presupposition is not granted to Plantinga, then the Satan hypothesis is not up to the defensive job assigned it. Or perhaps the Satan hypothesis could be modified to accommodate van Inwagen's point about nonculpable gratuitous^c or gratuitous^p NENP (of either type). In that case, Plantinga's defense would be a free-will defense against arguments from prima facie NENP^i—that is, a defense against arguments from *some* NERNP or *some* NE˜RNP, or both—and not from natural evil as such. At any rate, on Plantinga's defense, it must be possible for God to make a world in which there is either no natural evil at all, or no NENP (whether NERNP or NE˜RNP, or both) over and above a certain amount. And the same possibilities are essential to the concept of W^p, thus to the viability of the reformed argument. In one respect, then, I am conscripting a key assumption in Plantinga's Satan hypothesis in support both of an essential feature of my description of W^p, and thus in support of my subsequent use of that possible world in developing the reformed logical argument from prima facie NENP^i.

How is it possible for God to actualize a world that contains no NENP (of either sort), or none above a certain amount? Obviously, Plantinga and I are neither one in a position to say precisely. The circuit-breaker hypothesis with the override feature—in Plantinga's argument the override feature, in addition to applying to human beings, would also apply to nonhuman persons—seems to me to be as initially plausible as any other. At any rate, if Plantinga's free-will defense is allowed its implicit reliance upon the idea of a possible world in which no natural evil is a natural by-product of natural processes (NERNP)—and it *is* allowed that idea, as the widespread (and deserved) respect for Plantinga's defense testifies—so my description of W^p should be allowed the idea too. And if the point is disallowed to me, then likewise it should be disallowed to Plantinga, with the result that the extended free-will defense against arguments from natural evil would be stifled. To be sure, this is an ad hominem point, but it earns for my hypothesis that God could strongly actualize a world containing no NERNP the same acceptance that the hypothesis has in Plantinga's theory. And that is enough.

The question of how it is possible for God to actualize a world containing no NERNP at all, or none above a certain level, could be answered another way, too, namely, through serendipity. That is to say, there is no contradiction in thinking that it could just so happen that a God-made world would contain either no NERNP or none in excess of a certain amount.[16]

In sum, insofar as the existence of NERNP is concerned, W^P, in one respect, would be like the Garden of Eden in the Christian story, a world wherein brute nature itself produces no evil (or, adjusting the story to van Inwagen's arguments, none above a certain level). However, I make no claim to a resemblance between W^P and the Garden of Eden in any other respect: thus, there is no suggestion that W^P is a blissful place. In fact, it is very like the actual world in the sense that it contains vast amounts, varieties, and distributions of evils, natural and moral. The big difference is that none of the natural evils are NERNP (or NERNP above a certain level). Instead, as I explain presently, they are NE˜RNP, natural evils that come through, but never just from, natural processes, and NE˜RNP can be consistent with God on the grounds that it is necessary for NEM.

Form (a^{ii})

Here is a second description of W^P. This second description of W^P modifies (a^i) in order to accommodate van Inwagen-type points that gratuitous^P NERNP up to a certain level may be compatible with God. On this second description, W^P's natural evils fall into either or both of two classes: first, NE˜RNP, as in the first description; second, a certain level of NERNP compatible with God. In all other relevant respects, though, the description of W^P is unchanged.

NERNP and NE˜RNP

W^P contains no NENP^i and perhaps no NERNP at all. But this does not mean that it does not contain a vast amount, variety, or distribution of pain and suffering, as well as of other natural evils, too. And of course W^P is on a par with the actual world, insofar as the possibility of *moral* good and evil is concerned. The idea at the heart of this possible-world conjecture, thus at the heart of the reformed logical argument, is that W^P would contain NEM even though it does not contain NERNP, or none above a certain level: in W^P, NEM is provided by moral evil or NE⁻RNP, or both.

In order to see that W^P need contain no NERNP at all in order to provide for NEM, thus, that it need contain no NERNP to provide for the realizability of the divine plan, we need the distinction between NERNP and NE⁻RNP. The following illustration will establish the distinction. The cat, sitting contentedly at the open second-story window, monitoring the passing scene, is blown off the window ledge by a sudden gust of wind. Both his injuries upon impact and the pain, suffering, and discomfort associated with them are natural evils resulting from natural processes alone (NERNP), as are his feelings of panic and terror en route to the pavement. But if my young child—too young to realize the consequences of his action—pushes the cat from his place on the window ledge, or if I accidentally nudge him off, his injuries, pain, suffering, discomfort, panic, and terror are no longer NERNP, even though they are quantitatively and qualitatively the same as the injuries, pain, and so on that he suffers when his fall is the result of the gust of wind. Certainly, they are still natural evils—the raw feel of pain, its phenomenological dimension, is always a natural evil—but they are not now (in the second case) natural evils that result from natural processes themselves alone. Of course, they still come through, or by way of, natural processes: for, if the cat's neurophysiological system were not working right, or close enough to right, he would not have felt any pain at all. But the natural evils in this case do not result just from those natural processes themselves. For my or my child's morally nonculpable agency is a crucial part of their causal history. The cat's injuries, pain, suffering, discomfort, panic, terror, and so on, both individually and together, when I accidentally nudge him from the window ledge, are instances of NE⁻RNP, natural evils through (but not resulting just from) natural processes. Granting phenomenological sameness, the relevant difference is the two different relations between the natural evils—the pain and so on—and the natural processes involved. In the first case, the natural processes themselves (in combination) are sufficient (also necessary) for the occurrence of the cat's pain, while, in the second case, the relevant natural processes are necessary, but not sufficient.

This distinction between NERNP and NE˜RNP, together with the fact that there would be the same abundance of the latter in W^p, if it were actual, as there is in the actual world, together with the further fact that W^p provides just as well as the actual world for the occurrence of moral evil, gives us a core part of the reformed logical argument from natural evil: namely, that, in W^p, NEM is a subset of NE˜RNP or of moral evil, or of both, thus that NERNP is not necessary for NEM to be possible.[17]

In the actual world, there is a vast amount of natural evil, much of which is due to natural processes alone. And a vast amount of that seems to be inconsistent with God, which is to say that a vast amount of NERNP is prima facie NENP^i. Now, for van Inwagen-type reasons, some of this NERNP may be both gratuitous^p and consistent with God. But that still leaves a great deal of NERNP left over. And that is natural evil from natural processes that seems to be both gratuitous^p and inconsistent with God, thus making it the target class in the reformed logical argument, namely, prima facie NENP^i.

NE˜RNP and NEM

There is more to be said on the key question of how, in W^p, practical belief or knowledge, thus moral good and evil, are possible without the existence of any NERNP. For instance, in W^p, how could there be a first moral wrongdoer? This way of posing the question is Richard Swinburne's. It is a crucial question. Consistent with the divine plan as articulated in OT, God could actualize no possible world containing significantly free human persons in which moral good and evil are not possible. And moral good and evil are possible only provided certain epistemic conditions are met. In particular, moral good and evil are possible only provided there is NEM. But Swinburne maintains that NEM is impossible without NERNP. As my answer to Swinburne's challenge is closely bound up with discussion of his thinking on the subject, perhaps I can postpone answering it till the next chapter. The distinction between NERNP and NE⁻RNP is the lynchpin of my answer.

In a related vein of postponement, the reformed logical argument gets further fleshed out in competition with the defenses of theism offered by Swinburne, Plantinga, and Schlesinger. So, over the next three chapters, the argument will undergo additional development and refinement.

Two final points. First, it is not proposition 1 of OT alone that must be defended against the reformed argument, but the nine-part complex as a whole. A defense of proposition 1 is necessary for a defense of OT, but it is not sufficient. Second, on OT, the divine plan for human life emphasizes that human persons are to have the possibility, in a world where both success and failure (and, of course, *degrees* of success and failure) in soul making are possible, of developing into morally, intellectually, and spiritually mature agents capable of freely choosing their individual destinies.[18] But, while the kind of possibility of development called for in the divine plan is, presumably, live, and not just bare logical, possibility, it is the latter kind alone that will figure in the discussion of OT's defenses to which I now turn. And clearly this makes the task of the theistic defenders of OT easier than if possibility were understood as live possibility.

5

SWINBURNE'S GREATER-
GOOD DEFENSE

An action falling under the following description is morally justified. It is done with the intention to do good; the good intended is a good worth trying to do now, as opposed to later; the action is done neither negligently nor with any intention to cause harm; it is done in anticipation of causing or resulting in harm; the harm thus anticipated is outweighed by the intended good, or at least the performer of the action reasonably expects the intended good will outweigh the foreseen harm; he or she has a reasonable belief that no better means are available for now doing the good in question; the action does result in harm. We take our child to the doctor or dentist for treatment that we have very good reason to believe the child will find unpleasant or even painful, but we do so in the expectation that, by virtue of the treatment, our child's life will be better than it would have been otherwise. Our causing or permitting the natural evil which is the child's pain and suffering is justified in the circumstances by its being a necessary means, or at least by our reasonably believing it to be a necessary means, to a greater good that is both worth realizing now and that, to the best of our knowledge, is not otherwise attainable now. Prima facie we have a morally sufficient reason for either permitting or not preventing the pain in question. Obviously, many similar examples could be given, for the point is not a controversial one. Arguably it is a moral truism, although not unimportant on that account.

Generalized into a moral precept, the point is that we are not morally obliged either to eliminate or to prevent, or to decline to permit, all pain and suffering, or, more generally, all evil: on the contrary, we may have a strict moral duty to permit certain evils to occur, as means to otherwise unattainable greater goods. We are never morally justified, though, in intending an evil outcome or in intentionally bringing about such an outcome. Our obligation to eliminate evil, to prevent it, or to decline to permit it as much as we can, is bound up with our best understanding both of available greater goods and, in given situations, of the means available to realize them.

Much of our understanding of God and of God's relations with us and the world is an analogical projection based on our understanding of our dealings with one another and with the world. Analogically, then, as our permission of certain evil occurrences and our performance of certain evil actions is, in some circumstances, morally justified (and sometimes obligatory), so too it would plausibly appear to be with evils whose responsibility we lay at God's door. This analogy lies at the heart of the greater-good defense against arguments from evil. Arguably, Richard Swinburne's version of that defense is both the best and the most prominent contemporary version.

Like Plantinga, Swinburne states the problem of evil as a problem for restricted theism, but, unlike Plantinga, in the actual practice of defense, he tends to move to an expanded conception of the theory. For instance, he incorporates into his defense the notion of a divine plan for the world, and for human life in particular.[1] (It is the same notion of a divine plan that we find in orthodox theism.) As a result, Swinburne's conception of the theistic defender's task assumes a greater burden of proof on the defense than Plantinga's.

Acknowledging that among problems of natural evil, it is the specified as opposed to the unspecified problem that is especially "awkward" for theism, Swinburne sees the following as his task in defense, namely, to give "adequate reason why . . . God might bring about natural evil of the quantity and intensity which this world contains."[2]

Consistent with the minimal interpretation of the defender's burden of proof we have been working with, I read the terms "adequate reason" and "might" in this quotation in such a way that adequate reason why God might bring about natural evil of the quantity and intensity that this world contains will be given by showing that possibly God could not have otherwise actualized a world meeting the criteria of divine world making, c1 and c2, discussed in chapter 4. But Swinburne does not have to establish that possibility in order to be successful in defense of OT against the reformed logical argument. For his greater-good defense will succeed if it succeeds in the lesser task of showing that the reformed logical argument fails. In sum, then, my focus will be on Swinburne's success in establishing either of the following possibilities: first, the possibility that the natural evil at issue in the reformed logical argument, prima facie NENP^i, is necessary for a certain greater good or goods, thus, that it is not gratuitous in a way that is logically inconsistent with OT; or, second, and more weakly, that there is a disabling fault in the reformed argument. In effect, then, while Swinburne commits himself to bearing a greater burden of proof in defense than Plantinga commits *himself,* both philosophers are here held to the same, lower standard of success that Plantinga operates with.

A free-will defense is an important component in Swinburne's greater-good defense. He calls it the "central core of any theodicy."[3] For the most part, the free-will component's contribution to Swinburne's greater-good defense is to defend against arguments based on facts of moral evil in the world, while the non-free-will component is directed to arguments drawing upon natural evil, and, in particular, upon the quantity of natural evil arising from the operations of natural processes, although this division of labor is not exclusive.[4] This nonexclusiveness holds because Swinburne maintains that the free-will defense "can be extended to deal with much natural evil as well."[5] He is not here thinking of a Plantingalike extension whereby it is argued that possibly natural evil is really a special subset of moral evil due to actions of free, malevolent, nonhuman persons of enormous power and cunning—Satan and Satan's cohorts. Rather, and more mundanely, Swinburne's thinking on this point is that if human persons are free with regard to significant choices between good and evil, then it is a necessary precondition of such free choice that those persons possess "a certain depravity" to begin with.[6] By this, Swinburne means that significant moral choice presupposes genuine desire to do evil: "if [we are] to have a [significant] choice between good and evil, [we] must be subject to temptation."[7] And such depravity is natural, not moral, evil. In Swinburne's thinking, it is part of human nature.

Our principal interest here is natural and not moral evil, and in particular the merits of certain theistic defenses against arguments that draw upon the enormous quantity of inscrutable NERNP that the actual world contains—this being, first, an amount of natural evil far greater than the depravity spoken of and second, natural evil of a different sort to that depravity—yet, let us begin our examination of Swinburne's defense by briefly considering the free-will defense as a defense against moral evil.

The Free-Will Defense against Moral Evil

It is plausible to believe that if God exists and has a plan for human life along the lines described in chapter 4, then, of their very nature, human beings will have the capability of meeting God's expectations of them. For instance, a divine plan such as we find in orthodox theism requires that human beings possess freedom of choice. Swinburne's description of the significant freedom of human persons emphasizes that it is a freedom to decide our own individual destinies: without such freedom, that great good would be impossible. Furthermore, since our freedom is freedom in a strong libertarian sense, we are *responsible* for our own lives to a considerable extent, and also for the lives of others, such as our children. And this is long-term responsibility, arguably extending beyond our own life's term, for choices we make and actions we undertake may have important consequences far beyond the span of our own lives. But the freedom in question comes at a "substantial price."[8] It is a freedom that we can use for good or ill.

Here a free-will defender may make either of the following claims, relatively strong and weak, respectively: either a world with such free creatures is more objectively valuable overall than a world without, or it is possible that a world with such free creatures is more objectively valuable overall than a world without. Let us accept the point either way, as the difference in modality does not matter to my argument. As noted, free creatures in this context are creatures who can make free and significant choices, in a strong libertarian sense of freedom. By such a concept of freedom, I mean among other things that all determinist interpretations of freedom, whether hard or soft, are rejected. For purposes of our present discussion, consistent with taking OT and its defenses on the strongest version of their own terms, we will accept a strong libertarian conception of freedom.

On such an account of freedom, if God brings about a world with free creatures, God brings about a world over which God lacks full control. In such a world, God would, in particular, lack control over the intentions and choices of God's free creatures: in Swinburne's words, "a God who gives humans [free and responsible choice] necessarily brings about the possibility [of moral evil], and puts outside his own control whether or not that evil occurs."[9]

Like Plantinga, Swinburne maintains that there is no logical incompatibility between divine omnipotence and God's lack of control over free human choices. In response to "Leibniz's Lapse,"[10] Plantinga argues there is no inconsistency between divine omnipotence and the lack of such control, inasmuch as a determined free choice, in the relevant sense of "free," is a logical impossibility, and God's inability to do the logically impossible is no defeater of omnipotence, thus no falsifier of the proposition that God exists or of any other proposition of OT. Let us agree that if God strongly actualizes a world with significantly free creatures, God's control over that world is significantly limited. And let us agree as well that, overall, it is plausible to think that possession by human persons of significant freedom (given its being a necessary precondition of the possibility of serious moral development and choice of destiny) is both a good thing and worth its cost in moral evil. So, even if human beings possess such freedom as part of God's creation of them, God is not culpable, although God is indirectly responsible, for moral evil that might result: "my claim is that so good a thing is that deep responsibility [and freedom] that there is justification for God's allowing the evils caused by humans to each other (and themselves) to occur."[11]

In sum, then, a world populated by significantly free creatures is a world from which the possibility of moral evil cannot be excluded, and there is no logical inconsistency between God's existence and the existence of moral evil in that world.

In pleading "no contest" to this line of theistic defense, let us note two points. First, the analogies of divine to human goodness and of divine justification to justification for us come under strain here. For, while we rightly value human beings' respecting the freedom of their children to make up their own minds about things, say, we do not extend that to excusing complete parental noninterference with the exercise of that freedom. For instance, it may be morally permissible for me not to try to stop my young son from wishing to hit his friend, but my standing idly by while he acts on his wish is, in many circumstances, morally impermissible. So a second argument is needed to justify God's not interfering with free human actions, perhaps by justifying an extension to our free *actions* of God's noninterference with our free *choices*. Second, there is J. L. Mackie's point in "Evil and Omnipotence," namely, given that there is no logical impossibility in the notion of a free human being who, as a matter of fact, never makes an evil choice, there is no logical impossibility in the notion of a possible world whose population of free creatures consists entirely of human beings who never make an evil choice; so, given this, and assuming that God has knowledge of future contingents,[12] what justification is there for God's not creating only *those* human beings from among all the possible human beings God could have created? This question focuses Mackie's challenge to the free-will defense, a challenge to which Alvin Plantinga, in particular, has responded at length.[13] Here though, given my stated concentration upon theism's defenses against arguments based in certain facts of natural—and not moral—evil, I shall, with the exception of Plantinga's proposed extension of the free-will defense against arguments from moral evil to arguments from natural evil, not get involved in discussion of moral evil—hence, the rather generic discussion in this section of the free-will defense against arguments from facts of moral evil. Let us now accept without further discussion the free-will defense against arguments based on moral evil.

The Knowledge Clause in Swinburne's Defense

Swinburne announces his defensive position as follows: "I am . . . inclined to think that the higher-order goods defense is an adequate defense to the argument from natural evil."[14] Among greater goods, he is ultimately interested in two closely related things: human moral and spiritual development to the point where human beings can responsibly choose their own individual destinies, and the conditions necessary for such development to occur. This raises the following transcendental question, namely, what kind of world must God actualize in order for human beings to be able to develop in this way? Swinburne's greater-good defense turns on his answer to that question. The key to his answer is both epistemological and ontological: it must be a world providing adequate opportunity for human beings to acquire the knowledge necessary for responsible choice of their own individual destinies to be possible; but that in turn requires the existence in that world of NEM as the ultimate source of those experiences from which the development of such practical knowledge is possible. Swinburne makes the point this way:

> [there is] . . . need for knowledge of how to bring about good or evil if men are to have a significant choice between good and evil, and . . . that knowledge can only come from experience of good and evil. My claim is not that such knowledge from experience is necessary for free and responsible choice as such, but that it is necessary for free and responsible choice of a deeper and far more reaching kind which I call "choice of destiny."[15]

Knowledge of how to bring about good and evil is not knowledge in the abstract. It is not just knowing the difference between the concept of good and the concept of evil. Swinburne emphasizes that *practical* knowledge is what is needed. In his view, practical beliefs are insufficient for choice of destiny to be possible: it is practical *knowledge* that is required. From now on, the term "practical knowledge" will be used here only with the meaning Swinburne gives it, which is, knowing "what morally relevant features [a particular action] has . . . ([for example] causing pain, being a lie, extending life, enriching experiences of life)."[16] The contrast is with what he calls moral knowledge, the knowledge of moral principles or general moral propositions; for instance, "that causing pain is, other things being equal, wrong."[17] From now on I will also limit my use of the expression "moral knowledge" to this meaning.

But what conditions have to obtain in order for practical knowledge to be possible and for human beings to obtain enough of it to make possible the kinds of free, informed choices prized in OT's concept of the divine plan, and emphasized in Swinburne's defense? And where, between absolute ignorance and omniscience must a human knower's practical knowledge be in order for him or her to be well informed enough to be able to make responsible moral choices, and ultimately choices of destiny? The latter is a hard question. So it is fortunate that we do not need to answer it in detail, as it will be sufficient both for Swinburne's defense and our assessment of it to answer the former question, and, in answering it, to remain at the following level of generality, namely, that we do not have the right sort of practical knowledge unless some of our knowledge is "knowledge from experience of good and evil."[18] Thus, now to answer the first of the two questions just put: the condition that has to obtain in order for such practical knowledge to be possible is the world's including things and events from our experience of which we can learn what we need to know about pain, suffering, and other good and evil effects of our actions. Swinburne discounts the possibility that the knowledge needed could either be a priori or innate.[19]

Given this, the next question is whether that knowledge must come from firsthand experience. Specifically, must it come from direct acquaintance with the good or evil effects of various kinds of occurrences, actions, or omissions? Or could we acquire the necessary practical knowledge indirectly through testimony? This latter suggestion is that perhaps it could be a subclass of what Swinburne calls "verbal knowledge,"[20] for it is clear that acquiring a belief from testimony or hearsay qualifies as acquiring it from experience. But Swinburne argues that such experience is insufficient to account for the fact that human beings possess the kind of practical knowledge of good and evil under discussion. This is because testimony, when viewed in terms of a causal chain, relies in the last analysis for its epistemic justification upon direct, firsthand experience: in the present instance, firsthand experience of good and evil occurrences. For, Swinburne reasons, if our practical knowledge of good and evil does not come ultimately from direct experience of good or evil occurrences, the notion of a first moral wrongdoer is incoherent. Thus he argues that we cannot be content to halt at an epistemic level—testimony—but must press back to an ontological level; specifically, the actual existence of the good and evil phenomena that must be experienced.

Before addressing this point about ontology, there is another justification issue involved, distinct from the epistemic credentials of both the sources of our beliefs and the processes by which we acquire them. This second epistemic issue pertains to the availability of corroborating evidence for those beliefs we have acquired by reliable means from good sources. Consider the following situation. Jones is told by his good friend, Smith, that his (Jones's) wife is having an affair. Jones is very surprised to be told this, quite shocked in fact. The thought has never crossed his mind. He asks Smith for his evidence. Smith tells him that he (Smith) was told this by another person, Evans, who is a private detective. According to Smith, Evans, in the course of an investigation into something or other, comes upon information based upon direct firstperson experience that recently Mrs. Jones has been having an affair with a certain person. That is all that Smith knows. So, that is all he can tell Jones. Jones knows that Smith is a sober, careful, reliable person, and that he would not say such things frivolously. But Jones has noticed nothing unusual in his wife's recent behavior. She is as friendly and affectionate as ever, she keeps the same schedule as before, there have been no suspicious telephone calls, there are no unusual credit-card bills, she is not out in the evening any more than before, and so on. In short, Jones has no evidence whatever of his own that his wife is having an affair. But Jones believes what Smith has told him. Furthermore, what Smith told Jones is in fact true. Does Jones *know* that his wife is having an affair? I think it is clear that he does not. In his present situation he is not epistemically justified in believing that his wife is having an affair. He needs more information before he could be justified. So, in this case, although his source is good, and rightly believed by Jones to be a reliable and truthful person, and although what Jones was told is in fact true, Jones is not justified in believing what he was told. Arguably he is not epistemically justified in not believing it either, but that is beside the point. From an epistemic point of view, an open mind is called for—pending further developments—although, psychologically speaking, such open-mindedness may be difficult to achieve or sustain. The reason is that Jones's belief lacks appropriate corroboration. Applied to practical knowledge, we must, in addition to *acquiring* our practical beliefs in the right way from reliable sources, have adequate *corroboration* of those beliefs.

Now to Swinburne's ontological point, which is that in the case of our true practical beliefs about the good and evil consequences of our actions, appropriate justification means, in the last analysis, direct experience of good and evil occurrences in the world. So, either such occurrences must exist and be available to us, or to a first moral wrongdoer, in direct experience as either the sources of our beliefs about good and evil or as our corroboration of such beliefs, or they must be indirectly available to us as the ultimate sources of our verbal knowledge of good and evil. In the latter case, they must be directly available to at least the first person in the chain of testimony that leads to our verbal knowledge. For example, it is only from direct experience of sharp objects causing cuts to human beings and animals, coupled with experience of the pain that accompanies such injuries, that a first wrongdoer could be culpable, in the moral sense of culpability, for cutting a particular person or animal with a sharp object. Only thus could that first wrongdoer be a *moral* wrongdoer. Swinburne summarizes the position as follows:

> the argument . . . so far has been that God can give to men knowledge of the consequences of their actions only by telling men what he will intentionally bring about or by allowing them to infer what natural processes will bring about. Knowledge of the latter is to be obtained by observation of what natural processes have brought about in the past and generalizations therefrom. But if God is to give men knowledge by the latter route of which actions have bad consequences, natural processes must have operated in the past to bring about the bad consequences.[21]

And as, "a belief about the future requires to be justified by some other belief, such as a belief that one has had some past experience or perceived some event in the past,"[22] it follows that, "if God is to give us knowledge of the consequences of our actions in a way that allows us to exercise a free and responsible choice of destiny, that can only come through knowledge of many and varied past evils produced by natural processes."[23]

In this way, Swinburne argues that it is natural evil resulting from natural processes themselves alone, NERNP, which is necessary as the ultimate justificatory grid—in both senses of epistemic justification discussed—in a God-made world wherein the divine plan, with its provision for human moral development and individual choice of destiny, operates. And so, Swinburne concludes, the existence of NERNP—"the many and varied past evils produced by natural processes"—being necessary for that greater good, God has a morally sufficient reason for actualizing a world with NERNP in it. Swinburne does not mean here just that *some* NERNP is justified this way: he means the whole class of NERNP, which, of course, includes a vast amount of evil that appears to be NENP^i. In sum then, Swinburne's defense is this: NERNP provides NEM, the natural evil necessary for moral development and responsible choice of destiny to be possible; NEM could not occur by better means in a world wherein moral development and choice of destiny based on experientially acquired and corroborated practical knowledge is possible; thus, NERNP has a (God-)justifying reason to exist and so is not inconsistent with the world's being made by God.

Prima Facie NENP^i, the Need to Know, and the Reformed Logical Argument

The essence of Swinburne's position is that, given that any world containing free human beings that God actualizes will be a world in which the divine plan as articulated in OT will be realizable, and given that NEM is a necessary condition of that plan's realizability, any such world will contain NEM. The actual world, through its vast quantities and wide distributions of NERNP, contains NEM. But at what cost? The reformed logical argument is that the cost of NEM in the actual world is too high for God justifiably to pay, inasmuch as there is available for divine actualization a possible world, W^p, in which, at much less cost in evil, the same divine plan is fully realizable. In W^p, NEM is provided by the abundance of moral evil and by natural evils that do not result solely from natural processes, NE˜RNP.

Let us now test the strength of Swinburne's defense against that argument, and let us do so by picking up the question that, in my account of the reformed logical argument in chapter 4, I put off till now. The question is, how, in W^P, could a *first* moral wrongdoer learn about the harmful or helpful consequences of his or her actions, which is to say, how could he or she become a *moral* wrongdoer in the first place?

The question raises serious points. First, if moral evil is not possible in W^P, then W^P could not be a world that, consistent with OT's conception of the divine plan, God could actualize or permit. Second, if, as the reformed logical argument maintains, NEM is provided in part by moral evil, for instance the pain and suffering that free human persons culpably cause, then the reformed logical argument will fail if moral evil is not possible in W^P. For both of these reasons, then, showing how there could be moral evil in W^P will show (i) that NERNP is not necessary for practical knowledge of good and evil, thus, (ii) that NERNP is not necessary for either moral development or responsible choice of destiny, and so, (iii) that Swinburne's defense against logical arguments based on natural evil—a defense whose essential point is that NEM is impossible without NERNP—fails against the reformed logical argument.

In answering Swinburne's question about the possibility of a first moral wrongdoer, let us develop an idea that he rules out, namely, that we could acquire true practical beliefs nonempirically. It is logically possible that God could have implanted in us incognito both moral knowledge, as defined, and the requisite true practical beliefs—I do not say practical knowledge—about the good and evil effects of our actions, thereby removing any need for NERNP to exist as the source of either our practical beliefs or our practical knowledge of good and evil, or as the evidence by reference to which we corroborate those beliefs. The key question insofar as implanted, true, practical beliefs' becoming practical knowledge is concerned is the question of how we could be epistemically justified in believing them. After all, based on this implant hypothesis, we would not know that it was God who gave us these beliefs. If we *did* know that God was the source of our true practical beliefs, then surely we would be justified in believing them. But here we do not know this, so the question of epistemic justification, thus of knowledge, is open. As Swinburne maintains, the justification must be empirical, that is, it must ultimately come through somebody's direct experience of good and evil occurrences, for instance, pain and suffering. But how is that possible in WP, given the nonexistence of NERNP in WP?[24] That is the crucial question. If it can be answered satisfactorily, then, insofar as Swinburne's argument to the contrary is concerned, the way to WP's availability to God as a viable alternative to the actual world is open.

Swinburne accepts that knowledge of general moral principles does not require experience of good or evil occurrences or actions, or of the consequences of such occurrences or actions, in order to meet the justification requirement for knowledge. That is, he accepts that moral knowledge could be innate or implanted incognito by God. He puts the point as follows,

> I do not know of any satisfactory proof that experience is necessary either for the acquisition of concepts or for acquisition of knowledge of necessary truths of their interconnection. . . . God could ensure that men were given moral concepts and a deep imagination which would enable them to comprehend necessary truths about their application without their having any experience of harsh moral realities.[25]

Given this concession, we do not need to discuss moral knowledge further. But, immediately following the lines just quoted, Swinburne goes on, "with practical knowledge it is different, at any rate for agents, such as humans, who have a choice of destiny in that they can grow in knowledge of the nature and consequences of their actions."[26] Swinburne frames the issues concerning the justification component in practical knowledge in the three following passages:

> If an agent is to have a free and responsible choice of destiny, his beliefs must be true and justified.[27]

> Why can't I just know what will happen if I do so-and-so tomorrow? I can indeed have such a belief, but it would not amount to knowledge, because it would not be justified.[28]

> *God cannot give to men the sort of belief needed for a free and responsible choice of destiny without producing natural processes which bring about natural evils, and letting men observe and experience them. . . .* The more and more varied are the evils observed and experienced, the surer is the knowledge of the consequences of natural

processes gained, and so the greater is the opportunity for informed choice of action. The more that knowledge is made available to man by any other route than the observation of natural processes, the more his freedom and choice of destiny is reduced.[29] (italics added)

On the implant hypothesis, we would be born with true practical beliefs, a possibility that Swinburne accepts.[30] Of course, we would not, just by having those true beliefs, know that those beliefs are true, inasmuch as just by our having true beliefs we would not have true, justified beliefs, that we acquired in a justified way.

Suppose, on the implant conjecture, we are born with a true belief about the ill effects of a certain class of actions, reckless actions, let us say. We would not thereby be justified in that belief. However, upon acting recklessly or by experiencing others acting recklessly, we would see pain, suffering, and other ills result. Furthermore, by accidentally causing pain or suffering to a sentient being, or damage or destruction to the natural environment, we and others would witness or undergo those evils. In either or both of those ways—that is, as a consequence of our experience of certain kinds of moral evil (due to ourselves or others) or as a consequence of our experience of NE⁻RNP—our true practical beliefs would be justified. In these ways—that is, ultimately through directly encountering certain kinds of evils, whether moral evils or NE⁻RNP—we would come to know that such-and-such actions have such-and-such consequences. The knowledge we would acquire in that way would be practical knowledge of good and evil, in Swinburne's sense of the term.

To take a different illustration of the same point, suppose we are born with implanted true practical beliefs about the sometimes harmful consequences of negligent actions. Then, in WP, we or others sometimes behave negligently, that is, without due regard to the possible harmful effects of our actions and omissions on persons, animals, property, or the natural environment. And, as a consequence, we sometimes cause pain and suffering, among other ills. This pain and suffering is a form of moral evil. We experience it as do others. Thus, recognizing that the behavior that resulted in this pain and suffering is negligent behavior, our implanted, true, practical belief about the sometimes harmful consequences of negligent behavior becomes a justifiably arrived at, justified true belief.

Two qualifications are needed at this point. The first is purely terminological. I referred to some of those actions from experience of which we learn about the evil effects of our behavior as reckless actions, and I referred to others as negligent. But the terms "reckless" and "negligent" connote culpability, whereas, when first done by a first wrongdoer those actions would obviously not be culpable at all. The point is this: that, in W^p, upon observing the effects of certain actions that are of a sort with those that, in the actual world, we call reckless or negligent, the first wrongdoer (who is not yet a *moral* wrongdoer) would learn about the ill effects of such actions. Or that first wrongdoer (not yet a moral wrongdoer) would learn about pain and suffering, dangers of various sorts, and so on, from experience of NE˜RNP. Thus, with the lesson learned in either or both ways, on subsequent occasions, his or her behaving in that way *would* be reckless or negligent behavior, as the case may be.

The second qualification is also terminological, but, in addition, a point of substance turns on it. This qualification concerns two senses of "negligence." The first is that involved in our failing to intervene to stop something that causes harm—an occurrence in nature, for instance—when we could and should have intervened to stop it, while the second is the negligence that is involved in our own thoughtless or reckless actions. For want of better terms, let us call them passive and active negligence, respectively. Obviously, insofar as NERNP in sufficient quantities to provide for NEM is concerned, there could be no passive negligence in W^p, for there would be no such quantities of NERNP there in the first place. We could, however, be passively negligent in W^p with regard to actions and plans of action of other persons that result in harm, and that—anticipating that they would result in harm—we could justly have intervened to prevent. And, just as in the actual world, there would be active negligence in W^p, recklessness for example. In W^p, then, all pain and suffering would be due either to human malice or negligence, passive or active in the ways just described—again recall the Garden of Eden analogy—or to accidents or other unforeseen consequences of actions done without harmful intent.

By way of the implant hypothesis, I have made out a case for the availibility to God of W^p as an alternative to the actual world, an alternative that facilitates the divine plan at less cost in natural evil than the actual world. But the implant hypothesis is not necessary to my argument. An empirical case through and through could equally be made out for the same proposition, as follows.

WP is just as described above, except that God does not implant in us either moral knowledge or true practical beliefs. In respect of those, a human mind is initially a tabula rasa. The obvious question, then, is "how comes it to be furnished? . . . To this I answer, in one word, from experience."[31]

How might that work? In WP human persons, being the same as we are in the actual world, behave in the same sorts of ways that we do in the actual world. Some of this behavior results in pain, suffering, injury, damage, and so on, and these evils are either forms of moral evil or of NE~RNP. These outcomes of our behavior are objects of our experience and we learn from them, or at least, learning from them is both a logical and a live possibility for us. We form and test generalizations, both practical and moral generalizations. We acquire true beliefs from our experience, and we justify some of those beliefs by experience. In short, we acquire moral and practical knowledge just as we do in the actual world, or, more accurately, we have just as much opportunity in WP of acquiring moral and practical knowledge as we do in the actual world. The only difference, albeit a crucial one, is that in WP none of the evils from which we learn are NERNP. As we know from our experience of both moral evil and of NE~RNP in the actual world, there would be an abundance of pain, suffering, damage, and so on from which to learn. That is, in WP, there would be an abundance of NEM.

Either way, then, God could actualize a world reflecting the divine plan for human beings, thus containing NEM, without, for purposes of providing for NEM, actualizing a world that contains the NERNP that actually exists. This being so, Swinburne's defense of the proposition that the NERNP that actually exists is necessary for NEM, and thereby his defense of the proposition that prima facie NENP[i] is either not gratuitous or not shown to be gratuitous, fails. So the reformed logical argument from prima facie NENP[i] is not blocked or refuted by Swinburne's defense. That defense does not give us good reason to think that NERNP, thus a large quantity of prima facie NENP[i] is not inconsistent with OT. However, I do not here claim to show that such prima facie NENP[i] *is* inconsistent with OT.

My counter-argument to Swinburne does not entail that. Furthermore, recalling from chapter 1 that a minimal theistic defense, in order to succeed, does not have to show that prima facie NENP[i] is not inconsistent with OT, Swinburne does not have to undertake (and succeed in) that task in order to provide an adequate defense of orthodox theism.

Two Objections

Let us look at two objections. It will be possible to do this briefly because the points in question were largely covered in our discussion of Hasker in chapter 3.

Would it not become common knowledge in W[p] that God existed, and would this not inhibit (through fear of certain punishment in a hereafter, for instance) our freedom of choice and action, thereby defeating the main purpose of the divine plan itself? There are two lines of response to this. First, evil choices and other moral evils are not impossible in circumstances where the existence of God is known or claimed to be known. For instance, some believers in God are absolutely certain that there is a God and, for that matter, a God who will judge them on the conduct of their lives and then reward or punish them accordingly, yet these people are not thereby immune to moral evil. Furthermore, to recall an earlier point: in Christian mythology it is taught that Satan and Satan's cohorts knowingly and culpably rebelled against God and have been on a campaign of evil ever since. Thus, insofar as Christian thinking itself is concerned, sinning in the full knowledge of God's existence is possible. (Indeed, Plantinga's extension, via the Satan-hypothesis, of the free-will defense from moral to natural evil seems to presuppose it.)

A second response to the question is this: let us agree that, (1) even though God's implantation is secret, it would become recognized that, in W[p], nature itself—understanding nature here as excluding human nature, thus as brute nature—gives rise to no pain, suffering, or natural evil of any sort, and (2) that speculation about the cause or explanation of this phenomenon would result in the idea that God existed. There is no reason, though, to suppose as well that such speculation or its conclusion would be any more compelling or widespread than the rival speculation that natural evil's not being a natural by-product of natural processes themselves is a wholly natural phenomenon, explicable in naturalistic terms. After all, it is speculated in the actual world that there could be no world at all, and especially no world with the manifold sorts of order that our world possesses, apart from divine creation, but there is no intellectual sin committed by those who resist the explanans of divine creation. And even if the hypothesis of divine creation *were* compelling, the point made in the first response would still hold.

A second objection is that, in order to keep his activities secret—whether his activity of implanting in us true, practical beliefs or his actualization of a world without NERNP in sufficient quantities to guarantee the possibility of NEM—God would be put in the position of having to deceive us. But, as God could not be a deceiver, God could neither implant such beliefs in us incognito nor so arrange nature that there is no such amount of NERNP. But that is false. As we saw in chapter 3, keeping a secret does not entail deception. Presumably, on the theistic hypothesis of God's being the creator of the actual world, God keeps many things from us—there is no compelling, worldwide broadcast of the creation news, for instance—but this does not mean that God thereby deceives us or prevents us from figuring out the truth if we can. Likewise in W^p.

Summary

Here is a brief summary of the argument in this chapter. Two criteria govern God's actualization of a world containing human persons who possess significant freedom. The first of those criteria, $c1$, specifies that, consistent with the divine plan for human life, as we find that plan both in OT and in Swinburne's defense, God could actualize no possible world containing free human beings without adequately providing for the possibility of human beings' succeeding in meeting the plan's demands on them. Insofar as $c1$ is concerned, W^p is just as good as the actual world. But, when the cost in evil of providing for the realizability of that plan in the actual world is compared to the cost in W^p, we see that the cost in the latter is much lower. For there is natural evil in the actual world that we have good reason to think is $NENP^i$, while there is none in W^p. Given that W^p meets $c1$ just as well as the actual world, the upshot is that, insofar as Swinburne's greater-good defense is concerned, there is prima facie NENP[i] in the actual world, thus that the actual world is prima facie a world that God could not have actualized. Furthermore, insofar as the realizability of the divine plan is concerned, not only does Swinburne's defense not provide God-justifying reason for NERNP to exist, the reformed logical argument offers a good, God-justifying reason for such evil to *not* exist. Accordingly, Swinburne's defense fails to block or defeat the reformed argument.

6

PLANTINGA'S FREE-WILL DEFENSE

I t is an essential part of orthodox theism that, in any God-made world containing human persons, those persons have free will. The theistic conception of human freedom is a robust one in the main, a point crucial to Alvin Plantinga's version of the free-will defense. He explains his conception of freedom, a strong libertarian conception, as follows:

> What does the Free Will Defender mean when he says that people are or may be *free?* If a person S is free with respect to a given action, then he is free to perform that action and free to refrain; no causal laws and antecedent conditions determine either that he will perform the action, or that he will not. It is within his power, at the time in question, to perform the action, and within his power to refrain. Consider the state U of the universe up to the time he takes or decides to take the action in question. If S is free with respect to that action, then it is causally or naturally possible both that U hold and S *take* (or decide to take) the action, and that U hold and S *refrain* from it. Further, let us say that an action is *morally significant*, for a given person at a given time, if it would be wrong for him to perform the action then but right to refrain, or vice versa.[1]

He sharpens this account in the following way:

> The freedom of such creatures will no doubt be *limited* by causal laws and antecedent conditions. They will not be free to

CHAPTER 6

do just anything. . . . Of course my freedom is also *enhanced* by causal laws. . . . But if I am free with respect to an action A, then causal laws and antecedent conditions determine neither that I take A nor that I refrain.[2]

Let us continue to accept this conception of freedom as a basis for discussion, and so waive all considerations of either hard or soft determinism.

The Satan Hypothesis

The main thrust of the free-will defense against arguments from moral evil is described in chapter 5, so let us address here only the free-will defense against arguments from natural evil. For, unlike most apologists for theism, including those—Swinburne, for instance—who extend the free-will defense against moral evil to some natural evil,[3] Plantinga extends it to cover all natural evil. In essence, his extension is simple. Drawing upon the Christian mythology of good and bad angels, the bridge from a free-will defense against arguments from moral evil to a like defense against arguments from natural evil is built from a redescription of natural evil as possibly a subset of moral evil, "broadly moral evil," as Plantinga calls it.[4] The possibility thereby opened up is that what we tend to regard as natural evil is really the handiwork of certain undesirable members of a class of immensely powerful nonhuman moral agents. I refer to this as the "Satan hypothesis."

In this day and age, an ontology of angels, fallen or unfallen, is hardly credible, at least at first acquaintance. But, as Plantinga points out, in order to do the work he assigns it, the Satan hypothesis does not have to be true, offered as true, or believed by anybody to be true. It just has to be possible that it is true, in the bare logical sense of possibility. Furthermore, credibility and incredibility are relative matters. After all, if the notion of an omniscient, almighty, essentially spiritual, personal being is granted for the sake of debate on the problem of evil, and if, at least within the Platonic and Cartesian wings of theism, a multitude of lesser spirits—namely, us—is also granted for purposes of various philosophical debates, why in principle not Satan and Satan's cohorts?

Nor would an application of Ockham's razor justify us in pre-emptively depopulating Plantinga's defense of its devils, for, as described by Plantinga, the work of Satan and Satan's followers duplicates that of no other posited beings. So, given these things, and quite apart from the point rightly made by Plantinga that the credibility or incredibility of the Satan hypothesis is not relevant to the free-will defense against logical forms of the argument from evil, it is not illicit to argue, against arguments whose conclusion is that certain facts of natural evil are logically inconsistent with God, for the possibility of immensely powerful, intelligent, and cunning malevolent spirits who are morally responsible for natural evil. This is not to recommend an ontology of spirits, far from it. But if we are prepared seriously to consider theories that posit God, or that describe human beings as essentially spirits or immaterial substances,[5] then to balk at nonhuman, malevolent, spiritual beings is inconsistent. (This being said, however, in an appendix to this chapter, I shall raise a question about the credibility of Plantinga's description of the possible evil activities of Satan and Satan's cohorts.)

A fundamental question is this: is it logically possible that Satan and his cohorts exist? And the answer, plainly, is yes. As described by Plantinga, Satan is "a mighty non-human spirit who, along with many other angels, was created long before God created man. . . . Satan rebelled against God and has since been wreaking whatever havoc he can."[6]

Of its nature, a defense is a defense against a threat, actual or perceived, and a good defense is tailored to meet the particular attack or attacks made or anticipated. Plantinga has made it clear that he took up the task of defending theism against the logical arguments from evil that, in the mid to late 1950s, were brought forward by J. L. Mackie, Antony Flew, and several other atheistic philosophers. This had the following effect: that the theism Plantinga set about defending was restricted theism, for the antitheistic arguments in question were directed toward showing that the two propositions, "God, understood as an omnipotent, omniscient, perfectly good being, exists" and "evil exists" are mutually inconsistent in the strictly logical sense. In Mackie's seminal formulation of the logical problem of God and evil in 1955, the point is stated as follows:

I think . . . that a . . . telling criticism can be made by way of the traditional problem of evil. Here it can be shown . . . that religious beliefs . . . are positively irrational, that the several parts of the essential theological doctrine are inconsistent with one another . . . In its simplest form the problem is this: God is omnipotent; God is wholly good; and yet evil exists. There seems to be some contradiction between these three propositions . . . but . . . the theologian . . . at once must adhere and cannot consistently adhere to all three.[7]

As deployed, then, Plantinga's free-will defense is a defense against Mackie's argument, as well as against the roughly like-minded arguments of Aiken, Flew, and McCloskey,[8] that the conjunction of the two following propositions—"there is a transcendent and worshipful being, God, the omnipotent, omniscient, totally free, perfectly good creator of the world," and "there is evil in the world"—is necessarily false.

Notwithstanding Plantinga's focus on restricted theism, my question to his free-will defense is whether it is up to the task of defending OT, without doubt a formulation of expanded theism, against the reformed logical argument from evil. But it may be thought that to put this question to Plantinga's free-will defense is both unfair and at odds with my practice of taking theism's defenses on their own terms, for I am proposing to judge Plantinga's defense on its ability to do something that it does not try to do. For, unlike Swinburne, Plantinga does not conscript an expanded theism in defense of restricted theism. But what I am proposing to do is neither unfair nor inconsistent with the practice I have hitherto followed.

There are two reasons it is not unfair, and the first of them is also a reason it is not inconsistent with my previous practice. First, I *do* take Plantinga's defense on its own terms. I grant it all of its operating assumptions. It is simply a mistake to think that examining whether a defense is up to a task other than the specific one assigned it, when all propositions of the defense are granted for the sake of argument, is a denial to that defense of its own terms of debate. What I am proposing to do here is to test whether, precisely *on* its own terms, Plantinga's defense is able to defend a larger and more important target than restricted theism. Furthermore, suppose Plantinga's defense cannot successfully defend OT against the reformed logical argument from natural evil. Would that entail its failure to defend the limited target it was originally deployed to defend? No, and that point makes it clear that what I ask of Plantinga's free-will defense does not compromise its ability to carry out the task originally assigned to it.

Now to the second reason that what I propose is not unfair to Plantinga. It is that Plantinga himself has recently expressed a strong interest in showing that Christian, and not just generic, theism is both warranted and worthy of serious philosophical study: see his 1984 paper, "Advice to Christian Philosophers," and his recent announcement of a future book, *Warranted Christian Belief.*[9] So, as orthodox *Christian* theism is accurately represented in OT, my question of whether Plantinga's defense is up to the task of defending an expanded theism such as OT has a timely ring to it. Thus, for both of these reasons, there is nothing underhand about the experiment on Plantinga's defense that I conduct here. Furthermore, I think it is an interesting and important experiment.

In essence, Plantinga's extension of the free-will defense from moral to natural evil is the following: first, it is logically possible that no natural evil arises naturally or spontaneously just from the operations of natural processes, that is, there is no NERNP. Second, it is possible that all evils widely referred to in the literature as natural evils really belong to a subclass of moral evil, for which, in a way that is analogous to how significantly free human persons are responsible for moral evils, Satan or Satan's cohorts are responsible. Third, granting both a strong version of libertarianism and the viability of the free-will defense against arguments from moral evil, those evils—redescribed as either exercises or products of free will—are consistent with God. In light of this, Plantinga's task, in defense of OT against the reformed logical argument from natural evil, is essentially to establish the possibility that there is a God-justifying reason for actualizing a world containing free human beings, in which the Satan hypothesis is true. If he succeeds, he will have defended OT against the reformed logical argument from natural evil.

Before proceeding, let us agree on the following innocent restriction. Plantinga's Satan hypothesis is the suggestion that possibly all

NENP is really broadly moral evil. However, since chapter 3, the evil we have been concentrating on is prima facie NENP^i, in particular, the quantity of natural evil resulting solely from natural processes, NERNP, above a level that, for van Inwagen-type reasons, may be compatible with God. So, in discussing Plantinga's defense, let us agree to limit the class of natural evil that is addressed to NERNP above that level, whatever it is.

Which Worlds Could God Have Actualized?

Let us use the hypothesis of W^P to examine Plantinga's free-will defense, understood now as a defense of orthodox theism against the reformed logical argument from the prima facie NENP^i in question. In essence, the reformed argument is an argument for the following conjunction: that, all things considered, W^P is a better world than the actual world, W, in the sense that it has a much better balance of good and evil than W; that the divine plan is just as realizable in W^P as in W; and that God could, and should, have actualized W^P instead of W. If this conjunction is true, then God, if God exists, would have actualized W^P instead of W. Considered as a defense of OT against the reformed argument, the focus of Plantinga's argument is the third of the foregoing conjuncts: God could, and should, have actualized W^P instead of W. Let us stipulate then, as not controversial in our present context, that the first and second conjuncts are true, thus clearing the way for discussion of arguments for and against the third.

W^P has the two following important points in common with the actual world, when the latter is understood in terms of Plantinga's Satan hypothesis: first, in neither is there any natural evil resulting just from natural processes, or at least none in excess of a certain amount that, as van Inwagen argues, may result just from chance or from the initial state of the universe; second, both provide for NEM. In Hume's words from *Dialogues Concerning Natural Religion*, let us now compare these two possible worlds, W^P and the actual world on the Satan hypothesis, to determine, first, if either differs "from what a man . . . would, beforehand, expect from a very powerful, wise and benevolent Deity,"[10] and second, whether either is a world that God, consistent with the criteria in world making c1 and c2, could not justifiably actualize.

Recall Plantinga's distinction between strong and weak concepts of actualization of worlds:

> Let us say that God strongly actualizes a state of affairs S if and only if he causes S to be actual and causes to be actual every contingent state of affairs S* such that S includes S*; and let's say that God weakly actualizes a state of affairs S if and only if he strongly actualizes a state of affairs S* that counterfactually implies S.[11]

While both strong and weak actualization apply to God-made worlds containing significantly free creatures, the latter applies to such worlds only, inasmuch as many subsequent states of such worlds depend to a significant degree upon the free choices and actions of those free beings, thus putting those states beyond the power of omnipotence to determine. Those subsequent states of that world are then weakly, and not strongly, actualized by God.

Using Plantinga's terminology, let "T(W)" represent the largest state of affairs God strongly actualizes in W, the actual world as understood on the Satan-hypothesis.[12] Thus, T(W) includes a state of affairs making provision for the existence of Satan and Satan's cohorts, as well as for the existence of both non-Satanic angels and human persons. Furthermore, as there is either no natural evil in W or none above the van Inwagen line discussed in chapter 3, T(W) is such that it provides for either no natural evil at all or none over and above natural evil due to chance or the initial condition of the universe. But what does it mean to make provision for the existence of significantly free persons (human and angelic)? Principally it means that T(W) includes person-essences—diminished persons, in Richard Gale's term—such that,

> Each possible person contains a diminished possible person that is the largest possible subset of properties that is such that for any action A, it neither includes or entails freely doing A nor includes or entails freely refraining from doing A, in which a property F involves or entails another property G just in case it is logically impossible that F be instantiated and G not be. . . .

We will also refer to such a subset as a 'freedom neutral' set of properties. . . . God performs the same creative act when he endeavors to actualize P as he does when he endeavors to actualize P^1, namely, he supernaturally wills that the diminished person DP be . . . actualized.[13]

As Plantinga's extension of the free-will defense to cover arguments from natural evil tells it, it is logically possible that part of God's strong actualization of the actual world is God's creation of the person-essence DS (diminished Satan) as the proto-Satan, and so on in like fashion for each of Satan's cohorts, as well as God's creation of angelic person-essences for each of the "good" angels. Consistent with that, then, it is logically possible for DS to become the Satan of Plantinga's description (and Christian mythology). And that possibility means it is possible that certain subsequent states of that world—its containing evils that seem to us to be natural evils—are due to Satan or Satan's cohorts. That being so, and granting God's conjectured policy of strict noninterference with significant freedom, once granted, those evil states are consistent with God, after the fashion in which the free-will defense argues that moral evils are consistent with God.

Although Plantinga's Satan hypothesis does not require, or explicitly include, good angels as well as bad, let us stay close to the Christian story and say that, on that hypothesis, T(W) provides for their existence too and that the actual world W contains the archangel Michael and his cohorts, in addition to Satan and Satan's cohorts.[14] So T(W) includes DS and DM (diminished Michael). It is possible that DS will become GS, good Satan, and possible it will become ES, evil Satan (the Satan of Plantinga's extended defense), and possible that DM will become GM or EM, good and evil Michael, respectively.

The possible world WP differs from W in that Satan (good or bad) does not exist in WP. In order to weakly actualize WP, God must strongly actualize T(WP), the largest state of affairs God actualizes in WP. T(WP) differs from T(W) principally by virtue of its excluding DS. Thus, if God strongly actualizes T(WP), it is logically impossible for W, and Satan in particular, to come to exist, as W is not among the possible successor worlds to T(WP) and there is no proto-Satan included in T(WP).

Essentially, then, given our earlier stipulation, the reformed logical argument comprises the two following stages: an argument for the proposition that it is logically possible for omnipotence to strongly actualize $T(W^P)$, instead of $T(W)$; and an argument for the proposition that we have good reason to think that there is not a God-justifying reason for God to strongly actualize $T(W)$ instead of $T(W^P)$. In discussing the second stage, let us agree that $T(W)$ and $T(W^P)$ are the only viable candidates for strong actualization available to God. Thus, given that God will strongly actualize some diminished world—taking $T(W)$ and $T(W^P)$ to be world-essences, thus related to their respective successor worlds in a way analogous to the relation between person-essences and persons—God's having good reason for not actualizing $T(W^P)$ is tantamount to God's having good reason to actualize $T(W)$, and vice versa. This agreement will keep the discussion from getting intolerably unwieldy. Deployed against Plantinga's extended free-will defense, where that defense is understood in the broad sense of including Plantinga's arguments defending the free-will defense against attack, the thrust of the reformed argument is that the free-will defense does not provide good reason to think that possibly God could not have strongly actualized $T(W^P)$.

Plantinga's version of the free-will defense is predicated upon God's having middle knowledge.[15] If God has middle knowledge, then, among other things, God knows both future contingents and counterfactuals of freedom. So, for instance, first, in weakly actualizing the actual world with its mix of significantly free human and nonhuman moral agents, God knows both that sometimes their respective freedoms will be exercised in evil ways and what those evils ways will be, and second, God knows that if God were to have actualized W^P instead of the actual world, the free, rational beings in that possible world would have exercised their significant freedoms in such-and-such good and evil ways. In "Evil and Omnipotence," J. L. Mackie argued that as God, possessing middle knowledge, knows how things will work out in each of two weakly actualizable possible worlds containing free creatures, God is morally obligated to weakly actualize the less evil of those two possible worlds, W^P in the present instance, all other relevant things being equal. As Mackie thought that among the less-evil-than-the-actual-world possible worlds available to God for actualization was a possible world entirely free of moral evil, Mackie would not endorse my point that there is God-justifying reason for God to actualize W^p, for W^p does contain a great deal of moral evil. Notwithstanding that, though, my argument in this chapter is akin to Mackie's in some important respects, and for that reason it must address Plantinga's counterargument to Mackie's argument (and Mackielike arguments), a counterargument predicated on the possibility that every significantly free creature in any God-made world suffers from the condition Plantinga calls "transworld depravity."

This is a more robust concept of depravity than the one used by Swinburne in *his* extension of a free-will defense from moral to natural evil. For the depravity that Swinburne postulates as a necessary precondition of significantly free choice is our being seriously *tempted* to do evil. It does not include or entail our actually *doing* evil.[16] By contrast, transworld depravity is posited as possibly an essential property of each significantly free creature such that, in every possible world in which a particular significantly free creature exists, (1) there is an action that he or she regards as morally significant for him or her, and (2) he or she freely goes wrong with respect to that action.

Mackie's thrust against free-will defenses of theism is that if God is able to make significantly free creatures who sometimes freely choose good over evil, then God is able to make significantly free creatures who always freely choose good over evil. The salient point is that, "if there is no logical impossibility in a man's freely choosing the good on one, or on several, occasions, there cannot be a logical impossibility in his freely choosing the good on every occasion."[17]

Plantinga counters that possibly it is beyond the power of omnipotence to actualize a world in which all significantly free persons always choose the good, for possibly all such persons suffer from transworld depravity. This is to say that every significantly free creature could be depraved in all possible worlds in which it exists, with the effect that, in each of those worlds, he or she would choose evil at least once. If this is so, then it is logically impossible for God to weakly actualize a significantly free creature who always does right in all possible worlds in which it exists. If the possibility of transworld depravity is granted, then necessarily there is a possible significantly free creature that God, although omnipotent, cannot weakly actualize: a significantly free creature who always and only does right. Thus, on the transworld depravity conjecture, Plantinga's counterposition to Mackie is that, "there are possible worlds including God's existence that [God] could not have weakly actualized."[18] From that Plantinga goes on to the possibility that "all the worlds displaying a better mixture of good and evil than the actual world contains—all these worlds are among the worlds God could not have weakly actualized."[19]

Plantinga's most recent version of the argument for the proposition that there are possible worlds that include God's existence that God could not have weakly actualized is in his 1985 "Self-Profile," and, as he rightly regards this formulation as less "complicated, messy and hard to follow"[20] than the longer version he gave approximately a decade earlier in *The Nature of Necessity*, it is the formulation I follow here.

Plantinga's argument for God's being unable, notwithstanding his essential omnipotence, to weakly actualize many possible worlds is as follows. Lewis's Lemma is true. Lewis's Lemma, named for David K. Lewis, is what Plantinga calls the proposition that, for every world W in which God exists, God could have weakly actualized W only if $G(T(W)) \to W$ is true. As Plantinga uses certain formalisms in his argument, we need some terminological guidance before going further. Plantinga uses the following technical terms with the following meanings: "$T(W)$" represents the largest state of affairs God strongly actualizes in a world, W; "$\to$" expresses the counterfactual connective, thus "$\sim k \to t$" means that t is counterfactually implied by not-k—for instance, "if kangaroos had no tails ($\sim k$), they would topple over (t)," to use Lewis's example;[21] "$G(A)$" denotes God's strongly actualizing A.[22] I shall abide by Plantinga's usage. Here now, in his own words, is the remainder of Plantinga's argument for the proposition that there are possible worlds that God, although essentially omnipotent, could not weakly actualize:

given Lewis's Lemma it is easy to show that there are possible worlds God could not have weakly actualized. For consider a world W in which, say, Eve freely refrains from taking an apple, and consider T(W). T(W) does not include Eve's freely refraining from taking the apple (if it did, then in W it would be the case that God strongly actualizes Eve's freely refraining from taking the apple, which is impossible). It is therefore possible that God should strongly actualize the very same state of affairs that he actualizes in W, and Eve freely *take* the apple. . . . [T]here is another possible world W* in which Eve freely takes the apple and in which God strongly actualizes the very same state of affairs he strongly actualizes in W. But then $T(W) = T(W*)$. By Lewis's Lemma it was within God's power to actualize each of W and W* only if both $G(T(W)) \rightarrow W$ and $G(T(W*)) \rightarrow W*$ are true—that is . . . only if both $G(T(W)) \rightarrow W$ and $G(T(W)) \rightarrow W*$ are true. Since W and W* are mutually exclusive, the above counterfactuals can both be true only if $G(T(W))$ is impossible. By hypothesis, however, $G(T(W))$ is possible; hence either W or W* is such that it was not within the power of God to actualize it. Accordingly, there are possible worlds including God's existence that he could not have weakly actualized.[23]

I agree Plantinga has shown that possibly God could not weakly actualize a significantly free person who always does good, and also that there are possible worlds, including possible worlds whose overall balance of good and evil surpasses that of the actual world, that God could not have weakly actualized. But Plantinga's having shown those things does not blunt the thrust of the reformed logical argument. Plantinga's counterargument to Mackie does not show, or even give us reason to think, that God could not have strongly actualized $T(W^P)$ in preference to $T(W)$. Indeed, as Plantinga acknowledges, "[God] might have been able to create worlds in which moral evil is very considerably outweighed by moral good; but it was not within the power of omnipotence to create worlds containing moral good but no moral evil."[24]

It is not my claim that, in W^P, moral evil due to human persons is far outweighed by moral good due to human persons. We do not know that to be so, for we do not know how much of either kind exists in that possible world. But we do know that neither Satan nor Satan's cohorts exist in W^P, so we know there is in W^P no broadly moral evil (a.k.a. natural evil, NERNP in particular) due to them.

What we do know, then, is that in W^P there is far less moral evil, understood as *both* moral evil due to human persons and broadly moral evil, than in the actual world, W. But, according to the Satan hypothesis, there is no natural evil in W, or at least, if we temper that point with van Inwagen's argument, none in excess of some quantity due to chance or the initial state of things in the universe. And neither is there any natural evil above some quantity due to chance in W^P. Thus we know that in W^P there is less evil than in W and, as the quantity of evil that Plantinga's defense would attribute to Satan and Satan's cohorts is huge, we know there is *much less* evil in W^P than in W.

As deployed against Plantinga, the reformed argument for the proposition that God could and should have actualized W^P in preference to W has two stages, and I offer two versions of the second stage. Then I describe and endorse an argument of Richard Gale's, to which my argument bears a certain likeness.

Reformed Logical Argument: First Stage

The issue addressed here is whether it is within the power of omnipotence to have strongly actualized $T(W^P)$ over $T(W)$, and more specifically, whether there is anything in Plantinga's counterargument to Mackie blocking the idea that it is in God's power to have strongly actualized $T(W^P)$. The question in this first stage is not whether God should have strongly actualized $T(W^P)$, but simply whether God could have. The relevant difference between these two largest states of affairs, $T(W)$ and $T(W^P)$, is the absence of DS (as well as of the essences of Satan's cohorts) from $T(W^P)$ and the presence of DS (along with the cohort essences) in $T(W)$. Here I am taking the actual world to be as Plantinga, in his extension of the free-will defense, describes it. Without DS and its associated essences, $T(W)$ would be $T(W^P)$. The question before us is simply whether it is possible for God to actualize a world in which Satan never exists, or whether it is necessary for God to strongly actualize DS. Clearly, the answer is that it is possible, for it is plainly false that W^x is a possible world actualizable by God only provided that Satan exists in W^x. The existence of Satan is not a necessary feature in every possible world actualizable by God. Satan, in all worlds in which Satan exists, exists contingently, not necessarily. Thus, it is within the power of omnipotence to strongly actualize T(Wᴾ).

Reformed Logical Argument: Second Stage (First Version)

The argument in this second stage is that, given God's power to strongly actualize T(Wᴾ) instead of T(W), if God exists, God *would* strongly actualize T(Wᴾ) instead of T(W), thereby precluding the possibility of Satan's existence. This stage of the argument is directed at the "omniscience" and "goodness" clauses in the definition of "God."

God knows that if God strongly actualizes T(W), God actualizes DS and DM. God knows that DS is a particular combination of, among other things, psychological traits and capacities; for instance, capacities to cause and to enjoy causing pain and suffering on a huge scale over the whole of history. God knows that DM is another particular combination of traits and capacities. God knows that DS has the capacity to become the Satan of the Christian story (as well as of Plantinga's defense). God knows that if God strongly actualizes T(Wᴾ), God will not have actualized DS, thus that there is no possibility that Satan (as described in Plantinga's defense) will exist. Whether God strongly actualizes T(W) or T(Wᴾ), God strongly actualizes DM, as well as all the same human-person essences. And, given Plantinga's counterargument to Mackie, let us stipulate that each one of those essences suffers from transworld depravity, thus each whole person, angelic and human, who develops from each essence goes wrong at least once. Thus, whether DM becomes GM or EM, good or evil Michael, respectively, Michael goes wrong in both W and Wᴾ. The salient difference is that if DM becomes EM, then the amount of evil due to Michael will be considerably more than would be due to him if DM had become GM instead.

God knows the capacity for good and evil of DM. God knows that, while DM may possibly develop into EM, evil Michael, DM's pychological capacity for evil, as well as his taste for it, are much less than DS's. Thus God knows that if God strongly actualizes T(Wᴾ), it is logically possibly that the successor person to DM will go seriously wrong and become EM. But, knowing that DM's capacity for evil is much less than DS's, God knows that EM would do vastly less harm than ES. The question this raises, given that the divine plan is just as realizable in W^P as in W, is twofold: why would God take the risk of weakly actualizing ES and what God-justifying reason would there be for God to take that risk in these circumstances? Parenthetically, the knowledge God has in this version of the argument is not middle knowledge. It is the knowledge of the psychological makeup, the intelligence, power, and other capacities of various person-essences (human and angelic).

Plantinga's counterargument to Mackie does not block this argument. Arguably it does not even address it. For the thrust of the argument is that, knowing what God knows about each of T(W^P) and T(W), in particular the respective capacities for evil of DM and DS, and knowing that the divine plan is as realizable in the successor-worlds to T(W^P) as in those to T(W), God should have strongly actualized T(W^P). Its thrust, quite simply, is that God should not have created Satan: its thrust is not that God should create only human persons.

Here is an objection to the foregoing argument. God strongly actualizes T(W), knowing that it is logically possible that DS will become GS, good Satan, thus not the evil being of Plantinga's defense. Let us strengthen the objection by stipulating that good Satan would be very good. Knowing it is logically possible that DS will transpire to be a very good angel—let us say God knows that, logically speaking, there is an even chance that DS will become GS or ES—is not God off the hook? That is, is it not just a matter of bad luck that Satan (as described by Plantinga) turned out to be the successor-person to DS? It could just as well have gone the other way.

But this objection miscarries, for it could not just as well have gone the other way. True, the logical possibilities are as stated in the objection. But it is the psychological, not the logical, possibilities that are crucial. As noted, the essence of Satan has a certain psychological makeup: that is, DS is a certain combination of "freedom-neutral" properties, for instance, among other things, various psychological traits, tendencies, capacities, and so on. There is a gap between what God strongly actualizes—DS—and what God weakly actualizes—ES or GS—and the gap is bridged by Satan's exercise of Satan's significant freedom. But Satan's freedom is not just randomness or arbitrariness. It is the freedom of a being with a certain character, a certain set of traits, dispositions, capacities. Satan's freedom, like that of any other significantly free being, is freedom in character. But Satan's character—shaped in large measure by DS—inclines to large-scale, prolonged evil, indeed a campaign of evil over the whole of history. That is, Satan's psychological makeup means it is not an even chance that the successor-person to DS will be GS or ES: that psychological makeup means it is likely that if God strongly actualizes T(W), which includes DS, that ES will result. And knowing DS, God knows this.

Reformed Logical Argument: Second Stage (Second Version)

This version of the second stage of the argument is also directed at the "omniscience" and "goodness" clauses in the definition of "God." It differs from the foregoing version in that it presupposes, with Plantinga, that God possesses middle knowledge. Thus God knows that if God strongly actualizes T(W), either the conjunction of ES and GM or the conjunction of ES and EM is the weakly actualized result—given that God foreknows that Satan is evil in W. Given transworld depravity, GM goes wrong in W but is nevertheless predominantly good, and God foreknows that too. But God also knows that if God strongly actualizes T(W^P), neither of the conjunctions, ES and GM or ES and EM, will result, and that the outcome will be either GM or EM. Furthermore, God knows which of GM and EM it will actually be. And, as before, all other relevant factors are the same in both worlds, including the full realizability of the divine plan in W^P. As before, then, the question is, what God-justifying reason is there for God to strongly actualize T(W)?

Here is an illustration of the foregoing version of the argument. You are a renowned physician and the head of the cancer unit at a large university medical center and teaching hospital. Among the interns under your supervision are two specializing in surgery, Dr. Alltheway and Dr. Partway. Each of them faces tenure and promotion review in the near future, so they are both in the situation of trying to show themselves worthy of a secure future (with you) at the hospital. As their supervisor and director you know them and their work well, and you give each of them a considerable amount of freedom in the performance of his or her duties at the hospital.

A patient at the hospital suffers from a particular cancer. It is your responsibility to assign the case. Your available choices are the following. You could give the patient to Dr. Alltheway who has told you she would perform surgical procedure #1. If this course of treatment is followed, the chances of a complete cure are excellent. Or you could assign the case to Dr. Partway, who has told you that he would perform surgical procedure #2. This is a less radical procedure than #1 and sometimes needs to be augmented with a certain limited regimen of chemotherapy. The chances of a complete cure from surgery #2 alone are less good than from #1, but they are still very good. However, when #2 alone does not yield a complete cure and is supplemented with the appropriate chemotherapy, the chances of a complete cure become excellent. As it happens, the chances are then the same as those on #1. And you know all of these things to be so. If #2 needs augmenting, you yourself would introduce and control the supplementary chemotherapy. The last option is for *you* to assume primary responsibility for the patient's care and to use no surgery, but a mix of radiation and chemotherapy instead. The chemotherapy in this radiation-chemotherapy combination would be more extensive and prolonged than that which would be used in augmentation of #2. As it happens, the chances of a complete cure from this radiation-cum-chemotherapy treatment are also identical to those from #1.

Dr. Alltheway's proposed course of treatment, being major surgery, is riskier to the patient than any of the other treatments, that is to say, the chances that the cure will kill the patient are greater on #1 than on any of the others. However, surgery #1 is not very or unusually risky, as major surgeries go, but it *is* riskier than the other options for this patient. And you know all of this, too. These are the only courses of treatment that are appropriate, and you know it. You discuss the case with Drs. Alltheway and Partway and they each tell you clearly what they would do if given it. As a result, you are justifiably confident that you know what each would do and what the respective outcomes would be. For all practical purposes in this example, you have the equivalent of middle knowledge.

This whole situation is taking place in the future. It is a future where medical and neurophysical knowledge is much greater than at present. Compared to things at present, great advances have been made in the understanding, calibration, and control of pain, and highly accurate predictions are commonly and routinely made of the pain and suffering due to surgery and prescription medication. Now factoring in the risk to the patient of each course of treatment, along with the expected pain, suffering, and discomfort to the patient of each treatment, and expressing their conjunction on a grid—a practice both reliable and common in this medical future— the results are as follows: with Dr. Alltheway's approach, the combined level of risk, pain, suffering, and discomfort is quite high on the Pain/Risk Index (as it is called), being in the range p^9; with Dr. Partway's unaugmented approach, it is in the range p^3; with Dr. Partway's augmented approach, it is in the range p^4; with your own radiation-chemotherapy approach, it is in the range of p^3 to p^4. The Pain/Risk Index operates with a rating scale of p^0 to p^{15}.

Yours being a teaching hospital, you factor into your decision about assigning this case your obligation to the medical education of all the interns in your unit. It so happens, though, that all your interns need exposure to all of the above courses of treatment. Furthermore, as it happens, their need is the same for all the treatments mentioned that involve surgery, slightly less for the radiation-chemotherapy mix, while being greater for no other kind of treatment than for those involving surgery. One final happy coincidence, the financial costs of surgeries #1 and #2 (supplemented), and the mixed radiation-chemotherapy approach are identical, while that of the unsupplemented surgery #2 is less. All are fully covered by insurance. The risk that #1 will lead to a lawsuit against doctors or the hospital or both is somewhat higher than the risk that any of the others will, and there is an equal risk among all of those others that a lawsuit will be brought. The lawyers have explained all this to you. As the patient has no family, friends, or other representative to speak in the patient's behalf, and as, for an objectively good reason, the patient is unable to make a choice, you must choose the treatment. Let it be noted that, as both a doctor and the head of the cancer unit, your objectives in the present case are these: to do the best possible for the patient; to provide good training to your interns; and to avoid unnecessary costs and risks to the hospital. And you take very seriously your responsibility in each of these areas.

The pressing question before you in the present situation is this:

which doctor and which procedure should you choose? From a moral point of view, which is the right choice? Or, to come at the issue from another direction, which course, if any, should you not choose, that is to say, are any of these possible courses of treatment morally impermissible choices given the availability of the others? In the terminology of strong and weak actualization of states, your decision is between the strong actualization of various states, whose successor states are known to you: that is, your equivalent for all practical purposes of middle knowledge means you know which states you will weakly actualize. The answer to the last question is clear: you ought not to choose Dr. Alltheway's surgical treatment. Given the availability of the other options as described, in giving this case to Dr. Alltheway you would be bringing about a situation in which the patient would suffer unnecessarily and avoidably. That is, you would knowingly be weakly actualizing a situation in which there is more (avoidable) evil than in another situation you could have knowingly actualized instead, while there is no outweighing or even balancing good in the former situation, indeed there is no good in the former situation absent from the latter.

Just about equally clear is the answer to the first formulation of the question: Dr. Partway's proposed unaugmented procedure #2 is the right moral choice. You would be subjecting the patient to less risk, pain, suffering, and discomfort than you would if you chose another available treatment instead, the hospital to a lower risk of legal trouble than in the case of #1, and all other relevant factors are the same as in the other available options. True, the chances of achieving a complete cure using #2 alone are less than if you chose another treatment instead, but the chances are still very good and, without making the total package of risk, pain, suffering, and discomfort exceed that for #1, indeed without making it even come close to the level of #1, you could subsequently augment #2 if need be, and then have a chance of complete success just as good as with any of the alternatives to #2 (unaugmented). In choosing to begin with the unaugmented #2, your obligations to your interns and to your hospital's reputation and bottom line are met just as well as they would be if you chose another option instead.

How does this test case relate to the free-will defense as a defense against a logical argument based upon the existence in the world of a vast amount of evil, NERNP, that seems to be NENP[i] (in the Satan hypothesis, a subset of broadly moral evils)? Recall that, in Plantinga's estimation, the free-will defense is "simplicity itself,"[25] namely, that if an evil occurrence is due to the free agency of a free being, and if God so values the freedom of God's free creatures that God does not interfere with it, then that evil occurrence is not inconsistent with God's existence. This is because "[God] could forestall the occurrence of moral evil only by removing the possibility of moral good,"[26] inasmuch as the possibility of moral good presupposes freedom with respect to morally significant actions, and if God "causes [God's creatures, for example Satan] . . . always to do only what is right, then they don't do what is right freely."[27] Let us see how these points fit your situation in deciding to which doctor you should assign this patient.

You value the freedom of choice and action of Drs. Alltheway and Partway. You value those freedoms equally. Furthermore, you adhere to a strict policy of noninterference with their respective significant freedoms in treating their patients, once you have granted them those freedoms. But those points, whether alone or together, do not entail a moral carte blanche in your granting them such freedoms *in the first place*. If you weakly actualize W^a—the possible world in which you assign the case to Dr. Alltheway—the chances of your principal desideratum's being realized, that is, the patient's being cured, are excellent. If you weakly actualize W^b instead—the possible world in which you assign the case to Dr. Partway—the chances of your principal desideratum's being realized, in two installments, are equally excellent. The principal morally relevant difference is in the cost, as measured on the Pain/Risk Index, of these two courses of action. And the question is, which of W^a and W^b should you choose, knowing what you know? The question that is relevant is *not* whether or not the relevant evils in W^a—that is, the patient's score on the Pain/Risk Index—are due to free choices of Dr. Alltheway's, or whether, once you have given Dr. Alltheway the case, that is, granted her the freedom to treat the patient her way, you should take the case away from her or interfere in some other way. The choice, that is, is *not* between freedom and determinism, or even between more and less freedom, for, in W^b, Dr. Partway has just as much freedom as Dr. Alltheway does in W^a. A modified version of our test case will bring the main point at issue here into clear view.

The patient suffers from the same cancer as before. Dr. Alltheway recommends surgery #1. Suppose, however, that surgery #1 is the standard treatment in cases such as the patient's, and that both you and the majority of doctors involved in cancer treatment are familiar with surgery #1 and with its being the standard procedure in such cases as this. The chances of success are excellent. No doctor in your unit proposes another course of treatment, nor does the relevant medical literature. You duly assign the case to Dr. Alltheway. She operates. The patient's score on the Pain/Risk Index is in the range p^9, as in the earlier version of this scenario. The patient's postoperative pain and suffering is NE~RNP—natural evil not resulting solely from natural processes—due to certain freely done actions of Dr. Alltheway, actions that both you and Dr. Alltheway knew in advance would result in p^9-range postoperative pain and suffering. Surely, in this instance, nobody would second-guess your assignment of the patient to Dr. Alltheway for surgery #1. That is, nobody would or could reasonably second-guess your having weakly actualized W^a, the possible world in which she freely performs surgery #1 on the patient, resulting in p^9-range postoperative pain and suffering.

The free-will defender will claim a telling parallel here between your role in assigning the case, under the circumstances just now described, and God's weakly actualizing the actual world on the Satan hypothesis. The supposed parallel is this. The actual world contains NERNP, the largest class of prima facie $NENP^i$. We are all familiar with it. We accept it as a fact of life. If such evil is due to the free agency of a significantly free being, and if God, for good reason, follows a policy of strict noninterference in the exercise of the significant freedoms of God's creatures, then, granting the Satan hypothesis, Satan is to blame for NERNP, not God, and God is off the moral hook, insofar as such evil is concerned. Applied to the variation on our test case just described, this is the thinking in the free-will defense. And if God's actualization of the actual world on the Satan hypothesis were akin to the variation and not to the original test case itself, then the free-will defense would be in the clear. But the real parallel to God's actualization of the actual world on the

Satan hypothesis is the original version of the test case, not the variation.

To see this clearly, let us, in a variation upon the variation just described, go back much closer to the original version. Suppose now that, while surgery #1 is the standard treatment for cancers such as the patient's, you, being a doctor well-read in current cancer research and treatment, know there are also treatment options that are not yet as widely known and well established as #1; in particular, those alternative treatments earlier described—Dr. Partway's unaugmented and augmented approaches, your own nonsurgical regimen. Furthermore, you know that the chances of success for unaugmented surgery #2 are very good, that the chances on the augmented #2 are excellent and the same as for #1, and that the same is true of the combined radiation-chemotherapy approach. In addition you know the scores on the Pain/Risk Index of each of these are much lower than the score for #1. Yet, knowing these things, you assign the case to Dr. Alltheway for surgery #1. Is it now unreasonable or far-fetched to second-guess your choice, that is, your weak actualization of W^a? Surely not. But Dr. Alltheway acted freely, you say, and your policy of noninterference is overall beneficial and well known, and furthermore, surgery #1 is the most familiar of the options—just as the actual world with all of its many forms of NERNP is more familiar to us than the possible world W^p. All of these things are true, but they do not now even begin to get you off the moral hook for giving Dr. Alltheway the case to begin with, when you had equally viable and far less painful alternatives available.

At issue here in the variation upon the variation of our initial illustration is your choice among the possible worlds available to you for actualization, not Dr. Alltheway's freedom, not your policy of noninterference with freedom once freedom is granted, and not the wider familiarity within the medical community with treatment #1 than with either alternative. If you assign the case to Dr. Alltheway in the variation upon the variation of the story, your challenger need dispute or deny none of those points in order to press his or her argument that your assignment of the case is, at a minimum, second-guessable, for none is relevant to the situation as described.

And so it is with Satan's significant freedom and God's noninterference. Our challenge to Plantinga's defense need dispute or deny neither God's strict policy, both with OT and Plantinga's defense, of noninterference with significant creaturely freedom once granted, nor the relative greater familiarity to us of the actual world (with its abundant variety of evils, including NERNP) than the proposed alternative, W^P. To be sure, the actual world *on the Satan hypothesis* is not widely familiar. That is, it is not the way the actual world is widely regarded, but that is beside the point at present. The relevant point is that a world with extensive NERNP is a commonplace of our experience. (Of course, Satan's freedom would be moot if W^P were God's chosen world, as Satan never exists in W^P, but that is a different point.)

Here is an objection based on the notion of transworld depravity. You know both Dr. Alltheway and Dr. Partway very well. You have been a mentor to each of them, and you have examined their work and temperaments very closely since their respective residencies at your hospital began. You know their respective strengths and weaknesses.

Things sometimes go wrong in surgery; the unforeseen occurs, and virtually without warning there is a crisis and the life of the patient on the table is in serious danger. You know that both doctors are capable of handling such emergencies well. They would not be on your staff otherwise. But you know that, in such situations, when split-second decisions will mean life or death for the patient, Dr. Alltheway has a tendency to overreact and that, in certain circumstances, this could be disastrous. Unlike Dr. Alltheway, Dr. Partway is not prone to overreaction, but, in such crises, he is sometimes short-tempered with the attending nurses and hurts their feelings. This rounds out the account of what you know before you assign the case. Is Dr. Partway's tendency to occasional hurtful snappishness under pressure reason for you to not assign him this patient, reason to suppose that the moral pros and cons of both putative assignments of the patient work out to be, for all you can tell, even? If they do work out to be even, then, from a moral point of view, it does not matter to which doctor you assign this patient. But surely the factors that bear on your decision do not work out to be, for all you can tell, even at all. Perfection is improbable either way. But the risk involved in giving the patient to Dr. Alltheway is far greater than that involved in giving the patient to Dr. Partway. Under the circumstances as described, it is both not clear what would justify an assignment of the patient to Dr. Alltheway and reasonably clear that there is good reason to not assign the patient to her, with Dr. Partway available.

The actual world contains, in great abundance, evils that outside the Satan hypothesis, we think of as resulting just from the operations of natural processes themselves. Possibly it also contains Satan and Satan's cohorts who, unbeknownst to us, are causing those evils. Furthermore, with the Satan hypothesis, the divine plan is realizable in the actual world. That is not contested here. What *is* contested is the cost of its realizability. For the divine plan is also realizable in W^p, but at significantly less cost in evil. In W^p, there is neither Satan nor Satan's cohorts, thus, in the Satan hypothesis itself, no NERNP, or at least none that is prima facie NENP^i.[28]

Your decision to give the case to Dr. Partway and not to Dr. Alltheway would be parallel to God's choosing to weakly actualize W^p in preference to the actual world. Thus, in light of OT's proposition 8—in a God-made world there could be no NENP^i—in light of the world-making criterion, c2, that proposition 8 begets, as well as in light of the fact that it is the actual world and not W^p that actually exists, the reformed problem of evil is OT's problem of defending the proposition that the actual world could be God-made, given the availability of W^p as an equally viable and superior alternative. In this chapter that problem has been subcontracted to Plantinga's extended free-will defense, thus making OT's problem of self-defense Plantinga's problem.

In essence, the central question is not as the free-will defense would have us frame it, namely, either (1) how could God, consistent with the grant of significant freedom to all created persons, possibly interfere with his creatures' significant freedoms? or (2) granting the possibility of transworld depravity for all significantly free creatures, how could God weakly actualize any world in which there is no moral evil? Instead of (1), the central question is this: what viable possible worlds, in addition to that which we know as the actual world, were available to God to choose among *prior* to God's actualization of any one of them? And instead of (2), the central question is this: given that the divine plan is as realizable in W^p as in W, and that W contains no surpassing good lacking in W^p, what God-justifying reason is there to actualize a world containing so much avoidable evil (that is, broadly moral evil due to Satan or Satan's cohorts), when its avoidability involves neither any abridgment of freedom in W^P (compared to W) nor W^P's being an impossible and unconducive-to-soul-making utopia, compared to W? In sum: with W^P available as not just a viable but, to all intents and purposes, a superior alternative, what is the God-justifying reason for the actual world to exist instead of W^P, if God exists?

Gale's Argument

In one respect, both versions of the second stage of my argument presuppose the following point emphasized by Richard Gale: the freedom of a significantly free creature always reflects that creature's character. Significant freedom is never arbitrariness. My freedom is always *my* freedom: it both issues from and reflects who and what I am. An essential component of what I am is my psychological makeup, and to a large degree that component is part of my person-essence, as strongly actualized by God.

Going on from this point, Gale argues that the following conditions are sufficient to cancel significant freedom: "if M_1's actions and choices result from psychological conditions that are intentionally determined by another [person] M_2, then those actions and choices are not free," and "M_2 has a freedom-cancelling control over M_1 if M_2 causes most of M_1's behavior."[29] He then goes on to argue that God's relation to created persons in Plantinga's version of the free-will defense satisfies one or both of those conditions: "it is clear that [God's relation to created persons in Plantinga's free-will defense] satisfies [the first condition], since according to [Plantinga's free-will defense], God intentionally causes a created free person to have all of her freedom-neutral properties, which include her psychological make-up,[30] and "the God-man relation in [Plantinga's free-will defense] also satisfies [the second condition]; for, when God instantiates diminished possible persons or sets of freedom-neutral properties, he does have middle knowledge of what choices and actions will result, and thereby sufficiently causes them."[31]

By this analysis, the upshot of Plantinga's version of the free-will defense is that, by virtue, first, of God's creation of the essence of each person and, second, of the fact that each person's free behavior issues from (and reflects) his or her essence, God has a freedom-cancelling control over created persons, thus that Plantinga's defense is not, despite its name, a *free-will* defense. But if Gale is right, it is not just that Plantinga's free-will defense is misnamed, that it is really a kind of defense other than a free-will defense. If Gale is right, Plantinga's defense entails a denial of the significant freedom of human persons. Thus, if Gale is right, Plantinga's defense is inconsistent with OT and so cannot defend it.

Further Objections

Let us turn now to the following five objections.

1. Maybe God could not actualize W^p for the following reason: that, if God weakly actualizes a world without Satan or Satan's cohorts in it, supposing for the sake of argument that they exist in the actual world, then God would thereby have wronged Satan or Satan's cohorts by the omission, thus that God could not actualize W^p. But that is false. Prior to God's choice between possible worlds, none of the free beings, with the exception of God, who would populate those worlds, if those worlds were actualized, exists. But God is under no obligation to any possible being to actualize that possible being. Thus, no wrong is done to Satan—who, of course, would then be only a possible being—if W^p were actualized by God.[32]

2. Here is a second objection to my position. It is that, notwithstanding my having shown that Plantinga's free-will defense fails to block or defeat the reformed logical argument from the prima facie $NENP^i$ that NERNP represents, I do not refute that defense. That is true. But it is also irrelevant, for I neither aim nor claim to refute Plantinga's defense. Nor does my position, in order to succeed, require its refutation, or the refutation of any defense for that matter. But, from the fact that Plantinga's free-will defense's failure to defend orthodox theism against the reformed logical argument does not entail that defense's failure to defend restricted theism against a standard form of the argument from evil, only cold comfort should be taken. Given the superiority, on a scale of verisimilitude, of OT to restricted theism as a representation of the propositional content

of religious belief in the Abrahamic tradition, together with the attendant superiority of the reformed to the standard version of the logical argument from evil, it is a defense of OT against the reformed argument, and not just a defense of restricted theism against the standard argument from evil that is required.

3. Although the foregoing objection does not, in itself, amount to much, we can use a variation on it to raise a more interesting objection. The variation goes as follows. For the sake of argument, let it be stipulated that Plantinga's defense is adequate to the task of defending restricted theism against standard (which is to say, unreformed) logical arguments from evil. But restricted theism's being successfully defensible is necessary for a successful defense of OT, inasmuch as restricted theism is proposition 1 of OT. Thus, a successful defense of restricted theism keeps open the possibility that OT is logically consistent with the facts of prima facie NENP^i in question, or, at the least, the possibility that OT is not shown to be inconsistent with those facts. Thus, my reformed argument fails, for a successful defense of OT need only show either that OT and the facts of prima facie NENP^i in question are not shown to be logically inconsistent with one another or that it is possible for OT and those facts to coexist. So, the objection concludes, since Plantinga's free-will defense succeeds in defense of restricted theism, that defense successfully defends OT, too.

But this objection is not successful. The reason is that my argument—indeed, the very essence of what I have been calling a reformed logical problem of evil—is that there is good reason to think that propositions essential to OT, *but that are not part of restricted theism*, are either inconsistent with certain facts of evil or that theism's defenses are not up to the task of showing that the propositions and facts in question are not mutually inconsistent. Among the propositions in question are propositions 4, 5, and 8 of OT. In proposition 8, there could be no NENP^i in a God-made world, while 4 and 5 say that in any God-made world containing free human beings, there is a divine plan of a certain sort. Thus, even a successful defense of restricted theism is no defense against an argument that targets the conjunction of those three propositions, or any of them singly, or any other proposition or propositions of OT, other than proposition 1 taken alone. Therefore, a successful defense of restricted theism, while necessary for defense of OT, is not sufficient to defend it in either the maximal or minimal sense of defense. Thus, the objection fails.

4. A fourth objection is to a central tenet of my case, namely, the entailment that I have claimed between, on the one hand, the epistemic condition of a human being's needing both to be able to learn, and to be justified in believing, certain practical (and other) beliefs and, on the other hand, the ontological condition of W^P's having to contain order and NEM. The quickest way to get to this objection is through a variation on a previously used thought experiment.

This objection's basic idea is very simple, namely, that it is logically possible that all our beliefs are implanted and all our experiences are caused incognito by some powerful agent—God in the present context. This could be done either in a once-for-all-time way or on an occasion-by-occasion basis. If the former, our practical beliefs would have to be on a time-release formula so as, consistent with God's implantation's being incognito, to have it seem to us that we were acquiring these beliefs along the way. If the latter, the situation would not be essentially different in any significant epistemic respect from Hilary Putnam's brain-in-the-vat idea. For present purposes, the mechanism of implantation is irrelevant. The essential point here is that, by means of implantation, we would have practical (and other) beliefs, all the while justifiably (but falsely) believing that we were acquiring and testing them by veridical experience of events in the external (to our minds) world. Thus, we would be justified in believing those beliefs, and so the epistemic conditions necessary for the divine plan to be realizable would be met. But, given implantation, W^P would not have to be orderly or contain NEM. So, the objection goes, the epistemic conditions could be met without the ontological conditions' having to obtain. (In addition to its being an objection to the reformed logical argument, this is also an objection to Swinburne's defense, for that defense is committed to NEM's being necessary for the same reason.)

Is this objection successful? The answer depends on the question that is before us. If the question is whether practical knowledge, in Swinburne's sense of the term, could be acquired through such implantation as this, the answer is that the objection is successful. In this case, unlike the concept of implantation that was used in the previous chapter, it is not just practical beliefs that are implanted by God. Now the whole of what seems to us to be our sensory experience of a world whose existence is not logically dependent on us is implanted as well. If it were not, the justification condition for practical knowledge could not be met on the present implantation conjecture, and so the fourth objection could not be coherently formulated.

But the relevant question in considering this objection is not whether there are *any* conditions under which practical knowledge could be implanted. Instead, the question that is relevant is whether the implant conjecture is possible in W^p, or in any other God-made world, containing free human beings, in which the divine plan for human life is in effect. And the answer to that question is that it is not possible. Why not? Because God, as defined, is perfectly good and worthy of worship, but the implant conjecture in use in the present objection—unlike the original implant conjecture used in chapter 5, which conjectures only the implantation of true practical beliefs, not practical knowledge—would involve a massive and permanent specieswide deception of human beings that God could not possibly engage in. Why not? Because it is deception. Why is it deception? Because, as the whole of what seems to us to be our sensory experience of a world beyond experience is implanted, for all practical purposes we would be in the same epistemic position vis-à-vis God as the brain in the vat is in vis-à-vis its programmer. But would this deception necessarily be wrong for God to engage in? Yes. Why? Because, in OT—proposition 4, in particular—human beings, in their divinely given nature, are seekers after, and potential discoverers of, truth. So for God to engage in such deception is inconsistent with the perfect goodness clause in the definition of "God" and also, in OT, with God's having created human beings to be potentially successful seekers of the truth. Thus, the present implant conjecture does not break the epistemic-ontological entailment in any God-made world containing free human beings, and so the objection is not successful.

Perhaps, though, the objection could be reformulated. Suppose it is not God but some other very powerful and knowledgeable agent who is responsible for the implantation, and suppose also that all the earlier points about significant freedom still hold. Is not the claimed epistemic-ontological link now broken even in a God-made world? Yes, it is. But that the link is broken in this way does not avail the free-will defense against the reformed logical argument. For now, supposing (with the objection) that the deception is necessary in order for us to possess practical knowledge in a world without NEM, thus that God would want the deception to be made, then, unless God were prepared to perpetrate the deception, God would be dependent upon that other very powerful agent to do so. But such dependence as this is not consistent with the omnipotence clause in the definition of "God" or with the equally deep theistic notion that God is an essentially free being.

But, the objection might be further reformulated, what if it just so happened that the other powerful agent deceives us in the right ways? Does not this serendipity, which is not beyond the bounds of logical possibility, get God off the hook? No, for two reasons. First, given that, on the objection, the implant and its essential deception are necessary in a world where we possess practical knowledge without benefit of NEM, God would still be dependent upon that other agent unless God was prepared to do the deceiving, and the fact that God got lucky does not change that. Second, God would now be in the position of wanting the other agent to deceive us, or of being glad that the agent had deceived us, given the objection's own stipulated need for the deception. That is, God would be in the position not just of *tolerating* that agent's deception (her sin), but of having *wanted* her to sin in the first place, or of being glad that she had sinned. Tolerating sin is one thing, but either wanting an agent to sin or welcoming her sin is quite another. The former is compatible with perfect goodness and with being worthy of worship, but the latter two are not. Thus, a serendipitous (or otherwise) deception caused by another would not do the trick.

5. A fifth objection targets WP. As described, this is a possible world in which no natural evil (or none above a certain level granted for van Inwagen-type reasons) results from natural processes themselves alone. This fifth objection is that if God arranges things in WP so that there is either no NERNP in that world or none above the level mentioned, and if God makes this arrangement secretly and if, as a result, we erroneously and systematically believe there is NERNP

in W^p, then God is guilty of deception, albeit in a way different from the deception discussed in response to the previous objection. But it is impossible for God to be a deceiver. Therefore, this objection goes, there could not be the kind of secret arrangements in W^p that my description of the possible world included, and so W^p is not a possible world that God could actualize, and so my argument, needing W^p to be actualizable by God, collapses.

This objection was discussed in the previous chapter as an objection to the reformed logical argument when deployed against Swinburne's greater-good defense, and so I shall only briefly repeat the earlier-given reason for the objection's failure. But, before doing that, let us look at a different response that applies to the present objection when the objection is made in behalf of Plantinga's free-will defense, but that does not apply to the objection when it is made in behalf of Swinburne's greater-good defense. This unique-to-Plantinga response to the objection is as follows.

Plantinga's Satan hypothesis can function as a possible account of what seems to us to be natural evil only provided it is logically possible for God to actualize a world that, while containing free human beings, contains no indigenous natural evil, or at least none of the sort at issue in the reformed argument, in the amounts in which that sort is at issue in the reformed argument. The possibility of a world with free creatures but without indigenous natural evil (or at least without indigenous prima facie NENP^i) is a condition of the very possibility of the Satan hypothesis itself, thus of Plantinga's extension of the free-will defense from moral to natural evil. But if, as the present objection would have it, it is logically impossible for God to actualize a possible world that does contain free creatures but does not contain indigenous natural evil, without thereby engaging in deception of those human beings, then the Satan hypothesis itself is precluded, and so Plantinga's extension of the free-will defense is precluded, too. Thus, this objection cannot, self-consistently, be made in behalf of Plantinga's extended free-will defense. Now, briefly, I turn to the substantive response to the objection.

The presumption on which this objection turns is that we would not, indeed could not, know there is no indigenous natural evil (NERNP) in W^p. But it is not necessarily the case that we would not know, and false that we could not. We might or might not be in the dark about the true state of things in W^p, that is, it is not necessary that God's arrangement of things in W^p be secret. But even if we are in the dark, even if God arranges things in W^p in secret, that is not to say that we are misled or deceived by God. The concept of doing something secretly is not identical to the concept of doing something deceptively, nor does the former entail the latter. To suppose otherwise is just an error. For instance, God keeps us uninformed about the origin and fate of the universe, but there is nothing deceptive or morally shady about this. The reason is that although God keeps silent, we are free to discover the truth, and the fact that we do not, if we do not, is not because of deception. Likewise in W^p. In principle, we, the inhabitants of W^p, could learn the truth of how things are in that possible world: and if we do not, it is because we are not intelligent, perceptive, insightful, diligent, imaginative, and so on, enough. But it is not because we are deceived. There is no deception for which God is responsible inherent in, or consequent upon, God's arrangement of things in W^p, as described. Thus, there is no basis for the present objection, and so the objection fails.

The cognitive credentials of the reformed logical argument are stronger for having met the foregoing objections, and the upshot is that, so far as Plantinga's free-will defense is concerned, orthodox theism is undefended against that argument.

Appendix: What's a Devil to Do?

A reader not wishing to deviate at all from the development of the reformed logical argument should skip this appendix. Here I dig a little deeper than I did in the body of the chapter into Plantinga's Satan hypothesis. I begin digging with a question about what behavior it would be reasonable for a being such as Satan to engage in, and I speculate about the answer. These speculations are not objections to Plantinga's hypothesis, for they do not threaten its logical possibility. But I think they do raise questions about its credibility relative to the credibility of the other supernaturalist posits of theism.

According to a certain portion of Christian mythology, God created powerful, knowledgeable, spiritual beings—angels—long before creating human beings. Satan is among the most powerful and knowledgeable of angels. All of the angels lived in the knowledge and presence of God. Then, so the story goes, at a time before the creation of human beings, Satan and Satan's followers among the angels rebelled against God. Following a struggle, won by God and the angels loyal to God, Satan and Satan's followers were banished from the presence of God. Ever since they have been causing all the trouble they can. Given their powers, that is a considerable amount. In Plantinga's hypothesis, it is all of the so-called natural evil in the world.

In this story, Satan has known from the beginning that God exists and made the world. Given Satan's vast knowledge and intelligence, as stipulated in the Satan hypothesis, Satan knows God's plan for the world, or at least knows God's plan for the lives of God's free, rational creatures. Satan knows that both NEM and a great deal of regularity in nature are needed in order for it to be possible for human beings to develop in the ways envisioned in the divine plan for free, rational beings. In Plantinga's Satan hypothesis, NEM is a subset of the broadly moral evil due to Satan and/or Satan's cohorts. And we know from experience that broadly moral evil (a.k.a. natural evil) is very regular indeed: all things being equal, if I cut my finger with a sharp knife, blood will flow out and I will feel pain in the place where the cut is made, and so on for a virtual infinity of occurrences across the whole of our experience of the world.

Now put yourself in Satan's place. Why would you cooperate in God's plan for human life? You are extremely intelligent, so you would not attempt to thwart God's plan by not supplying broadly moral evil at all, for, presumably, God would compensate by actualizing NERNP and you could be expected to know this. (An analogy is to your augmenting Dr. Partway's course of treatment #2, if that treatment, unaugmented, proved unable to supply a complete cure.) No, what you would do, surely, if you were Satan, is to either supply too much pain and suffering or to upset seriously the ubiquitous order in nature, or both. (The two are not mutually exclusive, but we will ignore that.) How? It is obvious how you could supply too much pain and suffering, so let us look at some ways that you might possibly disrupt the natural order.

I go into the Virginia Museum of the Fine Arts in Richmond and spend a pleasant afternoon. I emerge from the museum only to find myself upside down in Fitzgerald's Park in Cork, Ireland. How? Satan, feeling mischievous, and taking a leaf out of "Star Trek," beamed me there. Imagine my disorientation. Imagine my increased disorientation, moments later, to find myself alone in a South American rain forest, then, shortly after, in Hyde Park in Sydney, Australia. Now imagine this occurring randomly throughout the whole human population. Imagine Satan's pleasure. Imagine now a whole range of such disruptions. I open my mouth to speak but no words come. I am mute. And so are you. But not all the time: sometimes I can speak when I want, sometimes I cannot. And the same for you. Or we are reduced to Language Game (2) as described by Wittgenstein in *Philosophical Investigations*.[33] So reduced, our language consists of only the words "block," "pillar," "slab," and "beam." We can imagine two versions of this reduction, less and more radical, respectively. The less radical is that my speakable words—the only words that come when I open my mouth to speak— are only those four; the more radical version is that these are my only words. And the same holds for you and for our whole linguistic community. Imagine the effects. Upon the conduct of science or diplomacy, say. In short, imagine Satan interfering seriously with the regularity we find and take for granted in nature. Once you get the hang of this, it is an easy and, if you possess a certain temperament, diverting, mind game to play.

In the actual world, when animals get too close to fire they feel pain, clearly a biologically useful occurrence. But Satan could easily interfere with the neurological system of animals so that, sometimes, upon getting very close to fire, they feel no pain at all, and feel only pleasure instead. Imagine the casualty rate from fire among animals as a result. Imagine as well a pet-owner's consternation when William, his elderly basset hound, ambles into the lit living-room fire and is consumed therein. It is quite easy to multiply the number and range of examples, using many kinds of causes of injury and death.

In short, what is odd about the Satan hypothesis is how well Satan behaves, how well Satan and Satan's evil followers cooperate with God by so faithfully, regularly, and dependably contributing necessary conditions for the realizability of the divine plan. The amounts, kinds, and distributions of evils in the world, as well as the ubiquitous orderliness in the world, as we find them in experience, are surely distinctly unworthy of a band such as Satan and Satan's followers. Satan, as described in the Satan hypothesis, would surely be quite a disappointment to Satan, if Satan existed. Satan might reasonably think that Satan was only a devil conveniently dreamt up by a theist, a devil-of-the-gaps, in order to further a certain kind of theistic concept of the world.

7

SCHLESINGER'S NO-BEST-POSSIBLE-WORLD DEFENSE

Gratuitous Evil in an Always Surpassable World

Can an essentially omnipotent being do his or her best? If the answer is yes, then is not God, being essentially omnipotent (as well as essentially omniscient and perfectly good), culpable for a great deal of the evil in the world, in particular, natural evil resulting solely from natural processes (NERNP) in excess of a certain amount? For, at an intuitive level (to begin with), it is hard to accept that the natural world reflects the best effort of a being answering to God's description. But if the answer is no, then the way to a conclusion of divine culpability for the amount of NERNP is not so clear. The question is the key to Schlesinger's thinking on the problem of God and evil, and his negative answer to it is the key to his defense of theism against logical forms of the argument from evil.

But the question, as it stands, is ambiguous, so clarification is in order. Broadly speaking, there are two senses of "doing one's best." There is the sense of the term that applies to the finished product: this is the best work you have done, the best table you have made. And there is the sense of the term that applies to the expenditure of effort: I tried my best to do what you asked. Often, but not always, the latter sense suggests failure: I lost the game, but I did my best to win. And sometimes the two senses are coterminous. You tried your hardest in making this table and it is the best one you have made.

Both kinds of doing one's best are limited by the capacity of the doer, but not just by that. In cases covered by the former sense of the term, a limit also derives from the nature of the thing itself: for instance, first, if this is a one-gallon container, then the most water I can get it to contain is one gallon; but second, hitting the best possible backhand may be impossible because, in principle, the concept is open-ended—that is, there may well be no such thing. (But, while there may be no such thing as *the* best possible backhand, this may still be *my* best possible backhand. For I am a limited being, with only this much tennis talent, this much athleticism, and so on.) In the case of the latter sense of the term, I cannot make my best effort to lift this pen. For in present circustances—the pen is very light (relative to the lifting capacity of an adult human being), the gravitational pull on the surface of the earth is no more than usual, I do not suffer from any serious physical disability that might have a bearing on my capacity to lift this pen, and so on—the very idea of my trying my hardest to lift this pen is absurd. It has no application. But it could have, if circumstances changed in certain ways, and so the notion's absurdity in present circumstances is not strict logical absurdity.

The limitation on "doing one's best" in the former sense of the term applies equally to omnipotence and to less-than-omnipotence. God cannot succeed any better than you or I can in getting more than a gallon of water into this one-gallon container. But the limitation in the latter sense does not apply equally to omnipotence and to less-than-omnipotence. For I can indeed try my hardest to lift this rock, but God cannot. To omnipotence, lifting this rock would tax God no more, indeed less, than my lifting this pen. In the latter sense of "doing one's best," then, human beings, sometimes, can certainly do their best: we can, and do, sometimes try our hardest. But in this sense, God, because God is essentially omnipotent, cannot. The upshot is that, in the second sense of the term, we can imagine God singing the line from the old Broadway song— "anything you can do, I can do better: I can do anything better than you"—to God's self and of God's self, and always being right.

Based on the applicability to omnipotence of the limits, in both senses, of doing one's best, Schlesinger's defense stands on a rejection of the Leibnizian idea that God, the being than whom none better or greater is possible, contemplated all possible worlds and then actualized the one with the overall best possible balance of good and evil. Schlesinger's rejection of that idea adds to the long and compelling theistic literature of dissent from the expectation that God could, thus would, actualize the best of all possible worlds. For instance, among influential contemporary theistic philosophers, Plantinga, Schlesinger, and Swinburne maintain there is no such thing as the best of all possible worlds, thus that God could *not* actualize the best possible world.[1] In the words of Bruce Reichenbach, "the notion of best possible world proves to be meaningless."[2] In Schlesinger's version of the contra-Leibnizian view, whether God tries hard or not, for any world that God actualizes, there is always another and better one God could have actualized instead. Or, to revert to the foregoing illustration, God's tennis game, no less than ours, does not accommodate hitting the best possible backhand. There are two reasons: first, arguably "the best possible backhand" is a nonreferring term, and second, unlike mine, presumably the tennis talent and athleticism of an essentially omnipotent being are not limited. Thus, while I could hit *my* best possible backhand, God could not hit God's.

In examining Schlesinger's defense let us accept both that "best possible world" is a term without a referent and that God cannot do God's best in the sense of putting forth the greatest possible effort God is capable of. Let us agree, then, that, for logical reasons, God does not actualize the best of all possible worlds. Thus we agree that God has God-justifying reason to not actualize the best possible world. As a consequence, any possible world God actualizes is always inferior to another that God could have actualized instead, and God is not culpable for the fact that the actual world (for instance) is not the best possible world. An obvious analogy is to your failure to name the highest even number: any even number you name is inferior to another you could have named instead, but to find fault with you on this score would be unjustified, because it would reflect a serious misunderstanding of why you failed, that is, through no fault of your own.

Natural evil is evil for which no human person is responsible, in the moral sense of "responsibility." In light of that, let us interpret the fact that any world God actualizes will be inferior to another God could have actualized instead as the fact that every actual world both contains natural evil and more natural evil than another world God could have actualized instead. Thus, any world God actualizes *nonculpably* contains natural evil, and more natural evil than another world God could have actualized instead. As the kind of natural evil that is the focus of the reformed logical argument is NERNP in excess of a certain level, let us say that, given the impossibility of God's actualizing the best of all possible worlds, any world God actualizes nonculpably contains such evil and contains more of it than another world God could have actualized instead.

But while based in that idea, Schlesinger's position is not limited to it. Instead, his is the considerably stronger point that, regardless of what natural evils there are, in whatever amounts, intensities, or distributions, no NERNP *whatever* either is or could be incompatible with God; that is, no quantity of NERNP could ever be NENP^i. So, while it may seem to us that such-and-such facts of evil are facts of NENP^i, in Schlesinger's theory they cannot possibly be. Since no world God actualizes is unsurpassable, on that theory, it is always possible to say of *any* God-made world, God could have done better. Thus, in that respect, a God-made world with 1,000,000 to the power of a 1,000,000 units of NERNP ($1,000,000^{1,000,000}$ units) is not a world with NENP^i, even though God, with no negative effect upon any of God's goals in world making, could have actualized a world with $1,000^{1,000}$ units instead. For it is true of the world with $1,000^{1,000}$ units of NERNP, too, that God could have actualized an overall better world, say a world with $1,000^{999}$ units, instead.

The difference between the two amounts of NERNP is gratuitous^P natural evil, gratuitous natural evil that is preventable without loss of any greater good. Schlesinger does not deny that. But, in his position it is never gratuitous^P natural evil for which God is culpable, that is, it is never NENP^i. No amount could be. In essence, Schlesinger's position, like Hasker's and van Inwagen's, is committed to the view that gratuitous^P evil, per se, is not logically inconsistent with God, although each one of the three arrives in a different way at this conclusion, and the conclusion is weaker in van Inwagen's case than in either Hasker's or Schlesinger's. For, as we saw, van Inwagen does not rule out the concept of excessive quantities of gratuitous[P] NERNP, that is, he does not rule out the possibility of some evil's being NENP[i].[3]

The novelty and interest of Schlesinger's position come from a conjunction of two things. They are his acceptance of a point typically denied by defenders of theism, namely, the world's being improvable by God, and his denial of the antitheistic conclusion standardly drawn from that improvability, namely, that the world's being the ways it is is evidence in the theism-versus-atheism debate over the existence of God.[4] Recall Hume's seminal expression of the improvability of the world as it is reflected in the thinking behind the standard debate,

> if a very limited intelligence whom we shall suppose utterly unacquainted with the universe were assured that it were the production of a very good, wise, and powerful being . . . he would, from his conjectures, form *beforehand* a different notion of it from what we find it to be by experience; nor would he ever imagine, merely from these attributes of the cause of which he is informed, that the effect would be so full of vice and misery and disorder, as it appears in this life.

And Schlesinger's denial that the fact of the improvability of the world by God, if it is a fact, is evidence in the first place obviously entails a denial that it could be evidence against OT.

Schlesinger's unorthodoxy, relative to those substantive defenses of OT I have been examining—Plantinga's and Swinburne's—raises an important point about my enterprise here. Given the deviation from OT that is implicit in his denial of the proposition that any fact of gratuitous evil is logically inconsistent with the world's being God-made—in effect, his denial of the *possibility* that any fact of evil could disconfirm or refute OT—you may well wonder how Schlesinger's defense can justifiably be examined as a defense of OT at all. For orthodox theism does not deny its own defeasibility in principle by arguments from evil. Given that, the justification for addressing Schlesinger's position as a defense of OT is twofold: first, he intends it as such; second, suppose he succeeds in establishing that no amount of gratuitous[P] NERNP is too much to be compatible with God, then the philosophical problem of evil would "vanish."[5] For the very basis of the standard debate is that either there cannot possibly be any gratuitous^p evil at all in a God-made world or, for van Inwagen-type reasons, there can be some but none above a certain level. So, if Schlesinger (or Hasker) is successful, that basis would be dissolved. And if that were to happen, no version of theism could be threatened by philosophical arguments from evil. So, if Schlesinger succeeds, orthodox theism would be among the beneficiaries. Unlike Plantinga's defense, then, which was devised specifically to defend restricted theism and which we adapted to defend OT, and unlike Swinburne's, which in practice is a defense of an expanded theism *specifically*, Schlesinger's (like Hasker's) is a one-size-fits-all defense.

Possible and Impossible Worlds for God to Actualize

Given that God can neither try God's hardest nor actualize the best of all possible worlds, is it Schlesinger's point that God is free to actualize any possible world at all? It might seem so, but it is not. A recent criticism of Schlesinger's position by Robert Elliot provides a good opportunity for the necessary clarification. Elliot criticizes Schlesinger's thinking on, among other grounds, its allowing God to just "create any world at all."[6] In one way Elliot is right, but in another not, and, in the interest of avoiding a misunderstanding concerning the countercase I make below to Schlesinger's defense, it will be useful before proceeding to clarify the latter point.

Elliot overstates Schlesinger's position a bit, inasmuch as it does not entail God's having a moral carte blanche to actualize just any possible world. For instance, God could not justifiably actualize a world in which God makes and breaks promises, or in which God does not want justice to win through in the end, even if that be in a hereafter,[7] or (assuming it is a world containing free human creatures) in which moral and spiritual development of the sort in question in the divine plan are impossible. But the reason God could not actualize any such worlds has nothing to do with the idea that there is no best possible world. Instead, they are impossible worlds for God to actualize because of certain essential aspects of the divine nature itself. It is untrue, then, that, in Schlesinger's position, God could actualize any possible world at all. But, while a bit off target,

Elliot is not completely, or even very far, off target. To see this, suppose we restrict his point about God's freedom in world-actualization to aspects of possible worlds themselves, specifically, to degrees of improvability or of surpassability of possible worlds, as opposed to aspects of the divine nature. And let us continue to interpret the concepts of improvability and surpassability of worlds in terms of their containing more or less natural evil resulting solely from natural processes.

Now, if there is no best possible world, Schlesinger's point is that, in respect to NERNP, and apart from restrictions due to God's own essential nature on what worlds God can actualize, God may justifiably actualize any possible world.[8] Thus restricted, Elliot is right. In that context, Schlesinger's conclusion is that we are unentitled to any expectation of which possible worlds God could, would, or should actualize and which he could not, would not, or should not actualize. In this view, Hume's expectation, via Philo, of what kinds of worlds God could not or would not actualize is illicit, as is the philosophical debate over God and evil that is built on the supposition of that expectation's legitimacy.

Proceeding in this way, Schlesinger, in his defense, does not directly answer or attempt to answer the antitheist's question about prima facie NENP[i] so much as he attempts to finesse it. For his aim is to rob the question, thus the philosophical problem of evil that it drives, of its force, and he aims to do this by emphasizing implications for morally justified divine behavior of the two un-Leibnizian impossibilities discussed.

Viewing this defensive strategy within the framework of our two-part scheme of theistic defenses, defenses that operate by disputing the evidence and defenses that operate by providing an alibi, Schlesinger's defense belongs to both groups. It belongs to the former because of its denial that, owing to special circumstances, any facts of evil that might be cited as counterevidence to theism *are* counterevidence. And it belongs to the latter group because those special circumstances provide God an alibi—they are circumstances supposedly making it impossible for God to have done what the prosecution alleges, namely, culpably permitted or failed to prevent the world's being such-and-such.

Socrates, the Fool, and the Pig

The idea that God could have done better than God did in world actualization reflects a moral principle such as the following:

M: If everything is equal, a moral agent ought to endeavor, as much as possible, to increase, and never to either decrease or to be morally responsible for decreasing, the well-being of any thing.

The world-actualization criterion c2—God could actualize no world containing NENP^i—may then be seen as a specific instance of M. The antitheist's point in pressing the argument from evil is that in actualizing the actual world, or in permitting it to be as it is, God is deficient in God's moral duty, as that is reflected in M. As this line of reasoning goes, God did not make the world better than it is, even though God could have made it better, and, by not so doing, God is in breach of M. Schlesinger commits himself to a universal moral principle closely related to M, but the essence of his defense is a denial, based on the contra-Leibnizian ideas discussed, that either that principle or M applies to God in world-actualization.

Both the moral principle to which Schlesinger commits and his proposed solution to the problem of evil reflect the idea that John Stuart Mill famously expressed as: better Socrates dissatisfied than the fool satisfied; better the fool dissatisfied than the pig satisfied. As interpreted by Schlesinger, the moral principle at work in this maxim is the following:

O: If everything is equal, a moral agent ought to endeavor, as much as possible, to increase and never to either decrease or to be morally responsible for decreasing, "the degree of desirability of [the] state" of any being.[9]

What does this reformulation of M mean? More to the point, what does Schlesinger interpret it to mean?

In the years since 1964, when he first offered his no-best-possible-world proposal for solving the problem of evil, Schlesinger, in large measure, has explained the central concept in O—degree of desirability of state—and its associated moral duty by means of examples. The principal examples are the following.

Example 1. I have under my care a retarded child who is completely content in his condition. The opportunity exists to let him undergo a risk-free operation guaranteed by the best physicians to endow the child with normal intelligence. If I should leave him as he is, and not surgically correct his brain, he will remain incapable of acquiring even the most basic skills and thus will never be able to support himself by earning a livelihood; nor will he ever have a social or cultural life. Unfortunately, however, if he is subjected to the operation then, like any normal person, he will be subject to the ups and downs of life, sometimes suffering and therefore no longer completely happy. In his present state, he is assured of life-long contentment and hardly any suffering.

Example 2. Fred is an adult of normal intelligence, with an average amount of problems and worries, and a normal lack of complete happiness. I have the opportunity to hook him up to a machine which will stimulate electrically the pleasure [centers] of his brain, putting him, without his prior permission, into a state of perpetual, supreme, passive bliss. I have also the means to see to it that all Fred's bodily needs will be met for the rest of his days, without his ever being unhooked from the machine.[10]

As Schlesinger sees it, the morally right and the morally wrong things, respectively, to do in the first case are these: to see to it that the child has the appropriate operation that will fundamentally alter the kind of person he is; and to not do that. In the second example, Schlesinger's analysis is that we would be morally to blame if, without first getting his permission, we hooked Fred up to the pleasure machine. I have no quarrel with Schlesinger's reading of either example.

What makes the morally right responses to these cases right and the morally wrong responses wrong? In the first case, the reason is that, while the child was happier overall before the operation than after, "he is more than compensated for this by having become a better-accomplished person," while, in the second case, Fred is "being lowered from the state of a normal human being to the state of an inferior, quasi-hibernating inert existence."[11]

Implicit in these evaluations is a distinction between what Schlesinger terms the subjective and the objective desirability of a state. According to Schlesinger, the former corresponds more or less to the contentment or happiness of a person or persons, at least on one conception of happiness—for instance, the child before the operation and Fred after—while the latter reflects a "higher criterion"[12] than a person's happiness. This is an "absolute"[13] criterion, external to the subjective desirability of a state.

As used by Schlesinger to characterize the subjective side of this contrast between subjective and objective desirability, "happiness," for all practical purposes, is synonymous with "pleasure" or perhaps with "enjoyment" or "contentment." Given this, if we were to interpret happiness along the lines of *eudaimonia*, as Aristotle uses that concept in his *Ethics*, we would seriously misread Schlesinger. For, if so read, arguably happiness would be more a kind of objective than of subjective desirability, in Schlesinger's use of those terms.

Further light is shed upon Schlesinger's notion of the objective desirability of a state by noting his emphasis upon the possibility that, beyond Socrates, there is a super-Socrates, much wiser and more intelligent, possessing more than five senses through which to experience the world, who stands to the historical Socrates as Socrates does to a pig. The idea is that to be super-Socrates is much more desirable than to be Socrates, all other things being equal, which is to say that super-Socrates is higher up on the scale of perfection for human beings than Socrates. And then there is the possibility of a super-super-Socrates. And so on. On the same basis, then, that we agree with Mill that it is better to be Socrates dissatisfied than a fool satisfied, we may be led to agree that, objectively speaking, it is better to be super-Socrates, even if dissatisfied, than Socrates satisfied, everything else being equal. (I have two reservations about whether this is indeed so that I shall get to presently.) In all of these gradations it is understood that the dissatisfactions in question pertain more to the high-order capacities and functions of Socrates (or super-Socrates, and so on as appropriate) than to the low-order aspects.

Roughly, and I hope it is not misleading to say this, there is a mind-body distinction in play here. The underlying idea is that, for human (and super-human) beings, the pleasures of the body do not equal or exceed the cultivations or refinements of the mind, nor could enjoyment of the former pleasures compensate for the lack of the latter qualities in a being fitted to possess them. This mind-body distinction is only an explanatory device, and so, metaphysically speaking, it is quite benign. That is, by using it we are in no way committed to Cartesianism, for instance, or to any other particular dualist substance-ontology.

Schlesinger's point presupposes that we can usefully compare bodily states with mental states. Granting the possibility of such a comparison for the sake of argument, and subject to the reservations I voice below, I agree with Mill about Socrates, the fool, and the pig. Thus, still subject to those reservations, I agree that to be super-Socrates is more objectively desirable than to be Socrates, all other things remaining the same.

Here is the first of the reservations I mentioned. Suppose Socrates' dissatisfaction transpired to be extreme agony for the rest of his life, whereas the fool's satisfaction were to be an abundance of good friends, good health, good food, good wine, good movies, good books, good sex, and so on. And suppose the fool is not a dolt, but an unphilosophical person of somewhat lower than average intelligence, or perhaps an unphilosophical person of normal or above-normal intelligence whose intelligence or mental cultivation only seems low compared to Socrates'. In these circumstances would we automatically elect to be Socrates, and would we automatically be acting against our own long-term, rational self-interest if we chose the lot of the (relative) fool? I think not. But maybe, in choosing to be the happy fool, our choice only reflects greater subjective, but never objective, desirability of the fool's anticipated state than Socrates'? Again, I think not. It seems to me not at all obvious that Socrates in unremitting agony is overall better off, all things considered, than the (relative to Socrates) fool enjoying herself in the ways mentioned. Now possibly the ceteris paribus clause in the initial formulation of the Socrates-fool-pig point could be unpacked to cover this reservation, but it is not clear to me that the unpacking would be unproblematic. Be that as it may, though, the point highlighted by the reservation is that Schlesinger's distinction between objective and subjective desirability of a state, especially the distinction between objective and subjective desirability of a person's life, is not either quite clear or absolute. (I shall get to my second, and more important, reservation in the fourth section when presenting the third of three arguments I bring against Schlesinger's defense.)

Perhaps Schlesinger's point would be clearer if, instead of couching the comparisons of states at issue in the language of objective and subjective desirability, we were to say that super-Socrates is higher up on a scale of human development than Socrates. This does not mean just that super-Socrates has accumulated more properties or kinds of properties than Socrates, although he may have, but that super-Socrates is further along than Socrates in the kinds of developments appropriate to human beings: he is vastly more perceptive, intelligent, wise, compassionate, just, and so on than Socrates, possessing more than the five senses possessed by Socrates, and so on. So, if high intelligence, say, is truly a positive, objectively desirable, trait in a human being, higher intelligence is more so. For two kinds of reasons, further refinement would be needed to get Schlesinger's point clearly, distinctly, and completely in view. First, refinement is needed to take account of cases like the one above where a Socrateslike being could be rational in choosing the life of the fool. Second, refinement is needed because, for instance, weight is a desirable, indeed an essential, trait in a human being—I pass over the Cartesian objection—but, beyond a certain point, the accumulation of weight is no longer a positive attribute. In fact it becomes a negative attribute. Yet, notwithstanding these points, Schlesinger's idea is clear and serviceable enough to merit and repay serious consideration, and the need for refinement, although objectively desirable, does not block serious discussion of Schlesinger's proposed final solution of the philosophical problem of evil.

Schlesinger rounds off his account of objective and subjective desirability with the point that, conceptually, there is no upper limit to the degree that the objective desirability of a state of being may reach:[14] in effect, then, projecting the point on to the plane of possible worlds, for any possible world W, there is always an overall better possible world W^1, and so on to infinity.

Restated now to pick up the distinction between subjective and objective desirability that is crucial to Schlesinger's defense, the moral principle that Schlesinger extracts from Mill's illustration is the following:

P: If everything is equal, a moral agent ought to endeavor, as much as possible, to increase the degree of objective desirability of the state of a being and never to decrease, or to be morally responsible for decreasing, a being's objective desirability.

Let us now, without further ado, grant the distinction between objective and subjective desirability and, in so doing, stipulate that principle P is clear. The essence of Schlesinger's defense, now, is that P, or something very like it, is at the basis of the problem of evil and so drives philosophical arguments from evil, but that P is inapplicable to God, thus, that the problem of evil dissolves. Needed clarifications in place, let us turn to an assessment of this defense. In essence, the criticism I make of Schlesinger's position is that P does not fully reflect the moral duties of moral agents, that it is not P but another, albeit related, moral principle—in effect, a different refinement of M—that is at the root of the philosophical problem of evil and drives philosophical arguments from evil, and so the inapplicability to God of principle P does not justify the existence of the actual world, given the availability to God of W^p as an alternative to it. In effect, this amounts to the point that, contra Schlesinger, the inapplicability to God of P does not dissolve the reformed problem of evil or otherwise defend orthodox theism against the reformed argument.

Moral Duty and Prima Facie NENP[i]

I bring three arguments against Schlesinger's position, designating them (a), (b), and (c), respectively. The focus of each one is some aspect of Schlesinger's principle P.

Argument (a)

The first argument, in which my aim is to show that P provides an inadequate account of moral duty regarding natural evil, is a variation on Voltaire's maxim that the best is sometimes the enemy of the good.

Keith Chrzan proposes an alternative to Schlesinger's principle P that better reflects moral duties regarding natural evil, thus that better reflects the moral intuition at the base of the problem of evil, than P itself does. That principle is

Q: If everything else is equal, one ought as much as possible to prevent states of affairs which diminish, and to promote states of affairs which enhance, a being's [degree of objective desirability of state].[15]

In essence, my first argument is that Chrzan is right. Thus I will show, first, that Q, and in particular the amended version of Q, Q*, that I develop out of Q, is superior to P as a reflection, first, of our basic intuition concerning moral duty and then second, and relatedly, that Q* is superior to P as a reflection of an important underlying idea in the debate on the problem of evil, namely, that God is not without obligation to avoid or prevent certain facts of natural evil, thus that such facts, if they obtain, would be facts of NENP[i]. Thus, if we have reason to think such facts obtain, we have reason to think there is NENP[i]. These things being so means that a theistic defense based on P is not an adequate defense against a logical argument citing the existence of prima facie NENP[i]—for instance, the reformed logical argument.

Let us get into argument (a) through the following example, also drawn from Chrzan, an example that, in effect, is a variation on Schlesinger's example of the retarded child with the unimaginably rich parents. Chrzan asks us to suppose that the parents of the retarded child are

in the extraordinary position of being able not only to cure their child's retardation, but to raise its [degree of (objective) desirability of state] to any possible level [except an unsurpassable level]. If Schlesinger is right, one's inability to maximize others' [degree of (objective) desirability of state] removes one from any moral responsibility toward them. But surely the parents still have duties toward their child: they clearly would be wrong to let it die from neglect, and I submit that they would even be culpable if they did not at the very least free the child of its defect. In removing the possibility of maximal [degree of (objective) desirability of state] it is clearly not the case that all moral obligations are thereby also removed. To borrow some terms from Judith Jarvis Thomson, while omnipotence necessarily eliminates one's duties of Maximally Good Semaritism, it in no way relieves one of the burden of Minimally Decent Semaritism. Schlesinger's ethical principle, then, does not have the intuitive support he claims for it.[16]

The key point in the example is not the child's retardation, or the obligations that you or I might have to the child if either of us were his parent, but his parents' ability, by virtue of their limitless riches, to open-endedly raise the level of his existence's objective desirability. If Schlesinger's principle P did fully reflect moral obligation insofar as prima facie NENP^i is concerned, taking it for granted that the retardation in question is an instance of such evil, then the parents of this child would have no obligation to their child in respect to that, or any, instance of gratuitous^p natural evil. But if anything is a moral fact, it is that parents—with obvious exceptions for the comatose, the severely retarded, and so on—have moral duties toward their children, for example, duties concerning their children's welfare, and that the parents in the example are no exception. These two things being so, we need a formulation of a universal moral principle that reflects them, and Q is more adequate to the task than P, for, with P, those parents would have no obligation to not leave their child in his present retarded state.

But Q itself needs adjusting to bring the basic point that is relevant clearly into view, namely, our moral obligation, all things considered, to avoid evil as much as possible, and, if possible, do good, that being the threshold condition in moral obligation. Modified to pick up this threshold condition, Q becomes

> Q*: (1) All things considered, and everything else being equal, avoid evil and do good, perhaps minimalistically interpreting this maxim as "do no harm" or as "do good by avoiding avoidable evil."
> (2) All things considered, and everything else being equal, do as much good and avoid or prevent as much evil as possible.

The second of these points closely approximates P. But proposition (1) of Q*, which falls outside the scope of P, reflects our most basic moral duty. Thus, if a moral agent's particular circumstances—for example, his being omnipotent, or rich without limit—make it impossible for him to discharge his moral obligation under $Q^*(2)$, which is to say P, this does not cancel his moral obligation under $Q^*(1)$. Thus, in comparatively analyzing the case of the retarded child in terms of P and of Q^*, we see the inadequacy of P. It not only does not reflect either the basic moral intuition—if possible, avoid evil and do good—it licenses a moral judgment inconsistent with that intuition, thus P conflicts with that intuition.

Apply this now to the reformed logical argument, that is, to the availability of W^p as a better alternative, with OT, to the actual world. With Q^*, if God actualizes W^p in place of the actual world, God will be doing good, arguably not the most good God could do, but good nonetheless, and God will be avoiding avoidable evil. And considering that in weakly actualizing W^p over the actual world God would be preventing a vast subclass of gratuitous evils, the good done—the avoidable evil avoided—would be considerable. Thus, with Q^* our basic moral intuition is upheld, and, by contrast, the inadequacy of Schlesinger's principle P is seen.

Furthermore, it is a basic and long-standing theistic idea that God is not without moral duties to God's creatures, inasmuch as there are some possible actions that no moral agent could be justified in performing or not preventing (when it is within his or her power to do so). This idea is a basic component of the philosophical problem of evil, insofar as that problem emerges from a context that presupposes various tenets of orthodox theism itself. Principal among those is the idea that not all logically possible actions or occurrences are consistent with the existence of God or the world's being God-made. But, allowing for the qualification made in the second section insofar as permissible divine actions and nonactions are concerned, P implies otherwise. By contrast, Q^* coheres with that basic theistic idea. Again, then, the inadequacy of P, relative to Q^*, is seen.

Argument (b)

Here is a second line of argument against P. Let us begin it by recalling that the concept of God that Schlesinger is working with is the traditional monotheistic one, according to which God is a personal being who, in certain respects, is unsurpassable. For instance, in the Abrahamic tradition, God is regarded as being, in God's essential nature, perfectly and unsurpassably good. Furthermore, God, uniquely, is understood as worthy of worship. It is this Anselmian notion of God that I will now show Schlesinger's position to call into question.

Consider the following possibility: Jove, an omnipotent, omniscient, extremely good being, is bent upon world making. In particular, Jove wishes to actualize a world in which, on their own initiative and largely through their own efforts, human beings are capable of developing into mature moral and spiritual agents responsible for their own individual destinies. In actualizing a world containing human beings Jove intends to abide by the world-making criteria $c1$ and $c2$ described in chapter 4. Furthermore, being omniscient, Jove knows that, in virtue of his essential omnipotence, he will necessarily fail to meet the standard reflected in principle P. Like God in Schlesinger's defense, then, Jove must fail in two ways to do his best in actualization of worlds.

Among the possible worlds Jove considers for actualization are the actual world and W^P. Jove elects to actualize W^P, and his principal reason is that it is a world in which human beings have full opportunity to develop themselves into mature moral agents able to responsibly choose their own destinies, while, at the same time, it contains none of the NERNP that, in the reformed argument, is cited as prima facie $NENP^i$. In making this choice, Jove recognizes other possible worlds objectively more desirable than W^P, for instance W^{P1}, W^{P2}, and so on, that he could actualize instead of W^P. And there is no prima facie $NENP^i$ in any of these better-than-W^P worlds either. But he chooses to actualize W^P nevertheless. The point of all of this is not so much what Jove does as it is what Jove does not do. Specifically, Jove does not settle for the actual world. But God does. Given their respective choices under the same conditions, it is prima facie clear that Jove morally surpasses God, that is, surpasses God in respect to one of God's essential traits. Under the circumstances, how could the god defended by Schlesinger be worthy of worship?, or, more worthy of worship than Jove? These things being so, the god defended by Schlesinger does not fit the Anselmian description and so is not God.[17] A parenthetical note:

argument (b), modified in various ways, could be deployed against Plantinga's and Swinburne's defenses just as well as against Schlesinger's, turning, as the argument does, upon the realizability in principle of a world better overall than the actual world, while accommodating the divine plan in world making that we have seen is an essential part of OT.[18]

Here is an illustration of the point at issue in argument (b). Socrates is one third of a trio of identical triplets. His brothers are Sokrates and Psocrates. As it happens, the three of them have been injured and are in terrible pain. As it further happens, their injuries are identical and so is their pain. In the medical future in which this is taking place, we have reliable means of verifying the latter. I come upon the scene. I have both the means and the capacity greatly to relieve the pain of each one of the triplets, although not to relieve the pain entirely. Furthermore, because of my extraordinary medical talents, I cannot make my absolute best effort. I set about my business as follows. Fully aware both of what I'm doing and what I could do, I elect to do nothing for Psocrates. Equally aware both of what I'm doing and that I could do more, I relieve Socrates' pain up to degree h, while, with full knowledge aforethought, I relieve Sokrates' pain to degree k, that is, to three degrees more than I do with Socrates'. Poor Psocrates is left as he is. Clearly, I have not fulfilled my moral duty on P: I have not endeavored, as much as possible, to increase the degree of objective desirability of the state of a being (Socrates, Sokrates, or Psocrates). Nor have I fulfilled my moral duty on Q*. That much is not in dispute.

If, in assessing rival moral principles, one more adequately covers a situation in which there is obvious moral culpability or malfeasance than another, then that greater adequacy is good grounds to prefer the one principle to the other, other things being equal. Let us compare P and Q* on that basis. My moral failure in the case of the Socrates brothers is twofold: I fail to do any good at all for Psocrates, when I could easily have done good; I fail to do more for Socrates (at least as much as I do for Sokrates), thus, for no good reason, treating similars dissimilarly. (The latter failure applies also to my dealing with Psocrates, relative to my dealing with his brothers.) Let us focus here only on the different levels of treatment that I give to Psocrates (none) and to Socrates (some, but less than to

Sokrates). I am culpable in both cases—possibly in the Sokrates case, too, but let us not pursue that—notwithstanding my nonculpable inability to do my best or to fully relieve their pain. And Q* picks this up better than P. For, while both P and Q* fault me for failing to improve the lot of both Socrates and Psocrates, Q*, but not P, faults me for failing to do any good at all in Psocrates' case, as such. Thus Q* is a better formulation than P of our moral obligation to avoid evil as much as possible *and*, if possible, to do good.

But on Schlesinger's application of P, I am no more culpable in Psocrates' case than in Socrates', nor in Socrates' more than in Sokrates'. Furthermore, consistent with Schlesinger's thinking, I am culpable in none of the cases. The reason is the same each time: I cannot do my best. But surely it is true that I *am* culpable in the case of Psocrates, and more culpable in the Socrates than in the Sokrates case. Let us apply this now to God's actualization of the actual world, given the availability of an overall better world, W^P.

In Schlesinger's defense, even if God had actualized W^P instead of the actual world, W^P would be no closer to the best possible world that God could actualize than the actual world is, and that is true. But it does not mean that W^P is no better or worse than the actual world, no more than ten's being no closer than eight to n in the infinite series of whole numbers means that ten is not greater than eight, and neither does it mean that, if I cannot help you the most that either I can possibly help you or that you can possibly be helped, it is a matter of moral indifference whether I help you this amount or that amount, or at all. That is, the basic counterintuition to Schlesinger's that I am urging is that, even when nonculpably I do not do my best, I do not have moral carte blanche to do, or not do, anything at all.

Argument (c)

Let us approach the inadequacy of Schlesinger's defense based on principle P, thus the case for my counterintuition to his, in another way. This other way turns on a distinction that has been implicit in the foregoing arguments and that I now make explicit, namely, the distinction between, on the one hand, moral duties concerning pleasure, pain, suffering, happiness, and the like, that is to say, states of feeling and/or mind, and, on the other hand, moral duties concerning the existence and operation of sentient (and cognitive) capacities. As defined, natural evil is possible in respect to both of these, but a tendency, such as Schlesinger's, to discuss natural evil wholly in terms of the latter suggests a conflation of the concept of natural evil with another Leibnizian concept, namely, metaphysical evil. Given this, the present argument is that, even on P itself, and so without invoking the inadequacy of P relative to either Q or Q*, Schlesinger's defense fails.

In Schlesinger's position, there is no maximal state of possible development of sentient and cognitive capacities, for Socrates could be upgraded to a super-socratic level and super-Socrates to super-super status, and so on ad infinitum. Thus, as God, on logical grounds, cannot actualize a creature with the maximal sentient or cognitive capacity, he has no moral obligation to try. This is granted. But, to grant this is not to grant that God has no moral duties concerning an already actualized sentient being's pain, pleasure, suffering, happiness, and so on. Why not? Because there is a limit to the pain and suffering a particular human being, Socrates, can endure. That is not open-ended and so it is not true that, in a given situation, God cannot succeed in actualizing the best relevant state, for example, fully relieving Socrates' pain and suffering.

Socrates is an actual human being just like you and me in that, among many other things, his nervous system is the same as ours. Like ours, his capacity to feel pain and to suffer is finite. Under torture of such-and-such a degree, he will black out just like us. After prolonged severe torture he will die just like you and me. That is, there is an upper limit to what physical pain he can endure, given that his nervous system is such-and-such. Furthermore, at the other end of the spectrum, it is possible, in fact it is often actual, that a person or animal feels no pain. There is no logical or physical anomaly in being fully conscious, not under anesthesia, yet completely pain free. So, while God can always make more objectively desirable human beings than Socrates, God cannot always make Socrates suffer more or always make him suffer less. To both of those there are limits. To say that Socrates could have had a different kind of nervous system does not blunt the point, which is that this particular suffering creature, Socrates, has the nervous system that in fact he has. And moral agents, as such, have certain moral obligations to Socrates, to this actual human being, as he is here and now.[19] An important one of those obligations is the obligation to prevent, as much as possible, excessive pain and suffering, for instance pain and suffering belonging to the class of prima facie NENP[i]. So, while God could have created super-Socrates instead of Socrates, and super-super-Socrates instead of super-Socrates, and so on, inasmuch as there is no upper limit to such beings, the relevant fact is that, ex hypothesi, he created Socrates toward whom he now has obligations. Given that, God's failure, even for good reason, to create the best possible human being—super[n]-Socrates, let us say—does not excuse a failure to prevent the preventable pain and suffering (prima facie NENP[i]) experienced by a creature he *did* create, Socrates.

The following objection may be anticipated. The foregoing argument operates on the basis of a distinction between (1) the improvability of human beings' sentient capacity, especially their tolerance for pain and suffering, and (2) the actual tolerance that a given person, Socrates, has for pain and suffering. It is granted in my argument that the former is open-ended and argued that the latter is closed-ended. But, the objection goes, the open-endedness of the former entails the open-endedness of the latter, too, in effect, that the distinction upon which argument (c) is predicated is a distinction without a difference. The key point in this objection is that (1) means it is always available to God to increase Socrates' tolerance for pain, and so that God, on conceptual grounds, cannot relieve Socrates' pain to the limit.

But the objection miscarries, first on logical then on metaphysical grounds. In the first place, from human beings' tolerance for pain's being open-endedly improvable, it does not follow that any given human being's tolerance is open-endedly improvable. To suppose that it does follow is the fallacy of division. In the second place, to suppose that the capacity of a given human being, Socrates, to tolerate pain is open-endedly improvable reflects an inadequate conception of the self. The point I shall now develop is also the second reservation about Schlesinger's concept of open-ended improvability of sentient beings that I announced, but did not develop, in the third section.

In its essence, the conception of the self embedded in Schlesinger's position is Cartesian or at least quasi-Cartesian, inasmuch as it is a conception of the self as essentially self-contained and nonsocial. What I mean is this. Schlesinger's position supposes that Socrates could be altered in ways significantly affecting his sentient capacities, which is to say that significant changes could be made in his central nervous system, and that, through it all, he would remain the same Socrates. But the kinds of changes that would have to be involved would be significant changes in his capacities for interaction with the world and with other people. For instance, unlike you or me, he would be able to do much more than before without being stopped by pain and suffering. Or again unlike you or me, he might, as Schlesinger suggests, possess more than five senses by means of which to experience the world, each one of which is much keener than before. And these sorts of differences would significantly alter his concept of himself and his dealings with the (compared to him, benighted) rest of us. For who Socrates is is inseparable from a complex web of social and other transactions, present, remembered, and anticipated. In significantly souping up his tolerance for pain, for instance, or in endowing him with both extra and enhanced (compared to us and to his former self) sensory powers, God would greatly alter Socrates, making him no longer himself. But for God to transform Socrates into a significantly different descendent version of himself, super-Socrates, has no relevance to the point of argument (c), namely, the limited capacity that the actual Socrates has to tolerate pain and suffering and thus the possibility that God could indeed successfully relieve Socrates' pain.

Applied now to Schlesinger's adaptation of Mill's illustration of the pig, the fool, and Socrates, as the second of two reservations I mentioned in the third section, the point is this: that while God could indeed open-endedly replace Socrates by super-Socrates and super-Socrates by super-super-Socrates, and so on, it does not follow that God could open-endedly improve *Socrates himself*, nor *could* Socrates himself, while remaining himself, be improved without limit. For Socrates' identity as the particular human person he is is not a pristine thing detachable from the web of involvements with the world, the Lebenswelt that Socrates shares with others.

Let us now apply argument (c) to the case of W^p and the actual world. There is no uppermost limit to the degree of objectively desirable possible worlds that God, in God's essential omnipotence, could have actualized. But the actual world actually exists and contains an abundance of natural evils for which we can discover no God-justifying reason, some of which are the actual sufferings of actual sentient beings. But those sufferings can be palliated. Furthermore, the whole class of prima facie NENP^i is one for which we cannot discern a God-justifying reason, inasmuch as we saw W^P is able to provide just as well as the actual world for the realizability of the divine plan in world making that is specified in OT, but without W^P's containing any such natural evil. In effect, then, in W^P, the same beings who inhabit the actual world suffer less than they do in the actual world, at no cost in terms of the realizability of the divine plan for worlds inhabited by human beings. By actualizing the actual world over W^P, then, God is standing idly by while Socrates, say, endures suffering for which we can discern no God-justifying reason, suffering that, given the availability of W^P, we have good reason to think is NENP^i.

Argument (c) challenges the logic of Schlesinger's position, namely, that just *because* God cannot do God's best, God has a morally sufficient reason for neither avoiding nor preventing prima facie NENP^i. The following (adapted) example of Chrzan's illustrates the point in argument (c)'s challenge:

Jones has literally no end of wealth. Every year he donates a zillion dollars to the Save the Dogs Society. Given Jones's infinite supply of money, no logical upper limit constrains the number of dollars he can give the Society. Unfortunately, as Jones drives away from this year's Save the Dogs fundraiser [he sees a fire in a forest near the road and Sparky trapped by the fire. From where he sits, Jones can see there is an escape route available to Sparky, but the dog himself does not see it. As Jones watches, Sparky is burned in the flames and, after lying in terrible agony, dies]. Now clearly the fact that Jones cannot give the Society a "greatest possible gift" does not justify Sparky's demise [or Jones's failure to do anything to help the dog]. [Perhaps] one can imagine explanations [and justifications] of Jones's [nonintervention] . . . but Jones's wealth is not one of them. Thus in spite of its ability to explain why Jones does not give the Society a larger gift, a "no greatest possible gift defense" does not by itself offer insight to Sparky's lamentable fate. Obviously, therefore, "God cannot create a best possible world" does not justify "[prima facie NENP[i]] exists" any more than "Jones cannot give Save the Dogs a maximum gift" warrants "Sparky must die."[20]

In developing the foregoing arguments against Schlesinger's defense, I drew upon Chrzan's criticism of Schlesinger. I did so with a qualification, though, that I will briefly mention. In the quoted example of Jones's generosity to the Save the Dogs fund, Chrzan made the following claim: "in spite of *its ability to explain why Jones does not give the Society a larger gift,* a 'no greatest possible gift defense' does not by itself offer insight to Sparky's lamentable fate" (italics added).

But the no-greatest-possible-gift defense does *not* explain why Jones does not give the society a larger gift, as the following counterexample to Chrzan's claim shows. For a very worthy cause, the society needs $2,500,000. Jones knows this and agrees that the cause is very worthy. He also knows that his helping this cause will not adversely affect any other good cause, or indeed anything at all. He pledges $1,000,000. The society itself raises $1,000,000. Jones knows that the society will be unable to raise the additional $500,000 by the deadline. He does nothing. There is no upper limit to the amount of money he could have given. So, he cannot give the most he could give. It is quite true he has no obligation to pledge or give anything at all. The society has no (initial) right to his money. But two things are clear: first, the fact that there is no greatest gift he could have given does not even begin to explain his not giving the $500,000 the society needed, and that rebuts Chrzan's quoted remark; and second, given his wealth, his devotion to the Save the Dogs cause, and so on, his failure to come through with the $500,000 is prima facie good reason to think that, in this case, his conduct falls short of some level of Decent Samaritanism, in Thomson's sense of the term.

The upshot of the foregoing arguments is that Schlesinger's no-best-possible-world defense does not hold against the reformed logical argument for W[p] as a divinely available alternative to the actual world, in that respect faring no better against the reformed argument than Swinburne's greater-good defense or Plantinga's free-will defense. Thus, as it did in the wake of Swinburne's and Plantinga's defenses, orthodox theism stands undefended by Schlesinger's defense against the reformed logical argument. What conclusion are we to draw from these failures of those three defenses? Let us turn now to answering that question.

8

THE EMPIRICAL PROBLEM
OF EVIL (1)

F rom three components now in place I propose to construct
an indirect empirical argument from evil. The first component is the taxonomy of relations between a philosophical
theory and its supporting arguments outlined in chapter 2. The second component is the fact that belief in God has an implicit set of
important cognitive and theoretical commitments. The third component is the failure of Plantinga, Schlesinger, and Swinburne to
defend orthodox theism against the reformed logical argument
from natural evil, given that the problem of evil survives Hasker's
(and with an important qualification, van Inwagen's) efforts to disal-
low it. In essence, my indirect empirical argument is the conjunction
of these three points. Before conjoining the components, let us
briefly look again at each one.

Three Components

Component #1

A philosophical theory and the arguments necessary to its support
or defense are not related to one another as two independent and
separate entities, notwithstanding the fact that, in principle, all such
arguments can be separated from their theory and discussed, post
partum, in their own right. Shorn of such supporting or defensive
argumentation, a philosophical theory is no longer a theory in the
relevant sense at all—namely, a unified system of principles, laws,

assumptions, stipulations, conjectures, analyses, data, and arguments, whose principal goals are to solve conceptual problems and to explain puzzling phenomena. Stripped of such arguments, a theory is reduced to being only a set of claims and analyses. A theory's relationship to the arguments necessary to support or defend its essential propositions is an internal or essential relation. So, if those arguments fail, the theory's epistemic standing is seriously compromised.

Within the framework of the standard debate, the defense of orthodox theism against the reformed logical argument from prima facie NENP[i] rests with the greater-good defense, the free-will defense, and the no-best-possible-world defense. So, given the internality to a theory of the arguments necessary to its defense; given that within the standard debate, it is plausible to think that at least one of these three kinds of defenses is necessary for OT; and given that Swinburne's, Plantinga's, and Schlesinger's versions of those kinds of defenses are the best, then, within the standard debate, it is plausible to think that OT has an internal relation to at least one of those defenses.

Component # 2

Given the distinction between belief in God and belief that God exists, the latter is possible without the former, but the former is impossible without at least the assumption or acceptance that God exists. Thus, the belief that God exists, or, more weakly, the assumption or acceptance that God exists, is an indigenous cognitive or theoretical dimension of belief in God. Consequently, the cognitive status of that propositional belief or acceptance is important to the cognitive status of belief in God, for both the truth-value and the degree of epistemic justification of the latter wax and wane with those of the former.

But in the Abrahamic tradition, belief (or acceptance) that God exists is really shorthand for belief (or acceptance) that there obtains a state of affairs more complex than just the existence of a particular being, even if God is that being. Specifically, within that tradition, the cognitive or theoretical dimension of belief in God is the nine-part complex that, in chapter 4, we saw to be OT. Thus, the cognitive status of OT—whether it is true or false, justified or unjustified—is crucial to the cognitive status of belief in God: if there is good reason to reject the former as being either false or unjustified, there is good reason to reject the latter as either false or unjustified.

Component #3

Given the basic assumptions of the standard debate, arguments from evil for which we are unable to discover any God-justifying reason challenge OT at its core. Thus, with those assumptions, OT can remain a philosophical theory in good epistemic standing only provided its defenses are able to defeat, block, or somehow disable, such arguments. For if the defenses cannot, and if, as a consequence, one such prosecuting argument goes through to establish that, for instance, certain evils are indeed $NENP^i$, then, regardless of the total evidence—arguments such as the argument to design in the natural world or an argument from religious experience, for example—orthodox theism would be refuted.

The crucial question, then, has two parts: first, whether the reformed argument from evil penetrates OT's defenses; and second, if it does, whether it goes on to establish that there is in fact $NENP^i$ in a world made by God. Within the framework of the standard debate, I have given an affirmative answer to the first part of this question. But, true to the Pyrrhonian gap implicit in the reformed argument, I do not thereby claim to give or to justify an affirmative answer to its second part as well.

The Indirect Empirical Argument

Let us now combine the failure of the three defenses mentioned with both our taxonomy of theories and their supporting arguments and with the essential cognitive dimension of belief in God that OT represents. Given that the failure against the reformed logical argument from the amount of prima facie $NENP^i$ in the actual world of Plantinga's, Schlesinger's, and Swinburne's defenses does not entail that there is $NENP^i$ in the actual world, that failure does not entail the falsity of OT. In light of that, let us switch from logic to

177

epistemology to find a conclusion about OT that *is* entailed by the failure of those defenses. The conclusion is that, within the framework of the standard debate, the failure of its best defenses against an attack on some of its essential propositions gives us good reason to reject OT. And given that OT is the cognitive dimension of belief in God in the Abrahamic tradition, thus an essential dimension of it, good reason to reject OT is good reason to reject belief in God, too. That is to say, in the context of the standard debate, the failure of those defenses to provide necessary support to OT, thus to belief in God, gives us good reason, if we are either agnostics or theists to begin with, to move toward atheism from those initial positions, although not necessarily *to* atheism. If we are atheists to begin with, the failure gives us good reason to stay put. Within the framework of the standard debate, that is the conclusion of the indirect empirical argument.

I said that if we are either theists or agnostics to begin with, the defensive failure in question gives us, within the context described, good reason to move in the direction of atheism. But how far in that direction do we have good reason to move? Obviously, I do not know precisely. Presumably nobody does. But, given both the stature of the defenses in question—their stature as both types and tokens—and the plausibility of thinking that OT's relation to them is an internal one, I would say that the defensive failure in question here gives good reason to theists and agnostics to move a significant way toward atheism. That is, the failure is a serious matter for OT. Thus, the conclusion of the indirect empirical argument from evil is that atheists are justified in staying put, while theists and agnostics have good reason to move a significant amount in the direction of atheism. In the latter cases, though, what does this mean in practice? My conjecture is this: for agnostics it means significantly *tending* toward atheism, thus giving their agnosticism a pronounced tilt, while for theists it means that belief in God is intellectually troubled to a significant degree.

Direct and Indirect Empirical Arguments from Evil

There are two related switches in the foregoing argument. The first is from a logical to an empirical form of the argument from evil, with the latter based on the former. The second switch is from one kind of evidence to another, namely, from evidence provided by certain facts of evil to evidence provided by the fates of certain defensive arguments. In the second switch, arguments employing evidence of the former sort are direct arguments from evil, whereas arguments that employ evidence of the latter sort are indirect. This is because the evidential base of arguments of the latter kind, being facts about arguments and not facts about evil, is at a remove from the phenomena of evil themselves. Thus, the capstone of the reformed logical argument is an indirect empirical argument.[1]

The contrast is with direct forms of the empirical argument, to discussion of which let us now turn. In doing so we pick up a new thread of argument, one that will force us to question the standard model's ability to be what it promises, namely, a framework, at least in principle, for settling the problem of God and evil one way or the other.

In its direct form, the empirical argument cites certain facts of evil in the world—in the case of the reformed logical argument, these are facts of the vast quantity of NERNP in the actual world—as good reason to regard orthodox theism as either false or unworthy of rational belief. And at face value it is quite reasonable to think that the existence in great abundance of multiple kinds and instances of inscrutable evils, especially natural evils, amounts to evidence that OT is either false or epistemically unjustified. The reasonableness of this point is considerably strengthened by the fact that God, if there is a God, is silent in the face of so much pain and suffering.[2] Thus, theistic philosophers by and large concede the point that the great abundance of evil, natural evil resulting solely from natural processes, in the present instance, is evidence against theism. But while conceding it, such philosophers are typically quick to stress as well that something's being evidence for a given proposition does not entail its being either strong or decisive evidence for that proposition. Thus, the philosophical debate over the direct form of the empirical problem of evil has, in the main, tended to focus not on whether, but on how much and how decisively, the facts of inscrutable evil in the world count as evidence against a particular formulation of theism.

But there is nowadays a strong theistic dissent from that tendency, and the implications of this dissent cut deep. In particular, those implications have an important effect upon the conclusion of the indirect empirical argument sitting atop the reformed logical argument, as well as upon the standard model of debate for the problem of evil. Pending discussion of that dissent and its implications, then, the conclusion of the indirect empirical argument is interim and provisional.

PART 2

9

THE EMPIRICAL PROBLEM
OF EVIL (2)

I n Hume's *Dialogues*, Demea claims that, "were a stranger to drop on a sudden into this world, I would show him, as a specimen of its ills, a hospital full of diseases, a prison crowded with malefactors and debtors, a field of battle strewed with carcases, a fleet foundering in the ocean, a nation languishing under tyranny, famine, or pestilence."[1] At a minimum, Demea's point is that the rich abundance of moral and natural evils in the world is an incontrovertible fact. In addition, he accepts without question that the phenomena of evil listed, as well as other facts of evil that could be added, constitute a philosophical problem for theism, albeit a problem he is confident that theism has the resources to solve. The particular solution in which he places his confidence is widely accepted among theists, namely, an eschatological theory citing "other regions" and "some future period of existence" in which "the present evil phenomena . . . are rectified."[2]

Demea's fellow-theist, Cleanthes, is less sanguine about theism's fortunes in the face of evils such as those described in the dialogue. In his view, should Demea's and Philo's converging descriptions of evils in the world be true, then "there is an end at once of all religion."[3] Thus, it is understandable that, rejecting Demea's favored solution as "arbitrary suppositions," inappropriate in response to an empirically based problem of evil, his own response is to deny Demea's and Philo's accounts of the evils of the world. In his words, "your representations are exaggerated; your melancholy views mostly fictitious; your inferences contrary to fact and experience."[4]

Notwithstanding this disagreement between the two main theistic characters in the *Dialogues*, there is agreement among all three main characters that the problem for theistic belief posed by the facts of inscrutable evil in the world, or, in Cleanthes' case, the problem that would be posed if the facts were as stated, is an evidential problem, and not, say, just a pastoral problem. This is to say that the main characters in the *Dialogues* all accept that the existence of inscrutable evil is (or would be) *evidence* against the existence of God. They differ, among other things, regarding the extent and significance of the evidence, and on the best way for theism to respond to it. And ever since this kind of assessment of the facts of evil in a supposedly God-made world has been more or less an article of faith on both sides of the philosophical debate on the problem of evil.

A First Look at Skeptical Theism

Against this background, to now emphasize that certain facts of inscrutable evil are counterevidence to theism would only belabor the obvious, were it not that, in recent years, there has been a radical departure from this approximately three-hundred-year consensus. Specifically, certain theistic philosophers recently have challenged the idea that inscrutable evil is evidence against theism, or for atheism, in the first place. In essence, their point is threefold: (1) that no good reason has been given to think that any facts of evil that we know of hold an evidential lien on theism; (2) that good reason can be given for thinking that the evils in the world—including those evils for which we are unable to discern any God-justifying reason— are not evidence against theism, or for atheism, at all, long-standing consensus to the contrary notwithstanding; and (3) that none of the evils we know of lend probative weight to atheism at theism's expense, and, given our cognitive state, no possible evil could do so either. Viewed against the background of Enlightenment and post-Enlightenment evidentialism, which so profoundly shapes the standard model of debate on the problem of evil, it is a radical and for that reason, interesting, position.

I refer to this kind of theistic response to direct empirical arguments from evil as skeptical theism. But, by use of this term, I do not impute general skepticism to adherents of the position, including those adherents who, like William P. Alston and Stephen J. Wykstra, offer a version of it as strong as that articulated above. It is skeptical theism in that strong version that I discuss here. The skepticism in question is limited to the idea that our inability to discern a God-justifying reason for certain, indeed for many, evil occurrences does not entitle us to believe those evils are inconsistent with God. Although I go some of the way with skeptical theism, perhaps even a long way, I also side with certain critics of it in maintaining that some facts of inscrutable evil justify atheists in the view that there are evils inconsistent with God, thus that there is no God. However, in arguing for this interpretation of those facts, I do not thereby commit, implicitly or explicitly, to the stronger view that the evidence in question is sufficient to establish that any evil occurrences are inconsistent with God, thus to win over to atheism someone "antecedently convinced of a supreme intelligence, benevolent, and powerful."[5]

In effect, and in a departure from the line hitherto followed in this book, I argue here in part 2, insofar as the direct form of the empirical argument from evil that we find in the work of William L. Rowe is concerned, for a detente. Specifically, I argue here for a mutually accepted coexistence, between a certain kind of atheism, a version of what Rowe calls "friendly" atheism, and a correspondingly friendly version of orthodox theism.[6] In part, this requires me to sustain a Rowe-style atheism in face of skeptical theistic arguments against it.

In recent years, the debate over skeptical theism and direct empirical forms of the argument from evil has been a growth industry within analytic philosophy of religion.[7] So, in the interest of manageability within the scope of this book, I shall confine myself to the debate over Rowe's formulations of this kind of atheistic argument. With suitable adjustments, though, the skeptical theistic response, as it is discussed here, would apply also to the direct empirical argument advanced by Paul Draper. This restriction to Rowe's version of the direct empirical argument does not place the atheistic side in the debate at any disadvantage. For Jeff Jordan is surely right in his recent characterization of Rowe's formulation of the empirical argument as "widely considered the most cogent presentation of the problem."[8]

CHAPTER 9

My argument in support of a Rowelike position against the skeptical theistic critics mentioned turns on our distinction between the two senses in which either evidence or argument lends weight to a theory. They are, first, to support a theory by *settling* a disputed issue in its favor and against a rival, and, second, to support a theory by *sustaining* it, but without necessarily downgrading the cognitive credentials of a rival theory. Furthermore, as I use the term, to sustain a theory in the face of attack falls short of settling the disputed issue one way or the other. Lacking better terms, I refer to these as hegemonic support of a theory—in the case of *settling* matters in favor of a given theory and so against a rival—and support-in-place—in the case of *sustaining* a theory while not *settling* the disputed issue(s) in its favor—and then argue in support (in the sense of support-in-place) of a Rowelike position.

Skeptical theism relies on a certain conception of our ability to make epistemically justified judgments about what evils are and are not pointless or gratuitous, in the gratuitous[p] sense of gratuitousness, while Rowe makes a different assessment of that ability. (Recall that gratuitous[p] evils are evils that could be prevented without thereby losing a greater good.) This raises an important question, namely, who are *we* in this context? Are we agnostics, atheists, or theists? And that question gives rise to others. How well informed are we? What background beliefs do we have? To what *degree* are we agnostic, atheistic, or theistic? Let us adapt some terminology of Wykstra's to address these questions and to focus our discussion in this chapter and beyond.

Using Wykstra's terms, let us stipulate that there are square agnostics, square atheists, and square theists. In each case, the adjective means that the position in question is stable. A square theist, then, is a theist who, without being a dogmatist, strongly believes in God: in Hume's language from the *Dialogues,* a square theist is "antecedently convinced" that theism is true. A square atheist strongly disbelieves in God, that is to say, he or she is convinced of God's nonexistence prior to exposure to a given argument or piece of evidence on the topic, while a square agnostic occupies a cognitive position equidistant between square theism and square atheism. Square agnosticism is a stable position in its own right, not just a layover on the way to square theism or atheism from the other. With

186

square aqnosticism, the initial probability of each of theism and atheism is 0.5, and its set of background beliefs is neutral between those polar positions. (Undoubtedly, the three positions, as just described, are somewhat idealized, square agnosticism the most, but they are useful for discussion purposes nonetheless.) To repeat an important point: squareness in these contexts does not mean irrationality or dogmatism, although it does mean firm conviction. Peter van Inwagen succinctly captures the relevant sense of "squareness" in the following lines: "these beliefs . . . are not ones that I hold in a tentative or halfhearted way. They are firm convictions about matters that I hold to be of the utmost importance, and it is almost certainly true that I should hold them no matter what metaphysical arguments I was presented with."[9]

The last point van Inwagen makes in the lines quoted is reminiscent of a point made by G. E. Moore in his counterargument to Hume's skepticism. Moore defends the commonsense view of the world against Hume by arguing that the view is far more certain than any argument that could be brought either for or against it.[10]

On the foregoing understandings of agnosticism, atheism, and theism, I am interested in the three following questions: first, is Rowe's evidence or argument sufficient to move a square theist to, or towards, one of the other positions? Second, is Rowe's evidence or argument sufficient (1) to settle the question of God and evil in favor of the atheist or (2) to sustain the square atheist in his or her square atheism? Third, is Rowe's evidence or argument sufficient to move a square agnostic either to, or in the direction of, square atheism? Before attempting answers, let us clarify the questions. By the term "sufficient to move" in the first and third questions, I mean to ask whether the evidence is such that, for instance, were a square theist who knew and understood it not to move to or toward either agnosticism or atheism on the strength of that evidence or on the strength of that evidence combined with other evidence, would he or she be epistemically unjustified in staying put? At their extremes both the first and third questions ask whether the argument offered by Rowe is sufficient to settle the issue in the square atheist's favor, as does the first part of the second question. The first and third questions ask whether Rowe's case is sufficient to move a square theist and agnostic respectively *to* square atheism (in both cases) or *to* square agnosticism (in the former case). Naturally, then, the questions dovetail to a large degree. But the questions may be taken in less extreme form, too: in the case of the first, whether Rowe's argument weakens square theism in the sense of moving a square theist toward—how far is a further question—agnosticism (thus toward atheism too). Among the questions asked, it is the first and second that principally interest me.

Now to the answers. My answer to the first question is no: the square theist who stays put is not, in the circumstances, necessarily committing any epistemic sin. To the second, my answer is that the evidence supports a Rowelike friendly atheism in the *sustenance* sense of support, but not in the other sense of the term—in effect, my answer to this question is no to (1), yes to (2). To the third question, my answer is, perhaps not. In so answering the third question, I acknowledge my position to be a weaker (thereby friendlier?) version of atheism than Rowe's. Let us turn now to an account of Rowe's argument.

Rowe's Empirical Argument from Evil

We have reason to believe that gratuitous^p NERNP above the van Inwagen line exists. So, given that any such NERNP would be NENP^i and that God, if he existed, would prevent or not permit it, we have reason to believe that NENP^i exists, thus that orthodox theism is false. In its essentials, this is the seminal argument set forth in 1979 by William L. Rowe, and subsequently modified in some respects.[11] I take two liberties with Rowe's argument. First, Rowe himself explicitly addresses only a restricted formulation of theism, while I direct his argument against OT, thus against an expanded version of theism. Second, I import into his argument my focus on natural evil resulting solely from natural processes and its associated jargon. I justify this redirection of Rowe's argument to a larger target than it was intended for in similar fashion to my justification for taking the defenses we have so far considered as defenses of an expanded and not a restricted theism. That is, I am interested in seeing if and how far Rowe's argument makes headway against a skeptical defense of OT. If it fails, or fails to go far, no inference about its fate against restricted theism would be warranted. (I believe Rowe's argument fares quite well against a skeptically defended restricted theism, but I do not argue the point here.) I shall not get into the details of the differences between Rowe's earlier and later versions of his argument, for that would be off point: instead, I emphasize the later version of the argument over the earlier versions.[12] Given both the truth of the second premise—NENP[i] would not exist in a God-made world—and the argument's validity, it is the first premise that is decisive to the argument's success or failure. The crux of the matter, then, is whether there is rational support for the idea that there exist evils that God has no morally sufficient reason to permit or not prevent.

Here is a formulation of Rowe's argument that is not as compressed as the one above:

1. We have reason to believe there exist instances of intense suffering that an omnipotent, omniscient being could have prevented, without thereby losing some greater good or permitting some evil equally bad or worse.[13]

Furthermore, it is a conceptual truth that

2. An omniscient, omnipotent, wholly good, personal being would prevent the occurrence of any intense suffering he could, unless he could not do so without thereby losing some greater good or permitting some evil equally bad or worse, which is to say that a being such as God would prevent gratuitous[p] evil in excess of a certain amount.[14]

So, we have reason to conclude that,

3. The God of the Abrahamic religions does not exist.[15] Rowe offers a conjunction of four reasons to believe that the argument's crucial premise, the first, is true. They are: first, our experience and knowledge of the vast amounts of suffering that exist in the world; second, our experience and knowledge both of the goods that actually exist and that we can imagine coming into existence; third, our reasonable judgment about what an omnipotent being could do; and fourth, our reasonable judgment about what an omnipotent, omniscient, wholly good being would try to accomplish with respect to the good,

and what such a being would permit and not permit with respect to the harm, of his human (and animal) creatures.[16]

In order to pick up the "prevention of worse evils" clause in the first premise of the argument, we might augment the second of Rowe's four reasons along the following lines: that, just as we can imagine further (and greater) goods existing in addition to the goods we know to exist already, there are nonexistent, possible greater *evils* we can imagine existing. For instance, there are possible evils worse than the following evil reported in the *New York Times* on 28 July, 1995, as having occurred in Rutherford, New Jersey:

> for a week before he died, officials said Barry Jacobs, who was mentally and physically handicapped, lay on his living room couch without food or water, unable to help himself as his parents lay dead in the same room.
>
> Mr. Jacobs and his parents were found dead on Tuesday at the Hastings Village condominiums after neighbors complained of a foul odor from their one-bedroom apartment.

According to the newspaper's story, the parents died of natural causes, probably of heart attacks due (at least in part) to the hot weather, and, seven to nine days after the deaths of his parents, their son died "as a result of not receiving food or water." Or consider Rowe's famous example of the fawn, trapped in a forest fire caused by lightning, horribly burned, lying in terrible agony for days before dying. Or his example, borrowed from Bruce Russell, of a little girl in Michigan who was savagely beaten, raped, and murdered.[17] Now we can easily imagine a terrible natural disaster, say an earthquake that kills thousands of people and leaves hundreds of thousands homeless, that might have occurred on 29 July, 1995, but did not. It is not at all easy, though, to suppose seriously that the torment (both mental and physical), and then death, of Barry Jacobs, or the suffering of Rowe's fawn, or of the little girl in Flint, Michigan, were necessary to prevent that (possible) disaster on 29 July, or to believe that any other serious natural evil on that date or another, was prevented and could only have been prevented by their respective sufferings and/or deaths, whether alone or in conjunction with other evils.

True, there is no contradiction in the idea that those sufferings and/or deaths prevented, contributed to preventing, or were necessary to prevent, some possible greater evil. But, in direct forms of the empirical argument from evil, it is plausibility, not bare logical possibility, that matters. Hence, the fact that there is nothing contradictory in thinking that Barry Jacobs's suffering was necessary to prevent a greater evil gives us no reason for thinking his suffering was not NENP^i. That is, to call on G. E. Moore, the fact that a given contingent proposition *could* be true (or false) does not, in and of itself, carry any *epistemic* weight: that fact in and of itself gives us no reason whatever to suppose that the proposition in question *is* true (or false, as the case may be).[18] The upshot is that, prima facie, the disjunction—either the evil in question is not necessary for the good in question, say the prevention of a worse evil, or, if it *is* necessary, the good is unworthy of the evil necessary to realize it—seems very plausible to a person not antecedently committed to the existence of God.[19]

Rowe's is a specified argument from evil. For it is not the fact there is evil in the world that drives his argument, but the quantity of evil, which he judges to be far in excess of what a being such as God would need to permit in order to make possible significant soul making. The type of evil Rowe principally cites is NERNP, although, from time to time, he also refers to the example of moral evil noted above, namely, the murder cited by Bruce Russell. Using the fawn example as a test case, Rowe's claim is that, "so far as we can see, the fawn's intense suffering is pointless . . . [it is an instance of] apparently pointless suffering."[20]

An important question at this point is, who does "we" refer to in this quotation? The answer is that "we" here refers not just to square atheists, or to square atheists and square agnostics, but to atheists, agnostics, and theists alike. Rowe grants the possibility that, contrary to appearances, the fawn's suffering is not pointless at all, and his argument does not require either the fawn's suffering to *be* pointless, sub specie eternitate, or proof that it is so. Instead, what his argument requires is good reason to think that the suffering in question is pointless in the sense of its being NENP^i, that being "the crucial point in the [present] version of the empirical argument from evil."[21] And this is the very point the skeptical theistic response denies.

It is agreed on all sides that we (whether we are theists, atheists, or agnostics) can see no God-justifying reason for the evils cited. Nor for the rest of the vast amount of NERNP that could also be cited. Those evils are inscrutable to us. But Rowe's argument is built on a stronger claim, namely, "we have good reason to believe that no good state of affairs we know of would justify an omnipotent, omniscient being in permitting [any of the cited evils]."[22] Rowe makes clear that this stronger claim is the one he means, that it is not the *inscrutability* of those (or other) evils that is here driving his argument: "I don't mean simply that we can't see how some good we know about . . . would justify an omnipotent being's permitting [any of the cited evils]. I mean that we can see how such a good would *not* justify an omnipotent being's permitting [those evils]."[23]

What follows from Rowe's point? Let us divide the question into two: (1) in conjunction with other relevant premises, what inference, if any, is epistemically obligatory for us to draw from our having good reason to believe that no good we know of is a God-justifying reason for the evils in question? (2) In conjunction with other relevant premises, what inference, if any, is epistemically permissible or justifiable for us to draw from our having good reason for that belief? But before answering, let us be clear who we are in these questions. That is, who are we who have good reason to believe that no good we know about is sufficient to be a God-justifying reason for the evils in question, or for the many others that could be cited as well?

This question is harder to answer with justified confidence than the question asked of those same evils under the description of (mere) inscrutability. For it is not clear to me that here, in Rowe's stronger claim, *we* are theists, atheists, and agnostics alike. That being so, let us stipulate the following, and answer accordingly: in (1) we are square theists, while in (2) we are square atheists. Now what are the answers? The answer to (1) is that there is no conclusion we must draw, for instance, no conclusion at odds with OT. The answer to (2) is that there is no God-justifying reason for the evils in question, that they are NENP[i]. In Rowe's words, "I have reason to conclude that: No good state of affairs is such that an omnipotent, omniscient being's obtaining it would morally justify that being in permitting [the evils at issue]."[24]

In essence, the rest of this chapter in conjunction with the whole of the next is my case for these answers. It is a case for a version of Rowe-style friendly atheism, albeit a version conceding more to skeptical theism than Rowe himself may be prepared to give away.

Briefly, a speculation before continuing. It may be notable that, in the portion of his text I have just been examining, Rowe goes from saying that *we* find the evils in question inscrutable, and that *we* have good reason to believe that none of the goods we know of (God-)justifies those evils, to saying that *he*, William Rowe, has reason to conclude that no good state of affairs—and not just no known good state of affairs—(God-)justifies those evils. My speculation is that here Rowe wants to restrict the class of persons who have good reason to believe that no good state of affairs at all (God-)justifies those (or other) evils. But restrict it how far? To himself alone? I think not. My speculation is that the switch in personal pronouns may signal a restriction to atheists of a certain kind. But the switch in pronouns may mean nothing of the kind: it may have been quite inadvertent. Hence, I rest nothing upon this speculation about that switch. At any rate, whatever we make of Rowe's switched pronouns, consistent with a point I made in the previous paragraph, I would tend to restrict more than does Rowe himself the class of persons who have good reason to believe that no good we know of (God-)justifies the evils in question. Now back to the argument's main line.

It is neither analytically nor (in experience) self-evidently true that the fawn's suffering is NENP^i, here treating that token of NERNP as proxy for the whole class of NERNP above the van Inwagen line. So, if it is to be epistemically permissible for us to believe that the fawn's suffering *is* NENP^i, we need adequate corroborating evidence. At bottom, the evidence offered is a conjunction of two kinds. The first is substantive, the second is a common, epistemically justified practice, namely, our practice of concluding about things in a general sense from information about things in a more restricted sense—the latter being things we know, know about, or have actually experienced. The substantive part of the answer is that we know of very many good states of affairs, and among them we have good reason to believe there is none whose actualization (either strong or weak) by an omnipotent, omniscient, wholly good being would be a morally sufficient reason for that being to either permit or not prevent the fawn's (or Barry Jacobs's) suffering. And let it be understood that we include among the good states we know of, evil states of affairs (known or plausibly imagined) whose prevention would be good.

Why would the actualization of none of these good states that we know of justify the sufferings in our examples (or the wider classes for which the examples are proxies)? As before, Rowe's answer is that, when we reflect on the good states of affairs we know of, we find that either they could be actualized by an omnipotent, omniscient, wholly good being without that being's permitting (or not preventing) the fawn's suffering, for instance, or, if any of those good states of affairs could not be actualized by such a being without permitting (or not preventing) that suffering, then that good state of affairs would not be worth it. It would not morally justify that almighty being's permitting or not preventing the evils in question. Nor, by extrapolation from what it is reasonable to believe about existent goods, is it reasonable for us to believe that nonexistent, but possible, greater goods would either be unrealizable without the fawn's suffering, for instance, or, if indeed otherwise unrealizable, would be worth the price of that suffering.

But perhaps we are wrong. Perhaps the fawn's suffering really is either necessary in the ways discussed, or otherwise unachievable results really are worth the price. And perhaps we are also wrong about the suffering and death of Barry Jacobs. Rowe's counterpoint is that even if we are wrong about those cases, in order for the first premise in his argument to be unsupported by sufficient evidence to epistemically permit our justifiably believing it, we would have to be wrong about all of the many other instances of intense and apparently pointless suffering that we know of. Furthermore, we may add to Rowe's argument the point that we would have to be wrong about those inscrutable evils, not just individually, but collectively, that is, about the vast amount, duration, and distribution of inscrutable evils in the world. But that is clearly beyond the pale of reasonable belief for anybody not antecedently convinced of the existence of God, which is to say, for all but certain square theists.

Taking those factors into account, then, Rowe's empirical argument may be compressed again, as follows: from "no good we know of justifies God in permitting or not preventing either the evils cited or others like them," we inductively infer "no good at all justifies God in permitting or not preventing those evils." Then, granting that the evils in question are in excess of the level of gratuitous[p] evil that, for van Inwagen type reasons, may arguably be compatible with God, and given the relationship of mutual exclusiveness between God and gratuitous[p] evil above the van Inwagen line, we deductively infer "God does not exist."[25]

Clearly, it must be granted that if reflection *does* show that either the evils in question are not necessary for the good in question or, if they are, that the good is not worth the price, and, in addition, if reflection shows that the amount of evil in question is above the van Inwagen line, then we are justified in believing that the evil at issue is indeed NENP[i]. A cure for cancer would be an enormously good thing. So would such improvement in treatment of burn victims that fewer than at present succumb to fatal infection or shock. The decomposition of animal remains in the forest contributes, as a source of fertilization, to the overall good of the forest as well as to that of the wider ecosystem. From among the many actual and possible goods we know of, let us ask of the last two examples if it is at all reasonable or plausible to believe that, for an omnipotent, omniscient, wholly good being, the fawn's suffering is morally justified by them. (I omit the good that a cure for cancer would represent, on the grounds that there is no credible linkage at all, even a far-fetched one, between the fawn's suffering and cancer, whereas, in the case of the two other goods, it could perhaps seem reasonable to think there might be linkage.) In asking this question, let us accept these instances of obvious and significant goods as representatives of the class of significant goods we know of, and let us take the evil cited as a representative test case of the evils, and sorts of evils, Rowe has in mind.

If we fail to discover good reason to think that one or more of these representatives of the goods we know of justifies the fawn's suffering, it will not follow by strict entailment that there is no God-justifying reason for it. For, from "all swans we know of are white" it does not follow by strict entailment (or, indeed, otherwise) that "all swans are white." But up to a certain point in history, that was an epistemically justified conclusion to draw from that premise; for the class, "all swans we know of," was, presumably, at the time and for the persons designated by "we," a very large class.

Nonetheless, putting aside strict entailment, long-term failure to find among those goods we know of such a reason for the fawn's suffering would not be nothing: after all, it is a failure that atheism predicts. Thus, long-term failure would be reason for an atheist to believe the fawn's suffering is NENP^i. That this is so can be seen clearly by reflection on the counterfactual point that, if God-justifying reasons for the evils Rowe is discussing *were* discovered, that discovery would count heavily against atheism and for OT. I return to these points below.

Now back to our samples of relevant representative goods. It seems utterly incredible that the fawn's suffering is in any way at all causally linked to our devising improved burn treatment, for the fawn's injuries were not studied and, even if they had been, how would his pain and suffering—in contradistinction to his burn *injuries*—contribute to improved burn treatment? It seems to strain credibility to the breaking point, if not actually beyond, to suppose the suffering in question is morally justified in that way. In the case of the other example of a significant good that is known to us, the fawn's decomposed remains presumably *do* contribute to fertilization of the forest, but again, his *suffering* does not contribute at all to that result. Once again, it does not seem at all reasonable to suppose the fawn's suffering even begins to be morally justified in that way. These goods are by no means exhaustive, so we cannot conclude from the fawn's suffering's seeming to be NENP^i with respect to each or all of those goods that it would either seem or be NENP^i with respect to some other good or to all other goods, or that, all things considered, there is a strict entailment that it is NENP^i with respect to the goods mentioned. But, in the circumstances of the example, it is not at all clear what a God-justifying good for the fawn's suffering might be.

Recalling G. E. Moore's response in *Some Main Problems of Philosophy* to Hume's skepticism, Rowe anticipates that, faced with an argument such as his own, theists could sustain, by means of the "G. E. Moore shift" (Rowe's term), the reasonableness of their theistic position, while conceding to the atheist the reasonableness of his or hers, too. Briefly, the shift is as follows. In response to Hume's position, distilled by Moore to the argument—if Hume's skeptical principles are true, nobody can ever know of the existence of any material object; Hume's principles are true; therefore you do not know that this particular material object (a pencil) exists—Moore offers the following argument of his own: if Hume's skeptical principles are true, nobody can ever know of the existence of any material object; but I do know that this pencil exists; therefore Hume's principles are false.[26] Granting that both arguments are valid, Moore goes on: "the only way, then, of deciding between my opponent's argument and mine, as to which is the better, is by deciding which premise is known to be true. My opponent's premise is that Hume's principles are true. . . . Mine is that I . . . know of the existence of this pencil."[27]

With this shift, Moore does not refute Hume's skepticism. Nor is that his aim, or so I would argue.[28] But, short of that, he does achieve a valuable result, insofar as the epistemic fortunes of nonskepticism (cognitivism) are concerned, namely, a degree of stalemate sufficient for him plausibly to maintain that the cognitivist position does not succumb, or has been shown to succumb, to Hume's skeptical attack.[29]

Rowe offers to theism a relativized detente of roughly the same sort. For, if I have reason to believe there are gratuitous[p] evils above the van Inwagen line, then, proportionately, I have reason to believe the atheistic argument's conclusion. If I am a square atheist, believing that there is no God remains epistemically permissible for me. But Rowe acknowledges that sauce for the goose is also sauce for the gander. Thus, the square theist, antecedently convinced that God exists, retains the following, Moorelike, viable response to Rowe's argument: if I have reason to believe that God exists, then, proportionately, I have reason to disbelieve there are gratuitous[p] evils above the van Inwagen line, I do have reason to believe God exists; so I have reason to disbelieve that there are such evils (i.e., NENP[i]). Reason for believing there is a God might come from a person's life experiences or from reflection and argument, or from a combination of these.

The kind of atheism in play here is friendly atheism. And it would seem that it should, and so would, elicit a matching friendly theism—a firm, reasonable belief that both the first premise and

197

conclusion in Rowe's argument are false, but at the same time an acknowledgment that a given atheist's belief, first in the argument's first premise and then, second, in the conclusion on the basis of that premise (given that the other premise is accepted), is epistemically permissible for him or her (the atheist), given his or her life experiences, reflection, argument, or all of them in combination. In other words (Nicholas Rescher's to be exact) it would seem that both sides could and would agree to accept and respect "the commitment of individual inquirers to the rational appropriateness of their own position."[30] Instead, a more interesting theistic response has emerged.

10

Skeptical Theism and Friendly Atheism

A Skeptical Theistic Response to Rowe's Argument

"**S**o far as we can see, the fawn's intense suffering is pointless." Thus Rowe. But, given who we are and where we are, how far *can* we see? In large measure our verdict on the amount of evidential support, if any, for Rowe's statement, thus for the crucial first premise in his argument, depends upon the answer to this question. To those skeptical theists who deny that evil gives us any evidence against theism, or who maintain that at most it gives us very little evidence against theism, the question opens the way into what they believe is the fatal flaw in Rowe's argument. In Wykstra's words in 1984, "the suffering in the world is not, as Rowe thinks, strong evidence against theism, and in fact isn't even weak evidence against it."[1] In his most recent contribution to the topic, though, Wykstra offers a more modest version, acknowledging that the suffering in the world *does* count as evidence against theism, but arguing that it does not count *much* against theism, that it is still not *strong* evidence against it.[2]

Wykstra's is no appearance-reality claim. He does not deny that Rowe's examples are examples of inscrutable evils. Not denying any facts of inscrutable evil, Wykstra's point is that we have no reason to think that any of them—the fawn's suffering or that of Barry Jacobs, say—is NENP[i], thus no reason to think any of them is strong evidence that God does not exist.

Wykstra challenges the core of Rowe's case: that, all things considered, the fawn's suffering appears to be an instance of pointless (specifically gratuitous[P]) suffering in excess of whatever amount of gratuitous[P] suffering that, for van Inwagen-type reasons, we allow is not inconsistent with God; and that we have no good reason to suppose, in this example or in any of the many others that could be given, that appearances are not reliable guides to what is the case. The challenge is predicated on a necessary condition for "appearance" claims that, Wykstra argues, is unmet in Rowe's argument. Wykstra refers to this condition as "the Condition of Reasonable Epistemic Access," CORNEA for short: "on the basis of cognized situation s, human H is entitled to claim 'It appears that p' only if it is reasonable for H to believe that, given her cognitive faculties and the use she has made of them, if p were not the case, s would likely be different than it is in some way discernible by her."[3]

Wykstra gives the following illustration of the point. I am looking for a table that may be in an airplane hangar the size of a Concorde hangar. I look through the doorway of the hangar. The hangar is chock-a-block with objects of various sorts and sizes, many of them obstructing my ability to see what is in the hangar. My looking through the doorway is the extent of my search of the hangar for the table. I see no table in the hangar. I now report that there does not appear to be a table in the hangar. Pressed to clarify by philosophers mindful of the difference between the two following interpretations of my report—"it is false that there appears to be a table in the hangar" and "it appears that there is no table in the hangar"—I specify the latter.[4] This specification fixes the sense of "appears" as what Swinburne, following Roderick Chisholm, calls its "epistemic" sense (as distinct from its "comparative," "phenomenal," or "hedging" senses).[5] Is my appearance-report epistemically permissible in these circumstances?

The table I am looking for is either in the hangar or it is not. Let us say it is not. That being so, the hangar would look to me just the way it does, that is, my cognized situation would be s. Now suppose the table *is* there, although not visible to me while standing in the doorway, because it is buried in the clutter. My cognized situation would still be s. Thus, the evidence I get from looking through the doorway is only evidence manque, in the sense that, in present circumstances, it is wholly incapable of settling the question either way, or even of counting toward a settlement. Wykstra's point is that, in the circumstances described, my seeing no table in the hanger is not evidence that there is in fact no table in there. Or, to accommodate his recent, moderated, version of the skeptical defense, it is not evidence that in any plausible way at all is sufficient to justify either my abandoning my prior belief that there *is* a table in there, my holding that belief more cautiously than before, or my tilting from that belief toward its negation.

Here is a parallel example of Wykstra's point. I make you a cup of tea and ask you to judge from the way the tea looks in the cup whether there is a grain of sugar, no more and no less than a single grain, dissolved in it. You have not seen me make this cup of tea, so you neither saw me put nor not put a grain of sugar in it. Nor did you inspect the cup itself beforehand to see if it contained a grain of sugar to begin with. Your first response to the question is to look into the cup. Suppose you say, based on how the tea in the cup looks to you, "it appears there is no grain of sugar dissolved in this tea," and you go on to say that you will base your judgment whether or not there *is* a dissolved grain of sugar in the cup on that appearance. Rightly, we would be unimpressed, for, whether there is a grain of sugar, no more and no less, dissolved in it or not, the tea will look just the same, at least to the normal, naked, human eye. And yours is such an eye. Thus, how the tea looks to you is not evidence entitling you to accept or reject the proposition, "there is no dissolved grain of sugar in this cup of tea."

Wykstra's point is that if I am to be epistemically entitled to claim "it appears that p"—for instance, "it appears that the fawn's suffering is NENP[i]"—then it must be reasonable for me to believe that the epistemic access condition, CORNEA, is in fact met in this case. Thus, it must be reasonable for me to believe that, if the fawn's suffering were not NENP[i] and instead had a divinely exculpating, morally sufficient, reason to exist, my relevant cognized situation would be different, in a way I would recognize, from how it actually is.

The next step in Wykstra's argument is that if God had a morally sufficient reason for permitting the fawn's or Barry Jacobs's suffering, there is no reason whatever to suppose that morally sufficient reason would be apparent to me or to anyone, that is, there is no reason for supposing the relevant cognized situation would have been different from what it is in a way that I, or anyone, would recognize. Why not? Wykstra's reason is that "the outweighing good . . . is of a special sort: one purposed by the Creator of all that is, whose vision and wisdom are . . . greater than ours."[6]

Wykstra suggests we can usefully think of the difference in wisdom between God and us as roughly akin to that between us—adult human beings—and a one-month-old infant. So, if divinely purposed outweighing (or otherwise justifying) goods exist for the fawn's suffering, or for any facts of inscrutable evil, in Wykstra's estimation it is not likely at all that we would ever discern them. He goes on:

> so for any selected instance of intense suffering, there is good reason to think that if there is an outweighing good of the sort at issue connected to it, we would not have epistemic access to this: our cognized situation would be just as Rowe says it is with respect to . . . the fawn's suffering.[7]

He concludes that, for an atheist who is familiar with this sort of application of CORNEA to what, hitherto, he or she has regarded as apparently pointless suffering, it is no longer reasonable to believe either that the suffering in question is NENP[i] "so far as we can see," or that, based on how far we can see, it is NENP[i] in fact. Thus, given CORNEA, Wykstra's conclusion is that it is not epistemically permissible for a square atheist to maintain that the way the fawn's (or Barry Jacobs's) suffering appears to us is evidence that the first premise in Rowe's argument—there is prima facie NENP[i], inasmuch as either certain facts of inscrutable moral evil, or certain facts of NERNP that are both inscrutable and that we have good reason to believe are not (God-)justified by any goods that we know of, give us reason to think that NENP[i] exists—is true. That is, Wykstra denies that our failure to discern a God-justifying reason for the fawn's suffering is much evidence[8] that there is no such reason for that suffering.

Wykstra filters through CORNEA Rowe's reasons to think that the first premise of his direct empirical argument from evil is supported by experiential evidence. But in doing so, Wykstra is not trying to establish that the evils in question are not in fact NENP[i] at all, even though, presumably, he believes they are not. Instead, his aim is to establish that, on the basis of the fawn example (or others like it), Rowe is not entitled to believe that there are evils inconsistent with the world's being God-made. In William Alston's words, this kind of criticism of the empirical argument from evil operates "on the grounds that our epistemic situation is such that we are unable to make a sufficiently well grounded determination that [Rowe's first premise] is the case."[9]

Covering more ground than Wykstra, Alston argues for the following six limiting factors in what we know, or can know, of what might be a divine purpose in permitting evils like the fawn's suffering: lack of data, complexity greater than we can handle, difficulty in determining what is metaphysically possible or necessary, ignorance of the full range of possibilities, ignorance of the full range of values, and limits to our capacity to make well-considered value judgments.[10] The upshot is that, insofar as matters pertaining to divinity and divinity's relations with the world are concerned, we are said to be quite unable in principle to appeal to how things appear to us in judging how things are.

Wykstra's Assumption, Restricted Theism, and Orthodox Theism

In his initial published response to Wykstra, Rowe points to an assumption in Wykstra's criticism, namely, that the God-justifying goods in question either have not yet occurred or, if they have occurred, that they are quite unknown to us both in themselves and in their connections to the sufferings in the world.[11] Each disjunct in this assumption reflects a certain concept of justification. Let us refer to them as the compensation model of justification and the suppression model of justification, respectively.

Within theism, the former is arguably the more common of the two. To the best of my knowledge, theistic eschatology in all its main varieties is rooted in it. The classic instance is the heaven and hell story told in most monotheistic religions. As we saw in chapter 4, the basic idea is a simple one—the world was designed and actualized by God in order (among other reasons) to be a proving ground for human beings. This required that the world be a difficult and challenging environment, without clear or distinct signs of its divine origin or purpose. The presence of such signs, at least their presence in large or unmistakable quantities, would rob people of much of their incentive to do evil and thus, proportionately, of the credit for doing good. In such a world injustices occur, and any injustice not rectified in the lifetime of a victim will be put right in a future beyond the victim's life span, for then and there evils will either be outweighed by good or balanced by good. In order to accommodate these provisions, the compensation model posits a life after death.

Like the compensation model, the suppression model tells a story of a possible world. But instead of looking to a future beyond this world, it looks to a past before it. Again, the basic idea is a simple one. Imagine, in addition to the actual world, there is a possible world, W^s. W^s and the actual world are mutually exclusive. W^s is never actual, but, prior to God's weak actualization of the actual world, it is a possibility that W^s would be actual. W^s is the same as the actual world except that it contains (which is to say that it would contain if it were actual) more evil than the actual world. Supposing for the sake of argument that proposition 8 of OT is true and there is no $NENP^i$ in the actual world, let us say that the natural evil that W^s, had it been actual, would have contained over and above the amount of natural evil in the actual world would have been $NENP^i$. God, having middle knowledge, actualizes the actual world over W^s in order to suppress W^s. In the circumstances, we have no experience of W^s, nor *could* we have any. Thus, insofar as empirical evidence is concerned, we neither have nor could have any that the supression hypothesis is true. It is, though, one of the two broad, nonmutually exclusive, possibilities to one of which, or to a combination of both, OT would seem to be committed.

Maintaining that Wykstra's assumption is not part of restricted theism, Rowe concludes that Wykstra's skeptical defense fails to defend restricted theism—the target of Rowe's argument—against his version of the direct empirical argument.[12] Depending on just how restricted restricted theism is, I think Rowe is right about this. But we, in the context of our project in this book, need not decide one way or the other about the restrictedness of the restricted theism that Rowe attacks. For, as it is certainly true that neither the compensation nor the suppression model exceeds orthodox theism—in fact one or the other, or both, of them may plausibly be seen as implicit in OT, in proposition 8 of that theory, say—Rowe's counterpoint is unavailable to us here, given that our focus is on OT, undeniably a form of expanded theism. Thus our defense here of a form of friendly atheism against Wykstra's skeptical argument will have to come another way.

In Defense of Friendly Atheism

We have identified two ways in which evidence or argument supports a theory: first, by *settling* the issue under discussion in favor of a particular theory and so against a rival, and second, by *sustaining* a theory in the face of counter-evidence, but without thereby settling the disputed issue in that theory's favor at the expense of a rival theory. The former reflects the goal at which, at least since Hume, the philosophical debate over theism and evil has principally aimed. However, even within the standard debate, the idea behind sustaining a theory (while leaving the contested issues unsettled) is not new. For instance, the basic objective of theistic defenses against negative evidentialist arguments from evil has been to ensure theism's survival of the evil-based attacks upon it; the basic goal of those defenses is not to refute atheism and establish theism as true. That is, the basic goal of the theistic defenses is sustenance, in the present sense of the term. But our deployment here of this sustenance line of response goes in a new direction.

The novelty lies in our attribution, in support of a version of friendly atheism, of a similarly limited, defensive goal to a direct empirical argument from evil. The aim in doing so is to show that, notwithstanding CORNEA and the skeptical theistic response to the direct empirical argument from evil, our failure to discern a God-justifying reason for certain facts of evil *does* give us reason to believe the evils in question are NENP^i, while at the same time conceding that this reason is not binding on all sides. In other words, the facts of evil in question, together with two failures (first, our failure, whether we are agnostics, atheists, or theists, to discern any God-justifying reason whatever for those evils; and second, both our failure to find among the goods we know of any good state of affairs that would (God-)justify those evils and our having good reason to believe that, among the many good states of affairs known to us, none *does* provide a God-justifying reason for such evil[13]) help to *sustain* square atheism. But, depending on other factors—for instance, a theist's reasons for believing in God—the conjunction of those facts and failures need not be "levering" evidence toward a *settlement,* that is, evidence that moves a square theist to, or even toward, agnosticism or atheism, or moves a square agnostic to or toward atheism.

The crux of the skeptical theistic response to Rowe's argument is the following point: "for any selected instance of intense suffering, there is good reason to think that if there is an outweighing good . . . we would not have epistemic access to [it]."[14] In assessing this point, let us do two things. First, let us distinguish among the three following degrees of discernment of a God-justifying reason for a selected instance of intense suffering—full discernment, partial discernment, no discernment at all. And second, let us add to the discussion the two models of justification available to a skeptical defense of OT, namely, the compensation and suppression models described above.

Applied, in the service of skeptical theism, to evils for which we fail to discern a God-justifying reason, the three-way distinction among degrees of discernment gives us the following: (1) there is good reason to think we would not fully discern a God-justifying reason; (2) there is good reason to think we would not more than somewhat discern a God-justifying reason; and (3) there is good reason to think we would not discern a God-justifying reason at all. "We" in all three cases refers equally to theists, atheists, and agnostics. Wykstra's point is the third, and strongest, of these.

Briefly, the stipulated difference between the first and second interpretations of our failure to discern a God-justifying reason is this: with (1) there is good reason to think that, while we would discern a fair bit of a God-justifying reason, we would not discern the whole of it; with (2) there is good reason to think that we would never be able to discern more than a little of any such reason. But which of the three interpretations, (1), (2), and (3), of our failure to discern a God-justifying reason for the fawn's suffering, say, is the most plausible, thus the one to be expected? Let us conjoin this question with the two models of justification.

If the suppression model is part of OT, then, in principle, we cannot discern to any degree at all the God-justifying reasons for certain evils, and if the compensation model is part of OT, we cannot *here and now* discern any God-justifying reason for those evils. However, the compensation model maintains that later on, in a hereafter, we will, or at least may, discern God's reasons for such evils. And clearly it is not illicit, with OT, to invoke either or both of those models. For with OT, those models represent live and not just logical possibilities of God-justifying reasons. So, if the atheist, in bringing a form of the direct empirical argument against OT, insists on a verdict based on what is now present to us in experience, or was in the past, or can reasonably be expected to be present to us in future experience in this world, then the question will be begged against OT. For, implicit in such an insistance is a preclusion of the compensation and suppression models of justification, to each or both of which OT can lay legitimate claim.

Thus, it is not clear how properly to play this expectations game of how much of a God-justifying reason we would discern. And so, it is not clear how to decide, on the basis of our nondiscernment of such a reason, the relative reasonableness of the theistic, agnostic, and atheistic interpretations, or between OT and atheism. Thus, Peter van Inwagen: "no one is in a position to know whether [the facts of inscrutable evil are] what one would expect if theism were true"[15] and,

> if one is not in a position to assign any epistemic probability to [those facts of inscrutable evil] on theism—if one is not in a position even to assign a probability-range like "high" or "low" or "middling" to [those facts] on theism—then, obviously, one is not in a position to say that the epistemic probability of [those facts] on [atheism] is higher than the probability of [those facts] on theism.[16]

But Rowe, to the contrary, argues that,

> there are two distinct intuitions at work concerning suffering and theism. First, there is the intuition that the magnitude and intensity of human and animal suffering disconfirms theism. It is hard to see that suffering of this magnitude and intensity is

just what we should expect on the hypothesis that [God] exists. Second, there is the intuition that the existence of so much suffering for which we are unable to see any point at all disconfirms theism. It is hard to see that the existence of so much suffering for which we can see no point whatever is just what we should expect on the hypothesis that [God] exists.[17]

Notwithstanding Rowe's point, it only seems fair that, on the conjunction of OT and either the compensation or the suppression model of justification, we should not insist on a reasonable expectation of discerning (to whatever degree) the God-justifying reasons for the evils permitted. This point, together with its implications, reflects what I referred to earlier as my going part of the way with skeptical theism.

But another question comes up here that, while different from the question of whether it is reasonable to expect to discern God-justifying reasons (if there are any) for various facts of evil, is both related to that question and important in the game of expectations. It is the question of divine silence in the face of widespread appalling pain and suffering. William L. Rowe, writing in the context of Wykstra's claimed analogy between God and a loving parent who permits (or does not prevent) his or her child to suffer intense pain that is inscrutable to the child, makes the point in the following way:

> what happens when a loving parent intentionally permits her child to suffer intensely for the sake of a distant good that cannot otherwise be realized? In such instances the parent attends directly to the child throughout its period of suffering, comforts the child to the best of her ability, expresses her concern and love for the child in ways that are unmistakably clear to the child, assures the child that the suffering will end, and tries to explain, as best she can, why it is necessary for her to permit the suffering even though it is in her power to prevent it. In short, during these periods of intentionally permitted intense suffering, the child is *consciously aware* of the direct presence, love, and concern of the parent, and receives *special assurances* from the parent that, if not why, the suffering (or the parent's permission of it) is necessary for some distant good.
>
> If we . . . apply the parent analogy [as do Wykstra and many

other theists], the conclusion about God that we should draw is something like the following: when God permits horrendous suffering for the sake of some good, if that good is *beyond our ken*, God will make every effort to be consciously present to us during our period of suffering, will do his best to explain to us why he is permitting us to suffer, and will give us special assurances of his love and concern during the period of the suffering.[18]

The fact of divine silence adds an important dimension to the game of expectations. For we do not discern any God-justifying reason for God's silence in the face of the vast amounts of inscrutable evils that are in question here. True, the compensation or suppression models of divine justification might possibly cover it—certainly divine silence is incompatible with neither one—but their application, if any, to the fact of God's silence seems distinctly ad hoc. Or the theist might counter that the divine plan requires an epistemic distance between us and God, and that is why God is silent in the face of the sufferings in the world. But, as we saw in our discussion of Swinburne's version of this point of Hick's, there is ample evidence of persons who sin even though they are convinced of God's existence and of God's eventual punishment of their sinning. The problem is made more acute for the theist by the fact that God/loving parent analogies are deeply embedded in theistic apologetics. The upshot is that, absent a good reason for divine silence, the conjunction of the facts of evil for which we discern no God-justifying reason whatever and the silence of God in face of those facts poses a serious challenge to OT. In his recent "The Argument from Inscrutable Suffering," Daniel Howard-Snyder endorses the point. As he puts it,

> even when those who love us are not causally relevant to our suffering, we rightly expect their comfort and care. For on such occasions we need both to be looked after and assured of their concern for our well-being. This need is magnified when they are the ones who permit or cause our suffering and magnified again when we don't understand why they are allowing or doing it. So there is a special urgency for God to be forthcom-

ing about His love, if He exists. Given inscrutable evil, His failure to manifest Himself and His love is all the more striking.[19]

Let us now pose a different question, in the process circumnavigating the game of expectations, understood, as it is within the framework of the standard debate, as a competition between OT and some form of atheism that, in principle, leads to a settlement of the problem of evil one way or the other. Instead, let us inquire now only into the predictability and surprisingness of the facts of evil in question, as well as into the predictability and surprisingness of divine silence in the face of those facts, *on atheism alone.* Our question now is about the relative predictability and surprisingness, *on atheism,* of our failure to discern a God-justifying reason either for the instances of inscrutable NERNP in question or for God's silence in the face of those evils. For, while van Inwagen may very well be right that nobody is in an epistemic position to say whether both the vast amount of inscrutable evil in the world and the silence of God in the face of it are just what we would expect if theism is true, that gives us no good reason to think that we are also or equally not in a position to say whether those facts are what we would expect if *atheism* is true. On the contrary, we have good reason to think that we *are* in an epistemic position to say whether those facts of evil and of silence are what we would expect on atheism. Let the fawn's suffering (or the suffering of Barry Jacobs) continue to be our test case.

The third of our three interpretations of failure to discern a God-justifying reason for certain facts of evil is that there is good reason to think we would not discern such a God-justifying reason at all. In this interpretation, it is obviously not surprising in atheism that we do not discern a God-justifying reason for the evils in question. For that is fully what to expect on that theory, as, in atheism, there is no God. This failure, in atheism, is neutral between the two following possibilities: (3[a]) if atheism is true, there would be a God-justifying reason for the evils in question (as well as for the others that could be cited), and (3[b]) if atheism is true, there would not be a God-justifying reason for those evils. The first conditional, as noted earlier, is unlikely in the extreme, although not logically impossible, whereas the second is extremely likely. And either way, to repeat, we discern no God-justifying reason.

With atheism, what we get in experience—brute nature in all its indifference to individual pain and pleasure—is just what we would expect. In (3), then, in atheism there is no need to mount any exculpatory campaign to reconcile facts (both of inscrutable NERNP, which we take to be prima facie NENP[i], and of divine silence in the face of inscrutable NERNP) and theory: there is a very good initial fit between them. The distinction between the conditionals (3[a]) and (3[b]) has no bearing on the point that there is a very good initial fit between atheism, on the one hand, and both inscrutable NERNP and divine silence, on the other. By contrast, either (1) or (2), each of which involves *some* measure of discernment by us of God-justifying reasons for the evils, and sorts of evils, in question, would be a surprise in atheism. Hence, the game of expectations is playable in atheism, and the upshot of our playing it is that, in atheism, the conjunction of the evils in question (as well as the other vast amounts, varieties, and distributions of evil in the world that could be cited as well), together with human beings' complete failure, as stated in (3), to discern a God-justifying reason for those evils, together with the silence of God in the face of inscrutable evil of the magnitude that the actual world contains, *sustains*, or confirms atheism as a theory with good cognitive credentials, even granting CORNEA.[20] Those three things—the magnitude of the quantity of natural evil in the world, no discernment whatever of a God-justifying reason that such evil, and the fact of divine silence in the face of so much inscrutable evil—both singly and together are just what atheism predicts.

But while those factors sustain atheism, they do not grant it victory over a skeptically defended theism, in the sense of *settling* the disputed issues in the atheist's favor. Nor, in principle, *can* the three things in question settle the issue against theism. On the basis of those facts, we cannot justifiably choose between the two rival theories, theism and atheism, in the sense that a square agnostic might choose between them, in the sense of choosing that would be reflected in forsaking square agnosticism for one or the other of them. Nonetheless, with those same facts, the square atheist is fully justified in preferring atheism to theism, which is to say fully justified in *remaining* atheistic. But it is not entirely clear what it means to say that the facts in question give support-in-place (sustenance) to atheism, and the following objection will help to bring clarity to the issue.

The objection is this: how can a set of facts support one theory *without* thereby supporting it at the expense of its principal rivals? For, is not evidential support of a theory always relative, and so doesn't the one thing entail the other? Or, even stronger, isn't the one the same as the other? Thus, isn't the distinction between the hegemonic support of a theory, on the one hand, and the support-in-place of a theory, on the other, a distinction without a difference, and, for that reason, doesn't the earlier concession to van Inwagen, "one is not in a position to say that the epistemic probabilty of [certain facts of inscrutable evil] on [atheism] is higher than the probability of [those facts] on theism," cripple my proposed defense of friendly atheism against a skeptical-cum-orthodox theistic response?

Specifically, the objection is that even the sustenance or support-in-place of a theory implies its objective preferment, that is, its preferment by all concerned, over its rivals: but, as the evidence adduced cannot, because of the skepticism in the skeptical defense, win the preferment of atheism to theism by all concerned, it therefore cannot sustain atheism. In response to this objection, a distinction is needed between, on the one hand, my preferment of atheism over theism on grounds *in addition to* the facts both of inscrutable evil (including our having good reason to believe that, among the many good states of affairs we know of, none provides a God-justifying reason for the evils at issue) and divine silence now in question; and on the other hand, my preferment of atheism over theism on just those facts *alone*, or principally on those facts.

In the case of sustenance or support-in-place, the preferment of atheism over theism is not just on the set of facts of inscrutable evil (including our having good reason to think that, among the many good states of affairs we know of, none provides a God-justifying reason for the evils at issue) and divine silence alone. That is to say, the claim made is not that, confronted with the facts in question, a square agnostic will commit an epistemic sin if he or she does not move to or toward square atheism. For it is in the very nature of support-*in-place* —which, after all, is support, *for an adherent to a theory*, of his or her adherence to that theory—that the preferment of the theory is not just on the disputed facts alone. Thus, no claim to preferment of atheism over theism on the basis of those facts *alone* is the issue here.

Under the meaning of the term, sustaining a theory is supporting it *in place*: the model is that of adding support to an already standing, already supported, structure. In that context, that a given theory is sustained by certain facts means, at a minimum, that the facts in question are substantive facts germane to the theory, that they are consistent with it, predictable on it, unsurprising on the theory when and if they occur, so that there is nothing in those facts that would require either an abandonment of the theory, its curtailment, or ad hoc repairs to it. In Bruce Russell's term, when the facts of evil in question are understood to give support-in-place to atheism, they "remind" atheists that "even before the data of inscrutable suffering"[21]—entered as evidence in behalf of a particular atheistic argument—they can be justified in believing there is no God. Thus, there is no boast here, on the strength of the facts of evil, of inscrutability (including our good reason to believe that, among the goods we know of, none would (God-)justify the evils in question), or of divine silence that are in question, of *settling* either the question of the truth-value of atheism and, by extension, of theism, or the question of their relative probabilities. The point in question here about theory sustenance (short of settlement of the contested issues) may be illustrated by reflection on an aspect of the rivalry between creationism and the theory of evolution.

Let old-earth creationism be a rival theory to the theory of evolution by natural selection. According to old-earth creationism, the earth, with all its species of animal and plant life already in place, was created by an essentially omnipotent and omniscient being. Furthermore, this creation occurred recently, paleontologically speaking. An obvious year that comes to mind in this context is 4004 B.C., but the actual year proposed does not matter. What does matter is that, with old-earth creationism, the earth is young, geologically speaking. An obvious problem for this theory is the fossil evidence. With carbon-dating techniques, paleontologists and others are epistemically justified in saying there are numerous fossils that are datable as millions of years old. Unfazed, the old-earth creationist announces in response that these are precisely the sorts of findings his or her theory predicts: it is *old*-earth creationism, after all. The basic idea is that the earth was created in the paleontological recent past with those fossils already present. We need not inquire into the alleged creator's motivation for doing this—theodicy's being both out of fashion these days and beyond the scope of our present interest. What matters to us is that, first, there is no contradiction in asserting that no fossil—carbon-dating results to the contrary notwithstanding —is much older in 1997 than six thousand years, and second, the old-earth theory *predicts* the fossil findings to be just what they are. Hence, in old-earth creationism, the fossils found are unsurprising.

Does the fossil evidence support our preferment of the theory of evolution by natural selection over old-earth creationism? Let us understand support here as sustenance or support-in-place. The answer is no and yes. No, if the question is the following: in complete isolation, thus only on the basis of the fossil facts and nothing else, are we epistemically entitled to believe the theory of evolution true and old-earth creationism false, or vice versa? In the question so understood, who are we? We are square agnostics insofar as old-earth creationism and evolution by natural selection are concerned. But the answer is yes, if the question is this: given that the fossil facts are what they are and not something significantly different, do those facts sustain or confirm our justified acceptance of the theory of evolution through natural selection? And, again, who are we? In this question we are no longer square agnostic about the theory of evolution: we are square adherents to it. If the fossil data were other than they are in various significant ways, then the theory of evolution would face a serious threat of disconfirmation and its cognitive credentials would be much less compelling than they are.

But while sustaining the theory of evolution for its square adherents, the fossil evidence does not give evolutionary theory a victory over old-earth creationism on neutral grounds. For, presumably, old-earth creationism would be far less troubled than evolution theory if future fossil discoveries turned out to be quite different in various significant ways from both the currently available fossil evidence and the *kind* of fossil evidence that, based on past findings, future fossil evidence is expected to be, inasmuch as an ad hoc adjustment would get the old-earth creationist theory off the hook: old-earth creationism is prepared to accommodate *any* fossil facts.

214

In a sense this is parallel to theism's stance vis-a-vis the facts of evil and of divine silence, in the skeptical defense made of it by Wykstra and others. For, with that line of defense, no facts of evil whatever are acceptable as, even in principle, lowering the probative value of theism for theists, or, accommodating Wykstra's less "impetuous" second formulation of his argument based on the condition of reasonable epistemic access (CORNEA), at least lowering its probative value for theists to any significant degree.[22]

But the same is not true of atheism, at least not of an undogmatic, Rowe-inspired version of it such as is under examination (and defense) here. The world's being as it appears to be—at best indifferent to the fate or happiness of human and other animals—is just what is to be expected with atheism, while a natural environment that was clearly otherwise would be contrary both to common experience and to a basic atheistic intuition.[23] Thus, if the world either were or appeared to be significantly different from its present indifference to the fate or happiness of human beings, that would carry significant epistemic weight against atheism. In short, friendly atheism allows that atheism would be disconfirmed by certain occurrences in the world, while, on the skeptical defense of theism, theism makes no matching concession about itself.[24]

But, while old-earth creationism is not disconfirmable by the fossil facts, evolutionists-by-natural-selection do not take the theory seriously. For instance, we do not let the possibility that old-earth creationism is true undermine the rationality of the theory of evolution by natural selection, and rightly so. Why not? Because there is no objectively good reason whatever to suppose old-earth creationism true. Its initial probability is very low. The sheer fact that it is not incompatible with any paleontological or geological datum is no reason to think it is true, thus, such compatibility does nothing to raise its level of probability. In this regard, recall the point made earlier about G. E. Moore's lesson to us that a proposition's logical classification—its being contingent or noncontingent—gives us no basis for judging whether, in fact, the proposition is true or false.

But, here at the end of the twentieth century, surely the prior probability that there exists an eternal, omnipotent, omniscient, personal, spiritual, and essentially immaterial being—thus, for instance, a being without a brain or central nervous system, in any sense in which those words have meaning for us, who yet has self-same identity through time and change, who has consciousness, intentionality, knowledge, and who, from nonmatter, created matter—is also very low. Likewise, the prior probability that individual human persons do not perish in death, nevermore to exist, notwithstanding all the evidence that we do, is very low, as is the prior probability of the supposition that, if we *do* perish in death, each of us is nonetheless later on reconstituted as the same person each of us was at some point before death. These theistic ideas are not logically incompatible with the best explanatory system for existent things that we have, namely, natural science, but they do not sit well with it in any sense that comes readily to mind, and, if they *do* sit well with it, to see that they do would require considerable argumentation. Hence, from that perspective, their low initial probability. The "surely" at the start of this paragraph reflects the broad and deep naturalistic perspective characteristic of science and most philosophy in the twentieth century. But to the antecedently committed orthodox theist these and other propositions about immaterial persons, souls, life after death, and so on, are, insofar as their truth is concerned, live possibilities and not just logical possibilities—assuming for the moment that the idea of nonmaterial (for example, brainless) beings having thoughts, intentionality, and knowledge *is* a logical possibility. Arguably, they are even more than live possibilities to the already-committed theist, for, presumably, he or she accepts them, or at least some of them, as not just possibilities, even live ones, but as actualities.

Does this mean, then, that an antecedently committed atheist is just being dogmatic in denying the status of live possibility to those propositions, given that, with OT, the empirical evidence rules out none of them? Only if, by parallel reasoning, the evolution-by-natural-selection theorist is also just dogmatic in not taking old-earth creationism seriously, or if physicists, committed to indeterminacy at the level of quanta, are just being dogmatic in thinking that the rationality of our best physics is not undermined by the possibility that there is "an incorporeal [personal] being [who] is essentially omnipotent and omniscient, and who, necessarily, ensures that every event has a causally sufficient reason."[25]

Let this hypothesized being be Schmod, as recently described by

John O'Leary-Hawthorne and Daniel Howard-Snyder. The claim that Schmod exists is inconsistent with the causal indeterminism at the quantum level to which contemporary physics is committed. Schmod, being omnipotent and omniscient, gets his kicks by guaranteeing, unknown to us and undiscoverable by us, that each and every event is causally determined. In schmodism, the odds that we could or would ever discern that every event is causally determined, given that our best physics claims causal indeterminism at the level of quanta, are, to say the least, pretty slim. Given schmodism, the experimental evidence is only evidence-manque, insofar as *settling* the schmodism versus antischmodism dispute is concerned. Is causal indeterminism's good cognitive standing as a theory now in serious question? To schmodists, unless they are friendly schmodists after the fashion of Rowe's friendly atheism, the answer, presumably, is yes. O'Leary-Hawthorne and Howard-Snyder put the issue before us well: "concede that the possibility of Schmod undermines the rationality of our best physics or else admit the failure of your arguments," that is, the skeptical theistic arguments to undermine arguments for atheism based on evil.[26]

Applied to skeptical theism, what admission, in the O'Leary-Hawthorne/Howard-Snyder position, is required? An admission that the skeptical defense fails to establish that the facts of evil do not provide the atheist support-in-place for thinking that God does not exist. The creature of such an admission would be friendly theism. Friendly theism would acknowledge the rationality of atheism and its good fit with our failure to discern any balancing or outweighing good for many seemingly pointless evils (including those for which we have good reason to believe there is no God-justifying reason among the many good states of affairs that are known to us), as well as its good fit with the silence of God in the face of the suffering in the world.

Friendly theism would represent a theistic acceptance of the detente proposed by the friendly atheist. That peaceful coexistence, notwithstanding mutual rejection of each other's position, would be based on reciprocal acknowledgment of Nicholas Rescher's point, that "[it is] altogether rational that we should endorse and rest content with the implications of the experiential perspective that is in fact ours,"[27] for, "even in informative rational disciplines, practitioners need not be compelled to consensus through the force of reason alone, considering that different data may be available to different people."[28] You, given your life experiences, may be justified in believing OT true, while at the same time, I, with mine—which include my failure to discern any God-justifying reason for the evils we have been discussing, together with the predictability of that failure on the atheism that I hold—may be justified in believing it false.

The analogy here is to Rowe's imagined survivor bobbing along in his life raft after all search-and-rescue efforts have been called off. The survivor on his raft is fully entitled to believe himself alive, even as his distraught family, when told that extensive searches have failed to turn up a trace of any survivors of the plane crash at sea, is also fully justified in abandoning hope that he has survived.[29]

Let us expand Rowe's example as follows. Suppose the bodies of all the other victims of the crash are recovered during the search-and-rescue operation. In addition, much of the wreckage of the plane is recovered. But among the items not recovered is a life raft. Three days after the crash, the search-and-rescue efforts are called off. But the survivor is alive when the search for him is abandoned, adrift hundreds of miles from the crash site. In fact he survives for ten days after the crash, then drowns. To date, which is to say weeks after the crash, neither his body nor his raft has been sighted. By now it is very probable, even if his body were recovered, that an autopsy would be unable to fix a date of death accurate enough to settle the issue whether he was dead or alive when the search was abandoned.

Most members of his family agreed with the cessation of the search, believing him dead by the time it was called off. But some of his relatives believed, or at least did not disbelieve, that, at the time the search was abandoned, he was still alive and that the search should be expanded to cover a wider area. Those agreeing with the abandonment of the search relied upon expert testimony, as well as on their own common sense. Those who disagreed cited the missing raft and the failure to locate the (at the time, supposed) victim's remains, and argued that the raft (with him aboard) might have drifted beyond the search area, thus that no failure to find a trace of either him or the raft within that area counted as decisive evidence against their belief. The relevant experts said it was possible, although not probable, that he could have drifted beyond the search area, but that there was no way to know for sure. As things stand, neither side can convince the other, and not just because of closed-mindedness. But, at the same time, each side's story is supported by reasons and argument. On the facts before us, each side has support-in-place for its account of things, and such support only. On the facts before us, epistemic detente—mutual acknowledgment, by adherents to deeply incompatible positions, of rational justifiability and of inability to provide disinterestedly compelling evidence for (or against) either position—is appropriate.

Hidden Costs of a Skeptical Defense of Orthodox Theism

The skeptical theistic response to Rowe and like-minded atheistic philosophers raises the question of how far skeptical theism goes. Without doubt there is an indigenous strain of cognitive diffidence in OT, reflecting a deep strain of such diffidence in the wider Abrahamic tradition, and the skeptical defense reflects this to some extent. For instance, it has always been emphasized by theists that, at the very least, the ways of God are difficult for human beings to fathom. In the words of Garth Hallett, "one wonders how a far-from-omniscient being is to judge what is possible for omnipotence."[30] Theistic faith stresses an important role for mystery: indeed the very concept of faith itself is arguably meaningless without significant epistemic distance between God and human persons, or, at least, without humans' belief that such distance exists.

But, while acknowledging all of this, it must also be stressed that the Abrahamic tradition has not been quietist. This may be truer of the Catholic stream within that tradition than the Protestant, but it is not untrue of the latter either. For instance, in Catholic thinking there is a long tradition of natural theology, although it is not exclusive to Catholic thought. Typically, a natural theological argument proceeds from some feature of the world available to us in experience to a conclusion about some supposed attribute of God. In the case of the design argument, for instance, an inference is drawn about a supreme orderer and purposer from certain facts of order in nature that, in the argument's crucial premise, are interpreted as instances of purpose. But now factoring in the skepticism to be found in Wykstra, Alston, and other theistic philosophers, how can theists who are inclined to natural theology rely on what seems to them to be (otherwise) ultimately unexplained order in nature in drawing a conclusion about a conjectured transcendent cause of that order? Using CORNEA, won't their cognized situation be the same whether the order in nature is, in the final analysis, just a brute fact of nature or the result of purposive action? Thus, consistent with skeptical theism's CORNEA, how could natural theology ever get started?[31]

Theodicy is a systematic effort to explain the ways of God to human persons, especially insofar as the evils in the world are concerned. Moral theology functions on the strength of what it regards as a divine moral law, and both philosophical psychology and philosophical anthropology—important parts of at least the Thomistic wing of the Catholic philosophical tradition —emphasize that no adequate understanding of human nature is possible in purely naturalistic terms. Orthodox theism is committed to a robust notion of a divine plan for human life. While in none of these is it claimed that human persons have access to complete understanding of divine intentions or actions, yet the operating presumption across all of them is that we are sufficiently in the know about what God wants, intends, or expects of us. The moral theologian, for instance, could not function as such without believing that there are objective moral facts and that we are able to know them, which is to say that we can have practical knowledge of right and wrong, in Swinburne's sense of the term "practical knowledge." Skepticism on that point on a par with the skepticism that Wykstra, Alston, and other like-minded theists are proposing in regard to our ability to discern God-justifying goods for the facts of inscrutable evil Rowe has been emphasizing would put moral theology out of business without delay. The overall effect would seem to be that the Wykstra brand of skepticism that is proposed with regard to our ability, if any, to discern God-justifying reasons looks to be either ad hoc, inasmuch as it is limited to the empirical problem of evil, or else, by inducing us to emphasize a serious weakness in the indigenous theistic analogy between divinity and humanity, to require a serious curtailment of traditionally significant intellectual dimensions of theism.[32] For, as we have been using the term from the start, theism is the cognitive dimension of religious belief in the Abrahamic tradition. As such, it has various support systems of argument, natural theology for instance, as well as various projections of some of its central ideas into the wider intellectual culture, for instance via moral theology and theodicy. But CORNEA raises serious questions about the availability to us in principle of any telling facts in any of those areas, that is, the availability to us of any facts that would be decisive or, short of that, even significant tilting evidence one way or the other.

A further hidden cost comes up when we consider that, traditionally, theism has often both understood and presented itself as an empirical theory: for instance, a theory that is well able to make out a convincing inductive case for itself.[33] Let us look at that in context of Wykstra's assumption that either the God-justifying reasons for seemingly gratuitous natural evils have not yet occurred or that, unknown to us, they have occurred and maybe are still occurring. In short, the assumption is that either the compensation model or the suppression model provides an account of the absence of such reasons from our experience.

In the suppression model, there could never be empirical evidence of suppression available to us to either establish or confirm the truth of that model. But what of the compensation model? Doesn't it hold out a promise of evidence in a world to come? John Hick comes to mind here as a notable proponent of the view that it does. At first sight it may seem plausible and natural to suppose that the compensation model provides both for justice and recompense, on the one hand, and for empirical evidence thereof in the future, on the other. But, upon examination, that turns out to be not so. I shall now argue that a promise of empirical evidence in a world beyond this world and in a time beyond any future time in this world is not a promise of empirical evidence in any sense in which the word "empirical" is used in science, philosophy, or common life. Thus, it is a promise to which, upon analysis, we cannot attach a definite meaning. The upshot, given both OT's and its skeptical defense's implicit commitment to either the suppression model or the compensation model, is that, in the skeptical defense of OT, theism's traditional self-understanding as an empirical position is jeopardized.

When we say ordinarily that "time will tell," we are implicitly (and maybe explicitly) trading on the fact that such predictions have been warranted (and perhaps true) in the past. Thus we are invoking the authority of those past successes in positing a future confirmation or disconfirmation of some disputed point. But for this to work we have to be entitled to say that the future we are postulating will be, in significant respects, akin to the past states allegedly parallel to it. Furthermore, we have to be justified in saying that the concept of evidence in the postulated future will be approximately the same as it is in the present or the past, as will the apparatus of observation, and so on. But, if the prophesied future that is in question is to be literally transcendent, not of this world at all, and if we, the observers, are to be constituted quite differently from our present state of "too, too solid flesh," then we are not entitled to believe that the postulation of such a future parallels, and is as warranted, or as warranted in the same ways, as mundane predictions that "time will tell." If, consistent with a deep strain within Western monotheism, OT purports to be, in significant respects, an empirical theory, and if it purports to be participating on equal terms with its nontheistic rivals in an empirical debate over the existence of God and the problem of evil, as well as various other things, but if, at the same time, crucial parts of its own positive evidence are in principle unavailable at all times and in all states of the only universe we have reason to believe actually exists, then OT is effectively saying that it is not really an empirical theory at all. That is among the effects of the conjunction of OT and the skeptical defense.

Here is an analogy. Two people, Tibbins and Acton, apply for membership in a club that charges monthly dues. It is a club statute that nonpayment voids membership. Acton pays the first month's dues at the time of application, but Tibbins pleads special circumstances and promises payment. Acton is duly registered as a member and uses the facilities of the club. Now Tibbins and Acton are the closest of companions. Where Acton goes, there too we find Tibbins, and vice versa. So it comes about that, from the first month, Tibbins is right there alongside Acton using the facilities of the club. This is a gentleman's club, and so nobody challenges Tibbins or seeks to bar his way. The club permits members to bring guests, and there is a guest-book provided for the signing in and out of guests. But Tibbins never signs this book, for he regards himself as a member inasmuch as (1) he wants to be, (2) he intends to pay his dues, and (3) he has promised to pay them. Every month the pattern of Acton paying and Tibbins not, while muttering something about a big payoff to come, is repeated.

Eventually, with Tibbins and Acton now in extreme old age, and the club having passed through so many stewards that later stewards have just taken it for granted, without ever thinking to actually look into the matter, that both Tibbins and Acton are equally members (that is, paid up), there is a shake-up in the administration, and the record books are consulted. Thereupon it is discovered that Acton and Tibbins, respectively, have most impressive records of payment and nonpayment of dues. Prompted by his committee, the new steward confronts Tibbins and demands payment (including back payment). Tibbins agrees to pay, indignant that his integrity or his right to participate in the club should in any way be impugned. He tells the steward that payment in full will be made after death. The steward supposes this to mean that Tibbins has arranged for the executors of his estate to make full payment, and he is inclined to accept the promise of a bequest as sufficient. After all, Tibbins is a very old man and so payment in full is unlikely to be long delayed. Furthermore, it is arguably true that such posthumous payment in full will be both less delayed and less expensive to collect than it would be if the club now sued Tibbins for the money due. But, when asked for clarification, Tibbins tells the steward that this is not quite what he had in mind. Instead, he meant that after his death, the death of the steward and all of his successors, and also long after the very club itself has ceased to exist, payment in full would be made, and that those then receiving payment would be well satisfied with the settlement. In brief, payment would be made in a time, a place, and a coin not of this world at all.

We need not, I think, speculate about our steward's reaction to this clarification. Instead, let us ask the following questions: are Tibbins and Acton both members of this club? If Tibbins is a member, is he anything more than a member-manqué? Is Tibbins's use of the word "payment" in his promise to pay the same as yours when you promise your grocer payment on Friday? I think the answer to all three questions is no.

The moral of the story is this. Tibbins uses the facilities of membership, talks the language of membership, but he does not belong to the club. Likewise, in the compensation model that represents one interpretation of Wykstra's assumption, although OT may invoke hereafter empirical evidence and thus the mantle of empiricism, and although it uses the language of empiricism, it is not really an empirical theory at all. For, in the compensation model, as in the suppression model, the alleged empirical evidence is accessible to nobody participating in the debate. And it will remain inaccessible to them, as well as to all of their descendents throughout the whole of their lives. And should it transpire that, in a future beyond any future state of this world, empirical evidence does become available, this will be evidence for (then) transcendent beings. But we have no reason to believe that evidence to them is strongly analogous to evidence to us.[34] In sum, in both models of God-justifying goods —the compensation model according to which God-justifying reasons for various evils have not yet occurred but will occur in some future beyond any time in this world, and the suppression model according to which God-justifying reasons for such evils already exist but are in principle inaccessible to us; for on the latter hypothesis the cited facts of evil (in the actual world) are (God-)justified as the price (or the unavoidable by-product) of God's prevention (suppression) of the possible world(s) in which, had they been actual and not just possible worlds, the quantity, variety, and distribution of prima facie NENP[i] would far exceed the quantity, variety, or distribution in the actual world—to at least one of which Wyktra's assumption is committed, if OT is an empirical theory, it is no more than an empirical theory manque.

Summary

We experience much NERNP for which we can discern no God-justifying reasons. Intuitively, we may be inclined to take this to warrant an inference, for a square agnostic, say, that there is no God-justifying reason for those evils, thus that they are NENP[i]. But, granting CORNEA, this inference presupposes satisfying CORNEA. Given that the God-justifying reasons in question would, if they existed, be God-purposed reasons, and given that there is a vast disparity between God's and our ability to understand divine reasons for things, CORNEA is unmet, arguably unmeetable. OT, as a version of expanded theism, is within its rights in using both CORNEA and models of God-justifying reasons on which our failure to discern any such reasons is a live possibility, even if restricted theism would not be justified in using them. Thus, the conjunction of the evils in question, our failure to discern their God-justifying reasons, our good reason to think that no good state of affairs we know of (God-)justifies those evils, and the fact that God (if there is a God) is silent in the face of vast amounts of inscrutable evil is unable to settle the problem of evil in atheism's favor. But the failure to discern God-justifying reasons both for the magnitude, duration, and distribution of evil in question and for the silence of God is just what atheism predicts—perhaps the skeptical defense of orthodox theism, too —while *success* in discerning such reasons would undermine atheism, although not OT. Of course, such success would make a skeptical defense unnecessary as well as untenable, but that is another matter. At any rate, the upshot is that the conjunction of inscrutable evil, the silence of God in the face of it, our consistent failure to discern God-justifying reasons for either the evil or the silence, and our good reason to think that no known good state of affairs (God-) justifies those evils, *sustains* or reaffirms atheism for atheists, while not finally settling or tending to settle the question of God and evil in the atheist's favor.

In part, this is a proatheistic conclusion. Nonetheless, it reflects a significant restriction of our conclusion in chapter 8. True, that earlier conclusion, mindful of Pyrrhonian skepticism, stopped short of claiming that, in a context set by acceptance of a strong reading of both basic assumptions of the standard debate, the theistic side was defeated. And so does the present conclusion, although the skepticism occasioning the stop now is no longer Pyrrhonian. But the fact to note is that the present conclusion stops much further short of claiming the defeat of theism than did its counterpart in chapter 8. The arguments we have been discussing here in part 2 issue in, or at least prescribe, detente between friendly atheism and friendly theism. That is, our present conclusion is that *both* sides are sustained, and that the issue of God and evil remains unsettled, and arguably cannot be settled (in the epistemic senses of both those terms given earlier).

The sustenance report on theism at the end of part 1 was bleak—that, on the standard model and against the reformed argument, the theory has available to it only an ad hoc logical possibility of sustaining itself. Compared to that, the current sustenance report is considerably less bleak.

11

A WIDER DETENTE

The friendliness between friendly theism and friendly atheism for which I have argued neither is nor entails a meeting of hearts and minds: the two sides' basic disagreement on the ontological question of whether God exists or not remains wholly unbridged by my argument. Mutual friendliness of the sort in question is detente: reciprocal acceptance of coexistence, on the strength of each side's recognition of failure to either refute the other or to gain decisive cognitive advantage over it.

As it was in discussion of Rowe's direct empirical argument from evil that we came to this detente, the question naturally arises whether it applies only to the relationship between friendly theism and friendly atheism, as the latter is focused in that particular argument. In this chapter we will see it does not, that it applies to all standard-model formulations of the argument from evil, and that each side's failure to settle the matter in its own favor is a failure in principle.

The Essence of the Skeptical Defense and the Essence of the Standard Model

In Stephen J. Wykstra's words, the essence of the skeptical defense is that it is "not especially surprising"[1] that we cannot discern a God-justifying reason for evils widely seen as powerful counterevidence to theism. He regards it as not surprising because, in the skeptical defense, the possibility that we would fail to discern any such reason is, from the start, both open and live. The essence of the skeptical defense, then, is this: we are justified by certain skeptical arguments tied to the reasonable epistemic access condition, CORNEA, in believing that

(i) if there is a God-justifying reason for inscrutable evil, it does not follow that we would ever discern it (either in whole or in part).

This is weaker than: we are justified by the same skeptical arguments in believing that

(i*) if there is a God-justifying reason for inscrutable evil, it follows that we would not discern it (in whole or in part).

But (i*) is too strong, for the arguments in question do not justify us in believing it, and the weaker formulation, (i), is sufficient for the skeptical defense of orthodox theism. Now, letting "r" stand for "there is a God-justifying reason for any and all inscrutable evil,"[2] and letting "d" stand for "over sufficient time we would discern that reason (at least in part)," the essence of the skeptical defense may be expressed as follows: we are justified by certain skeptical arguments tied to CORNEA in believing that

(i) $\sim(r \supset d)$.

By material implication, $\sim(r \supset d)$ is $\sim(\sim r V d)$, which, by De Morgan's Theorem, is $r + \sim d$. Thus, the essence of the skeptical defense is that we are justified by the arguments in question in believing that $r + \sim d$.[3]

Now to the standard model of debate on the problem of evil. Its two basic assumptions are,

1. In thought-experiments, and to a sufficient degree to make a judgment possible, the condition of the actual world can be compared, in terms of inscrutable evil, to how the world would be if God existed and to how the world would be if God did not exist.
2. On the basis of such comparisons, a justified verdict can, in principle, be reached as to which of the two sides, the theistic or the antitheistic,[4] has the stronger evidence and so the better of the argument about theism and inscrutable evil.

But the version of a Rowe-style friendly atheism proposed in chapter 9, and then defended in the previous chapter, does not commit to the assumptions of the standard debate in this, their original, form. Instead, it commits to a more modest interpretation of the first assumption, thus of the second, too. Those two weaker interpretations are these:

1ᵃ. In thought-experiments it is possible to compare, in terms of inscrutable evil, the condition of the actual world to how the world would be if God did not exist.
2ᵃ. On the basis of such comparisons, a justified verdict can in principle be reached as to which of the two sides has the stronger evidence and so the better of the argument about theism and inscrutable evil.[5]

Assumption 1 entails assumption 1ᵃ, inasmuch as a conjunction entails its conjuncts, thus a square atheist committed to the former is committed to the latter as well.

On the modest reading of the standard model, the essence of the friendly atheistic position is that we are justified in believing that

(ii) if we fail over a long time to discern a God-justifying reason for inscrutable evil, then there is no God-justifying reason for such evil.

Again letting "r" stand for "there is a God-justifying reason for any and all inscrutable evil,"[6] and "d" for "over sufficient time we would discern that reason (at least in part)," the essence of the atheistic position defended here—call it a restricted standard-model atheistic position—is that we are justified in believing that

(ii) $\sim\!d \supset \sim\!r$.

By material implication, $\sim\!d \supset \sim\!r$ is $d \vee \sim\!r$, which by De Morgan's Theorem and commutation is $\sim\!(r + \sim\!d)$. Thus, the essence of our restricted standard-model atheistic position is that we are justified in believing that $\sim\!(r + \sim\!d)$.

The foregoing extraction of essences is incomplete in an important respect, for it leaves a crucial question unanswered. That question is this: who are *we* in both cases? In particular, are we the same people both times? The answer to the latter question must be no.

This is because, assuming that there is sufficient understanding of the two propositions in question, no person can simultaneously be justified in believing both r + ~d and ~(r + ~d), as those propositions make a contradictory pair. The answer to the former question, "who are we?," is that, in the first case, we are square theists, while we are square atheists in the second case.

Let us now bring the two essences into the same picture. The essence of the skeptical defense is the square theist's justified belief that r + ~d. The essence of the atheistic position on the restricted interpretation of the standard model is the square atheist's justified belief that ~(r + ~d). But the restricted interpretation of the standard model is entailed by the original, unrestricted interpretation. Thus, the essence of the atheistic position in the original interpretation of the standard model is the square atheist's justified belief that ~(r + ~d). But, from the fact that the respective essences of the skeptical defense and the standard model are what they are, it follows that there is no mutually acceptable common ground on which to comparatively evaluate both essential claims, *with a view to disinterestedly choosing between them.* The last clause in the foregoing sentence, the qualifying clause, is the key to the sentence's meaning. Based on the available evidence, then, which is, on the one hand, the great abundance of inscrutable evil and the silence of God in the face of it, together with our long-standing failure to discover any God-justifying reason for either those evils or that silence, and, on the other hand, the epistemic conditions and limitations emphasized in the skeptical defense, we are unable in principle to establish the truth of one side and the falsity of the other, that is, to settle the question one way or the other.

To be sure, if dramatically new evidence became available, for instance, God's breaking silence in an unmistakable way or our discerning God-justifying reasons for inscrutable evil, then our epistemic situation would be different and we would, or at least in principle might, be able to settle matters.[7] (In that possible world, assuming disinterestedness, it would not matter whether we were square agnostics, atheists, or theists to begin with, or at any rate it would matter far less than it does in the actual world.) But in present circumstances, as well as in the circumstances we may justifiably anticipate based on them, we cannot settle the issue one way or the other between OT committed to a Wykstralike skeptical defense and atheism committed to the standard model of debate.

Thus, the skeptical defense sustains orthodox theism against *all* forms of the argument from evil committed to the standard model. In addition to Rowe's argument, those include both reformed and unreformed versions of the logical argument, other formulations of the direct empirical argument, as well as indirect empirical arguments such as the one developed in chapter 8, or, as noted in chapters 1 and 8, the version presented by Michael Martin.

But this success of the skeptical defense falls far short of a destruction of the standard model, although it does establish that what we have been calling the standard model is no longer *the* model for debate on the problem of evil, thereby robbing the word "standard" of much of its force in philosophical debates over the problem of evil. Given the skeptical defense's success off the standard model, the expressions "the standard debate" and "the standard model" retain descriptive accuracy in a historical sense, while losing their prescriptive power.

But we saw in chapter 10 that the cost of the skeptical defense is high, possibly too high for OT to pay, and so the standard model— and especially the restricted version of it—remains a legitimate and fruitful model for debate on the problem of inscrutable evil. Furthermore, that model has good fit with our initial (strong) intuition that those facts of evil for which we can discern no God-justifying reason count heavily against OT, requiring it to defend itself.[8] Arguably the standard model is an articulation of that intuition.

A further check on overconcluding in the skeptical defense's favor is that it does not show, or even give us any reason at all to think, that any of the facts of evil for which we can discover no God-justifying reason are *not* inconsistent with OT, in either the logical or epistemological sense of consistency. That is, it gives us no reason to think that any of them *have* a God-justifying reason. And in fact the skeptical defense *cannot* show this. Furthermore, its inability to do so is inability in principle. To do so would require the very comparison of worlds that the skeptical defense outlaws. Nevertheless, in order for OT to be true, those facts of evil must be consistent with it. So while, off the standard model, the skeptical defense can block OT's indictment (and thus conviction) on evil-based charges brought against it, that defense does (and can do) nothing to show either that OT is in fact innocent as charged or that the square atheist's belief that certain inscrutable evils (including evils for which we have good reason to believe that no good state of affairs known to us provides a God-justifying reason) are NENP[i] is not a reasonable or justified belief in his or her epistemic circumstances.

The upshot is that it is not the standard debate alone that is context relative; so is the conjunction of OT and the skeptical defense. Consequently, unable in principle to settle the issue of God and inscrutable evil in OT's favor, orthodox theism, committed to a skeptical self-defense, is unjustified in being unfriendly to at least a restricted standard-model atheism for which the enormousness of inscrutable evil, the silence of God, and our failure (both long-enduring and justifiably predicted to continue) to discern any God-justifying reason for either one are sustaining evidence.

Two Kinds of Skepticism, and Substantive and Technical Defenses of Orthodox Theism Compared

What is the relationship between the skeptical defense's skepticism and the Pyrrhonian skepticism put to use earlier? The first thing to note is that Wykstralike skepticism[9] is a distinctly mitigated skepticism, Humean and not Pyrrhonian. Hence, it is not as strong a skepticism as that offered by Sextus Empiricus and the other academic skeptics. Yet, ironically, it is able to support a stronger defense of theism than the stronger Pyrrhonian skepticism. There are two reasons for this:

1. The skepticism of Wykstra-minded philosophers, being skepticism about the admissibility as evidence of the facts of inscrutable evil and divine silence cited in antitheistic arguments, is a skepticism that, off the standard model, leads to both a mistrial and to OT's immunization from future indictment on the basis of those facts, whereas the Pyrrhonian skepticism comes into play at the *conclusion* of a trial in which OT's defenses fail and asserts, but without offering any new evidence, the logical possibilities that OT is true and that, at some unspecified future time, either this will be established or the particular, now-

triumphant, antitheistic argument in question will be defeated or blocked.

2. The possibility of escape from disconfirmation offered to OT by Wykstra and like-minded philosophers is, on OT, a *live* possibility, whereas the possibilities offered by Pyrrhonian skepticism are bare logical possibilities. The latter sort of possibility, while sufficient to preserve OT from being shown to be logically inconsistent with certain facts of inscrutable evil, fails to take the measure of empirical arguments from evil and, even against logical forms of the argument from evil, makes pretty thin gruel.

In part 1, we examined certain substantive defenses of OT against the reformed logical argument. Those defenses stand in contradistinction to the non-Pyrrhonian skeptical defense, which is based on a technicality involving the rules of admissibility of evidence for the prosecution. This difference prompts the question of the relationship between that kind of skeptical defense and theism's substantive defenses. In particular, does the skeptical defense's success mean that those substantive defenses, either alone or severally, are not necessary for OT after all? The answer to this question is yes and no.

Given that the CORNEA-based skeptical defense relativizes the standard model of debate on the problem of evil to a set of assumptions that is not self-evidently true and that in fact is open to question, it transforms OT's relationship, off that model, to its substantive defenses from an internal to an external relationship, in Moore's sense of those terms. That being so, off the standard model, OT does not have to address any fact of inscrutable evil or of divine silence per se, or offer any substantive defense against arguments based on any such fact.

In this context, a substantive defense is any defense purporting to do more than deny, on technical grounds, the admissibility of certain facts of evil or of defensive failure against arguments from evil as evidence against theism. That is the gist of the "yes" answer. But a "no" answer is also right, and sheds light on an important issue.

The skeptical defense's success in freeing OT from a commitment to the standard model of debate on the problem of evil may make it seem that OT is thereby freed from negative evidentialism as well, and that a theistic repudiation of negative evidentialism is also justified. If warranted, such a freedom would be from virtually the entire Enlightenment context of much contemporary analytical philosophy of religion. But the skeptical defense cannot, and could not, liberate OT from negative evidentialism. For what constricts the atheistic argument and conclusion in the way described, thereby sustaining OT, is a skeptical *defense* of OT. Furthermore, that skeptical defense is necessary for that constriction, or, if not that defense or kind of defense, another defense or kind of defense is needed instead.

A defense of OT is necessary to justify a theist in believing that ~(r ⊃ d), which is to say, r + ~d, for not only is this not self-evident, it is a proposition against which leans the consensus of agnostic, atheistic, and nonskeptical theistic thinking on the subject. But that a defense is necessary to justify a theist in believing that ~(r ⊃ d) means that negative evidentialism is justified. For negative evidentialism, essentially, is the idea that the cognitive credentials of a philosophical theory are, at least in part, a function of its ability to defend itself, which is, at a minimum, its ability to sustain itself in the face of attack. Thus, the skeptical defense's ability to extricate orthodox theism from the standard model of debate on the problem of evil does not extend to extricating it from negative evidentialism, too.

Summary

Now to summarize. On the skeptical defense of OT, if there are God-justifying reasons for inscrutable evils (including those about which we have good reason to believe that no good state of affairs known to us (God-)justifies it), it does not follow that we would ever discern them. And of course we do *not* discern them. Therefore that failure to discover such reasons does not entail that there are none. This argument—~(r ⊃ d) / ~d // ~(~d ⊃ ~r)—is valid. Thus, a square theist may justifiably remain squarely theistic, and a square agnostic, who understands the skeptical defense, is not epistemically obligated by facts of inscrutable evil to move either to or toward atheism. In this way, the skeptical defense succeeds, against all versions of the argument from evil committed to the basic operating assumptions of the standard debate, in doing what a defense aims to do first and foremost: it wins the survival of the defendant. It sustains orthodox theism.

Given the incommensurability of essences between the skeptical defense and the standard model, there is no mutually acceptable common ground on which, without question begging, victory or defeat can be warranted for either a skeptically defended OT or a standard-model argument from evil. An effect of this is that the skeptical theist is justified in regarding the problem of evil as the mystery of evil, in a sense of the terms "problem" and "mystery" tracing to Gabriel Marcel's use of them.[10]

But the skeptical defense is unable to provide disinterestedly persuasive reasons to prefer OT to a Rowelike atheism, that is, friendly atheism. Thus, notwithstanding the skeptical defense's success, it remains true that the inscrutability of the facts of inscrutable evil and of divine silence, as well as our having good reason to think that no good we know of (God-)justifies any of those inscrutable evils, is just what we would expect in atheism. But those inscrutable facts are not just not inconsistent or not shown to be inconsistent with atheism: they are among the very things, indeed among the most important things, that, on its justified reading of the basic operating assumptions of the standard debate on the problem of evil, the theory predicts.

And it is worth emphasizing that this prediction is not a no-risk proposition for atheism, because, if God-justifying reasons *were* discovered either for the types and tokens of inscrutable natural evil we have been using as test cases, or for that class of natural evil as a whole, or for the silence of God in the face of such evil, that discovery would, at a minimum, tend strongly to disconfirm atheism. If such God-justifying reasons were discovered, atheism would be forced either to concede defeat and admit that God exists, or to cling in self-preservation to one or both of the following logically possible, but nonetheless unappealing, options: a version of Pyrrhonian skepticism deployed in service of atheism, or a version of Rowe's point discussed previously; namely, that the existence of God-justifying reasons for every fact of inscrutable evil does not entail the existence of God. On the last point, in a (faint) echo of the Euthyphro problem, the possibility of atheistic self-preservation would be this: it is not the case that there exist God-justifying reasons for hitherto inscrutable evils because God chooses such reasons; rather, God, if God exists, chooses such reasons because they are God-justifying reasons to begin with. The basic idea is that it would be just coincidental to God's existence (if God existed) that such reasons obtain. At any rate, returning to the main point: atheism's prediction about the open-ended inscrutability of much natural evil and about the silence of God in the face of massive quantities of inscrutable evil is in principle an empirically defeasible proposition. So, mere logical possibilities to the contrary notwithstanding, the facts of inscrutable natural evil, read by the atheist as facts of prima facie NENP[i], together with the fact of divine silence, sustain that theory.

The denouement of this book, then, is a wider detente than the one I described in the previous chapter. And mutual recognition of this would make of the two sides versions of friendly theism and friendly atheism, respectively.

I believe, although I do not know, that this final position at which we have arrived fits quite well with a fairly common view of the matter among reflective, but nondogmatic, square agnostics, square atheists, and square theists, which is to say among nonmilitant believers and unbelievers alike who are not strong partisans on either side of the philosophical debate, standard or nonstandard, or who are simply not party to the debate at all. What I mean is that, in the last analysis, theism and atheism are rival Weltanschauungen, mutually inconsistent at a deep level, with neither one capable of either refuting the other or of seriously undermining it. If I am right about this, then, overall, the Hume-inspired, bilevel argument in this book has been, in its essence, an argument for that intellectually tolerant, live-and-let-live view. And if I am right about *that*, then there is a sense in which the following lines from T. S. Eliot convey the spirit both of the position at which we have arrived and of our journey to it:

> We shall not cease from exploration,
> And the end of all our exploring
> Will be to arrive where we started
> And know the place for the first time.[11]

Notes

Chapter 1

1. Alvin Plantinga, "Self-Profile," in *Alvin Plantinga*, ed. James E. Tomberlin and Peter van Inwagen (Dordrecht: Reidel, 1985), 42. Although the distinction between defense and theodicy is by no means original to Plantinga, arguably his description both of their difference and of the epistemic obligations of a defense is the most influential contemporary description. In large measure it is the one I follow here. Richard Swinburne gives qualified agreement to Plantinga's description of the difference between defense and theodicy. Swinburne's qualification is his observation that Plantinga's assignment to theodicy of the wider, but not the narrower, of the two apologetical tasks I mentioned earlier is a deviation from the traditional conception of theodicy. See Richard Swinburne, "Theodicy, Our Well-Being, and God's Rights," *International Journal for Philosophy of Religion* 38, nos. 1–3 (December 1995): 89–90 n.1. In addition, see Swinburne, "Some Major Strands of Theodicy," in *The Evidential Argument from Evil*, ed. Daniel Howard-Snyder (Bloomington: Indiana University Press, 1996), 30 and 46 n.2. As Swinburne's qualification suggests, neither concept, defense or theodicy, is homogeneous. For instance, Plantinga, in his *The Nature of Necessity* (New York: Clarendon Press, 1974), 193–95, extends the notion of defense from deployment only against logical forms of the argument from evil to forms of the empirical argument, too, and so does Peter van Inwagen in "The Problem of Evil, the Problem of Air, and the Problem of Silence," in his *God, Knowledge, and Mystery* (Ithaca, N. Y.: Cornell University Press, 1995), 73–75. (This paper was first published in *Philosophical Perspectives 5: Philosophy of Religion*, ed. James E. Tomberlin (Atascadero, Calif.: Ridgeview, 1991). Richard M. Gale gives the following succinct account of the distinction between defense and theodicy: "a theodicy . . . is a defense plus an empirical argument for the actual existence of the possible world articulated in the defense," *On the Nature and Existence of God* (New York: Cambridge University Press, 1991), 98. This point of Gale's testifies also to the priority, in one sense, of defense over theodicy, a point I develop in the paragraph after next.

2. Although theism would not necessarily *be* defeated. If a theory's defenses are

237

defeated, then the theory is exposed as undefended against a particular argument, but actual defeat is a separate matter. I say more on this below.

3. J. L. Mackie, "Evil and Omnipotence," in *The Problem of Evil*, ed. Marilyn M. Adams and Robert M. Adams (New York: Oxford University Press, 1990), 25. Mackie's interest is in logical, not empirical or evidential, forms of the problem of evil. (For discussion of the distinction, see the third section below.) Consistent with his position it does not seem to me to be logically impermissible to say that, if evil as such is logically inconsistent with God, then the existence of evil is improbable if God exists, however absurdly weak a formulation would be under the circumstances. But if x is impossible on y, then x is improbable on y.

4. See Richard Swinburne, *The Existence of God* (New York: Clarendon Press, 1979), 219. For more on the specified/unspecified distinction, see my "On the Problem of Evil's Not Being What It Seems," *The Philosophical Quarterly* 37, no. 149 (October 1987): 441–47. As my argument in this book is about the amount of evil in the world, it avoids the issue, much emphasized by van Inwagen, of how much or how little natural evil God would have to permit in order to achieve God's purposes in making a world containing free human beings. On that issue, see section 2 of van Inwagen's "The Problem of Evil, the Problem of Air, and the Problem of Silence," in *God, Knowledge, and Mystery*, 72–86, and section 4 of his "Reflections on the Chapters by Draper, Russell, and Gale," in *The Evidential Argument from Evil*, 234–35. For, as Howard-Snyder puts the point: "even if there is no smallest amount of horrific evil God had to permit in order to achieve His purposes, if he could have achieved those purposes with a *lot* less than there is, then surely He would have." See Daniel Howard-Snyder, "The Argument from Inscrutable Evil," in *The Evidential Argument from Evil*, 289. And of course the class of natural evils that interests me in this book, natural evil resulting solely from natural processes, constitutes a lot of natural evil.

5. David Hume, *Dialogues Concerning Natural Religion*, ed. Richard H. Popkin (Indianapolis: Hackett, 1980), pt. X, 66. Also see pt. XI, 74. I discuss Hume's distinction further in chapter 2.

6. Daniel Howard-Snyder, "Introduction," in *The Evidential Argument from Evil*, xiv, xvi.

7. See Paul Draper, "The Skeptical Theist," in *The Evidential Argument from Evil*, 176.

8. William L. Rowe, *Philosophy of Religion*, 2d. ed. (Belmont, Calif.: Wadsworth, 1993), 79. See also William L. Rowe, "The Problem of Evil and Some Varieties of Atheism," in *The Problem of Evil*, 126, n.1, for the following: "Some philosophers have contended that the existence of evil is *logically inconsistent* with the existence of the theistic God. No one, I think, has succeeded in establishing such an extravagant claim."

9. van Inwagen, "The Problem of Evil, the Problem of Air, and the Problem of Silence," 66.

10. "With a little imagination we can screw out of the essays by Mackie and McCloskey an inductive argument from complete enumeration, laced with a good deal of conceptual analysis, for the proposition that it is logically impossible that both God and evil exist. Attempts to show that some proposition is necessary or impossible through an inductive argument are not uncommon." Thus, Richard M. Gale, *On the Nature and Existence of God*, 108. See also Michael Martin, *Atheism* (Philadelphia: Temple University Press, 1990), chaps. 15 and 16.

11. I take the term from Peter van Inwagen. See his *Metaphysics* (Boulder, Colo.: Westview Press, 1993), 7.

12. Nelson Pike, "Hume on Evil," in *God and Evil*, ed. Nelson Pike (Englewood Cliffs, N. J.: Prentice-Hall, 1964), 89–90.

13. *Outline of Pyrrhonism*, bk. 1, chap. 13, in *Selections from the Major Writings on Scepticism, Man, and God*, ed. Philip P. Hallie (Indianapolis: Hackett, 1985), 43.

14. I develop this idea in the second section of chapter 2.

15. I adjust this point a bit in chapter 3. There, in discussion of Peter van Inwagen's response to the problem of evil, I distinguish two types of gratuitousness applying to natural evils from natural processes. From that point on I focus on only one of these types—although the two are not mutually exclusive—arguing that, within the framework of the standard debate on the problem of evil, none of the best theistic defenses is successful against a version of the logical argument that maintains that a certain class of natural evils from natural processes is a class of evils falling under the description of gratuitousness in question and that this class is instantiated. For the present, though, we do not need that distinction between types of gratuitousness. So, until the distinction is needed, I shall continue to use expressions such as "gratuitous evil," "evil for which there is no God-justifying reason," and the like, without qualification.

16. I agree with Swinburne that NENP is the largest class of natural evils, In the seventh subsection I explain the sense in which I use the term "moral evil" and the term "natural evil." Alvin Plantinga's extension of the free-will defense from moral to natural evil trades on the possibility that what we are wont to regard as evils arising just from nature itself are really due to the malign agency of certain very powerful nonhuman, nondivine persons. He then reclassifies natural evil as "broadly moral evil." See his *The Nature of Necessity*, 193. For my present purpose of sketching the gist of the reformed argument let it be understod that the term "NENP" covers broadly moral evil, too. When in chapter 6 we discuss Plantinga's free-will defense as a defense against arguments from natural evil, we will use his own terminology. But here nothing except prolixity is gained by doing so, while nothing is lost by not doing so.

17. The distinction between NERNP and NE⁻RNP plays an important role in the reformed logical argument, especially in defense of the argument against an objection made by Richard Swinburne. The gist of the objection is that, on the

reformed argument, it would not be possible for there to exist a first moral wrong-doer, thus for that reason in conjection with some others it would be impossible for God to actualize the possible world W^p, whose availability for actualization by God as an alternative to the actual world is a lynchpin of the reformed argument. I discuss Swinburne's objection in the third section of chapter 5, and I further discuss the distinction between NERNP and NE˜RNP both there and earlier in the third section of chapter 4. Between here and chapter 4, though, the undifferentiated concept NENP will often be adequate to our needs. So, to avoid complexity, we will proceed largely without subdividing it.

18. In the fourth section of chapter 3, in discussion of an argument of Peter van Inwagen's, we will see that possibly some gratuitous NERNP is compatible with God.

19. If some gratuitous NERNP is compatible with God, then NENP^i is gratuitous NERNP that is incompatible with God.

20. I do not argue for this assessment of Swinburne's, Plantinga's, or Schlesinger's formulations as the best of their respective kinds. To do so would add unacceptably to this book's length. Perhaps some philosophers will disagree with some of my assessments, preferring Hick's version of the greater-good defense to Swinburne's, say. That possibility notwithstanding, it seems to me immensely plausible to regard the three I have chosen for discussion as the best of their respective kinds in terms of intellectual and logical rigor, perspicacity, fruitfulness, and range of objections both countenanced and addressed. But, taking it for granted that nobody in the know would seriously suggest that each of these defenses is not a formidable argument for theism, agreement with my estimate of these three defenses, as, respectively, the best of their kinds, is not a necessary condition of my going further here: after all, as noted before, the reformed argument builds in from the start an admission that possibly other types of defenses or other versions of the defenses under discussion might fare better than the three examined here. So, as long as it is agreed that these are significant defenses, we can proceed. To guard against a puzzlement that might come up now, let me clarify a point in relation to my earlier account of a two-stage structure in part 1. Plantinga's, Schlesinger's, and Swinburne's defenses endorse the standard debate on the problem of evil, while the defenses discussed in chapter 3, Hasker's and van Inwagen's, to one degree or another, challenge it.

21. Mackie, "Evil and Omnipotence"; A. G. N. Flew, "Divine Omnipotence and Human Freedom," in *New Essays in Philosophical Theology*, ed. A. G. N. Flew and A. MacIntyre (London: SCM Press, 1955); H. J. McCloskey, "God and Evil," *The Philosophical Quarterly* 10, no. 39 (1960); Henry D. Aiken, "God and Evil," *Ethics* 48 (1957/58).

22. I take the terminology of restricted and expanded formulations of theism from William L. Rowe. See his "Evil and the Theistic Hypothesis: A Response to Wykstra," in *The Problem of Evil*, 161, and his "The Empirical Argument from Evil,"

in *Rationality, Religious Belief, and Moral Commitment,* ed. Robert Audi and William Wainwright (Ithaca, N. Y.: Cornell University Press, 1986), 239. As I see it, both of these terms, "restricted" and "expanded," used of theism, are elastic. The most restricted form of theism is a single proposition, namely, "God exists," but it is doubtful if, in practice, any version of the theory could be so frugal. In a recent article, "Rowe's Noseeum Arguments from Evil," in *The Evidential Argument from Evil,* 140, Stephen J. Wykstra, in a useful term, refers to theism so restrictedly understood as "Core Theism." Here, however, we do not need to get involved in the cartographical question of where precisely the respective borders of restricted and expanded theism lie, for it is clear that, relative to certain other formulations of the theory that are both possible and actual, the version of theism under discussion here is an expanded version. And that is all we need from Rowe's restricted/expanded distinction. Also in the same article, Wykstra raises a serious question of whether Core Theism could be said to equip us to make any judgment at all about what would or would not, or could or could not, exist in a world made by God. Wykstra's question will be a focus of our discussion in part 2. It may also be worth note that William Rowe defends a key part of his empirical argument from evil against a criticism of Wykstra's by appeal to the frugality of restricted (or Core) theism. See his "Evil and the Theistic Hypothesis: A Response to Wykstra," 165–66.

23. I retain this focus upon the fates of theistic defensive arguments, in contrast to theism's own fate, in part 2, although there it is a version of the direct empirical argument from evil, as opposed to the indirect empirical and the logical forms of the argument, that is under discussion, and the theistic defense then in question is a version of the non-Pyrrhonian skeptical defense offered by Stephen J. Wykstra and others.

24. Martin first advanced such an argument in 1978. See his "Is Evil Evidence against the Existence of God?" *Mind* 87, 429–32. In his recent book, *Atheism,* Martin puts the gist of his strategy as follows:

> Although Rowe does not develop the inductive argument from evil in terms of the failure of known theodicies to solve the problem of evil, it is possible to do so. The general strategy would be to maintain that since no known theodicy is successful, probably no theodicy will be successful. And since probably no theodicy will be successful, there is probably no explanation for evil. However, there must be such an explanation if God exists. So it is likely that He does not exist. I call such an argument an indirect inductive argument from evil. (341).

In this passage Martin is not operating with the distinction between defense and theodicy with which I opened this chapter. But we may read his point about the failure of known theodicies to apply equally to the failure of known defenses. A different point now: that I migrate in this way to what is uncontroversially an empirical form of the argument from evil is a further reason that, notwithstanding Howard-Snyder's criteria for logical forms of the argument, I designate my argument through chapter 7 as a logical argument. For, in contradistinction to the issues raised in chapter 8 and beyond, it is the logic of theism and evil that is in question through chapter 7.

25. Gale, *On the Nature and Existence of God*, 98.

26. For a good discussion of the difference between logical and live possibilities, and the implications of the difference for the debate over God and evil, see William P. Alston, "The Inductive Argument from Evil and the Human Cognitive Condition," in *Philosophical Perspectives 5*, 29–67. Note that to establish something, say the conjunction of e and t, as a live, and not just a bare logical, possibility, is not tantamount to establishing that conjunction as true. Live possibility is still *possibility*, and so to establish it as such still falls short of establishing that something is actual.

27. Richard Swinburne, *Is There a God?* (New York: Oxford University Press, 1996), 2. The publication data on the other books of Swinburne's cited are, respectively, New York: Clarendon Press, 1977; New York: Clarendon Press, 1979; and New York: Clarendon Press, 1981.

28. In Woody Allen's film, "Everyone Says I Love You," the Alan Alda character, in a memorably funny line, remarks that the sorry state of the world would justify a class-action suit against God, if God existed.

29. Richard Swinburne, "Theodicy, Our Well-Being, and God's Rights," 76.

30. Robert Audi, "Direct Justification, Evidential Dependence, and Theistic Belief," in *Rationality, Religious Belief, and Moral Commitment*, 139 and throughout. In his "The Argument from Inscrutable Evil," 293, Daniel Howard-Snyder refers to what he calls "the enormously problematic thesis that theism is a theory."

31. Nelson Pike, "Hume on Evil," 102.

32. Robert Audi, "Faith, Belief, and Rationality," in *Philosophical Perspectives 5*, 218. For a stronger claim than Audi's, see Robert M. Adams, "The Virtue of Faith," in his *The Virtue of Faith* (New York: Oxford University Press, 1987), 20, and J. L. Schellenberg, *Divine Hiddenness and Human Reason* (Ithaca, N. Y.: Cornell University Press, 1993), 30. Schellenberg makes the following point: "there is something logically amiss in the suggestion that I could display attitudes and perform actions of the sort in question [that is, specifically religious attitudes and actions, respectively] without being disposed to feel it true that God exists." (He tells us that he defines "belief that p" as "a disposition to feel it true that p.") Schellenberg cites Hebrews 11:6 (New International Version) in support of the basic point at issue: "anyone who comes to God must believe that he exists." Later on—(Schellenberg, *Divine Hiddenness*, 36, n.34)—he distinguishes between believing that p and accepting that p, defining "acceptance" as "a commitment to *act-as-if* some proposition is true," where this "does not necessarily involve belief that the proposition is true." For my

purposes here, it is unnecessary to side with Schellenberg, that is to insist on the stronger (unqualified belief) over the weaker (presumption or acceptance) epistemic stance: either will do. For my point is that the cognitive sense of religious belief is implicit in the life-guiding sense, and acceptance or presumption of God's existence supplies that as well as belief does.

33. Audi, "Faith, Belief, and Rationality," 218.

34. Gary Gutting, *Religious Belief and Religious Skepticism* (Notre Dame: University of Notre Dame Press, 1982), 1–3.

35. As noted in footnote 15, I will qualify this point in chapter 3, in discussion of van Inwagen's thinking on gratuitous evil in a supposedly God-made world. But, while qualified, the essential point about God and gratuitous evil will remain as I stated it just now in the body of the text.

36. This point is subject to two significant, and related, qualifications: the dissent from it of the non-Pyrrhonian skeptics discussed in part 2; and my restriction of its scope, given the reasons for those skeptics' dissent.

37. John Hick, *Evil and the God of Love* (London: Macmillan, 1966), 371.

38. David Hume, *Dialogues*, pt. X, 59.

39. This position is defended by Mark T. Nelson, "Naturalistic Ethics and the Argument from Evil," *Faith and Philosophy* 8, no. 3 (July 1991): 376. For criticism, see my "Ethical Naturalism and Evil," *Faith and Philosophy* 10, no.3 (July 1993): 389–93.

Chapter 2

1. Nicholas Wolterstorff, "The Migration of the Theistic Arguments: From Natural Theology to Evidentialist Apologetics," in *Rationality, Religious Belief, and Moral Commitment*, 38–81.

2. John Locke, *An Essay Concerning Human Understanding* (New York: E.P. Dutton, 1961), bk. 4, chap. 17, no. 24, 279–80. By reason, in the passage quoted, Locke means evidence. This kind of internalist account of epistemic justification (thus of knowledge) has recently fallen upon hard times, both as part of the contemporary dissatisfaction with foundationalism as well as in its own right. Among theistic philosophers, Alvin Plantinga is in the vanguard of the new/old externalism in epistemology. See, for example, his *Warrant: The Current Debate* and his *Warrant and Proper Function* (both New York: Oxford University Press, 1993).

3. See, for instance, Karl Popper, *The Logic of Scientific Discovery* (London: Hutchinson, 1959), 40, and Karl Popper, *Conjectures and Refutations* (London: Routledge and Kegan Paul, 1974), 36–37. Reverting to Locke, it should be noted that in the passage just quoted, he does say that a rationally justified faith "cannot be opposite to [reason]."

4. Hume, *Dialogues*, pt. X, 66; also see pt. XI, 74. Nelson Pike argues that Hume is being disingenuous here. See his "Hume on Evil" in *God and Evil*, ed. Nelson Pike (Englewood Cliffs, N.J.: Prentice-Hall, 1964), 97.

5. Hume, *Dialogues*, pt. XI, 69.

6. In part 2, in discussion of the skeptical theism of Stephen J. Wykstra and others, we will take up the question whether, disinterestedly, we are entitled to *any* expectation about what a God-made world would or would not be like in respect to evil.

7. Relatedly, the following point made by Richard Swinburne about theistic arguments that draw upon the regularity in nature testifies to the same initial plausibility and attractiveness of such thinking as we find in the design argument: in Swinburne's words, "[t]he argument to God from the world and its regularity is, I believe, a codification by philosophers of a natural and rational reaction to an orderly world deeply embedded in the human consciousness." See Swinburne, *Is There a God?*, 54.

8. J. C. A. Gaskin, *Hume's Philosophy of Religion*, 2d ed. (Atlantic Highlands, N. J.: Humanities Press International, 1988), 7. Although he does not call it attenuated deism, Keith Yandell, in his *Hume's "Inexplicable Mystery"* (Philadelphia: Temple University Press, 1990), 215–23, endorses a similar reading. On this point, also see M. A. Stewart, "Hume's Philosophy of Religion: Part 2," *Philosophical Books* 37, no. 4 (October 1996): 226.

9. J. C. A. Gaskin, "Hume, Atheism, and the 'Interested Objection' of Morality," in *McGill Hume Studies*, ed. David Fate Norton, et al. (San Diego: Austin Hill Press, 1979), 151. Gaskin puts the point as follows: "for the purposes of discussing the relation between morality and religion, the atheist will be anyone who denies the existence of any god *having moral attributes*. . . . Hume is an atheist in this restricted sense—which I shall call moral atheism—though not in the sense that he denies the existence of all gods whatever." In his *Hume's Philosophy of Religion*, Gaskin makes the point in these words: "[Moral atheism] is atheism as far as the Christian God is concerned just as belief in the Christian God was atheism as far as the classical Roman religion was concerned" (222).

10. In his recent essay, " 'Is it Wrong, Everywhere, Always, and for Anyone, to Believe Anything upon Insufficient Evidence,' " in *Faith, Freedom, and Rationality*, ed. Jeff Jordan and Daniel Howard-Snyder (Lanham, Md: Rowman and Littlefield Publishers, Inc., 1996), 137–53, Peter van Inwagen suggests that nowadays the shoe may be decisively on the other foot, that religious belief tends to be held to *higher* epistemic standards than other kinds of belief. See also Peter van Inwagen, "Quam Dilecta," in *God and the Philosophers*, ed. Thomas V. Morris (New York: Oxford University Press, 1994), 31–60.

11. G. E. Moore, "External and Internal Relations," in *Proceedings of the Aristotelian Society* 20 (1919–1920), reprinted (with corrections) in G. E. Moore, *Philosophical Studies* (London: Routledge and Kegan Paul, 1970), 276–309.

12. As I use it, the term "anti-theistic" does not discriminate between atheism and agnosticism, but covers both.

13. I use the qualifier "virtually" because, in chapter 11, I shall argue that a weaker reading of assumptions 1 and 2 is preferable, from the point of view of a Rowe-style friendly atheism, to the face-value reading of them, which, by comparison, is a strong reading.

14. Hume, *Dialogues*, pt. XI, 67–68.

15. In another region of the philosophy of religion, though, Plantinga belongs with the theistic critics of the standard model, inasmuch as he is sympathetic to the non-Pyrrhonian skeptical defense of theism against arguments from evil.

16. On the one hand, the majority of analytical philosophical writing on the problem of evil falls within the scope of the standard debate, while, on the other, the recent, non-Pyrrhonian skepticism of some influential philosophical defenses of theism—also belonging to the analytic philosophical family—rejects the grounds of the standard debate.

17. Hume, *Dialogues*, pt. X, 63.

18. Hume, *Dialogues*, pt. XI, 68.

19. Hume, *Dialogues*, pt. XII, n.27, 81–82.

20. Nicholas Rescher, *A System of Pragmatic Idealism, Vol. III: Metaphilosophical Inquiries* (Princeton: Princeton University Press, 1994), xiv.

21. For instance, and perhaps most notably, see Gaskin, *Hume's Philosophy of Religion*, chap. 12. In particular, see pages 213–18 of that chapter for Gaskin's response to James Noxon. Noxon's influential dissent from the Kemp Smith/Gaskin line of interpretation is in his "Hume's Agnosticism," in *Hume: A Collection of Critical Essays*, ed. V. C. Chappell (New York: Doubleday, 1966), 361–83. My relative preferment here of Philo as his master's voice does not conflict with another influential position on the matter, namely, Nicholas Capaldi's, notwithstanding Capaldi's sympathy to Noxon's interpretation. See Nicholas Capaldi, "Hume's Philosophy of Religion: God without Ethics," *International Journal for Philosophy of Religion* 1, (Winter 1970): 233–40.

22. Hume, *Dialogues*, pt. II, 14.

23. Hume, *Dialogues*, pt. XII, 77; Hume, *Dialogues*, pt. XII, 79.

24. See Norman Kemp Smith, "Introduction," *Hume's Dialogues Concerning Natural Religion*, ed. Norman Kemp Smith (London: Nelson, 1947), 37–44.

Chapter 3

1. Arguably, it is unnecessary for evil to actually exist in order for theism to face a philosophical problem of evil. Taking a hint from Richard Gale, maybe it is only the *possibility* of evil, specifically the possibility of gratuitous evil (of a certain kind

or amount), in a supposedly God-made world that is needed. However, I shall not develop this idea here. See Gale's *On the Nature and Existence of God*, 111, for the point, made against Plantinga's extension of the free-will defense from moral to natural evil, that "to neutralize the deductive argument based on natural evil, Plantinga must show not just that every alleged natural evil really is or could be a moral evil but that *it is logically impossible that there be a natural evil.*" If I interpret him right, the general point Gale is making here is that it is insufficient for Plantinga or a Plantingalike theistic defender to show that, as a matter of contingent fact, there is no natural evil (or no gratuitous natural evil) in the actual world (supposedly God-made), but that what the Plantingalike defender must show is that there could not possibly be any, over and above those natural evils that, interpreted by Plantinga as broadly moral evils, are laid at Satan's door.

2. William Hasker, "The Necessity of Gratuitous Evil," *Faith and Philosophy* 9, no. 1 (January 1992): 23–44; George N. Schlesinger, *New Perspectives on Old-time Religion* (Oxford: Clarendon Press, 1988); "Suffering and Evil" in *Contemporary Philosophy of Religion*, ed. S. M. Cahn and D. Shatz (New York: Oxford University Press, 1982); *Religion and Scientific Method* (Dordrecht: Reidel, 1977); "The Problem of Evil and the Problem of Suffering," *American Philosophical Quarterly* 1, (1964); Peter van Inwagen, "The Place of Chance in a World Sustained by God," "The Problem of Evil, the Problem of Air, and the Problem of Silence," and "The Magnitude, Duration, and Distribution of Evil: A Theodicy," all in van Inwagen's *God, Knowledge, and Mystery*.

3. Hasker, "The Necessity of Gratuitous Evil," 24.

4. Hasker, "The Necessity of Gratuitous Evil," 24. A point about terminology. Hasker's understanding of gratuitous evil is evil not necessary for the occurrence of a greater good. In chapter 5, in our examination of Swinburne's greater-good defense, we will find Swinburne arguing that NENP is not gratuitous in a God-made world because it is necessary in order for us to be able to acquire the kind of knowledge without which significant moral and spiritual development would be impossible. Depending on how we interpret a key term, there may or may not be a difference between Hasker's and Swinburne's respective concepts of gratuitous evil. For instance, if what Hasker means is that gratuitous evil is evil not necessary for the actual, as opposed to the possible, occurrence of a greater good, and the lines just quoted do suggest strongly that he *does* mean this, then their respective conceptions of gratuitous evil are prima facie different. But, insofar as evils that may or may not be necessary for human moral and spiritual development of the sort Swinburne is interested in are concerned, the expression, "evil not necessary for the occurrence of a greater good" may be read as either (1) evil not necessary for significant moral development to actually occur, or (2) evil not necessary for significant moral development to be possible. And, as noted, (1) seems to reflect the tendency of Hasker's position, while (2) reflects Swinburne's thinking. But a

rapprochement is not out of the question here, nor do we have to strain credulity either too far or in an ad hoc fashion to achieve it. For, if we view the *possibility* of significant moral development as a "greater good," and surely such a possibility *is* a greater good, compared to the contrary impossibility, then Hasker's definition is not at odds with Swinburne's position. This does no violence to Hasker's position, or to Swinburne's, so I shall not pursue differences between their respective positions on the issue.

5. Hasker, "The Necessity of Gratuitous Evil," 34.

6. Hasker, "The Necessity of Gratuitous Evil," 39. In order to avoid a possible misunderstanding, it will be worthwhile at this point to clarify a side issue. That issue is this. If we were discussing the place in a God-made world of gratuitous moral evil, then we would need to distinguish between, on the one hand, the question of whether God's permission of gratuitous moral evil is necessary for the possibility or occurrence of some high-order goods and, on the other, the question of whether the actual occurrence of gratuitous moral evil is necessary for the possibility or occurrence of those goods. For God's permission of gratuitous moral evil (supposing for the sake of argument that divine permission of such evil is not incompatible with any essential divine attribute) does not entail the occurrence of such evil. Thus, the former's being necessary for the possibility or occurrence of a good does not entail the latter's being necessary for that good's possibility or occurrence. But our interest here is in natural and not moral evil, and in particular in natural evil resulting just from the operation of natural processes. In the case of natural evil resulting from natural processes alone, a distinction between God's permission of such evils and their occurrence is a distinction without a difference. For, in their case, for God to permit (or to not prevent) them *does* entail their occurrence. Thus, in my text, to avoid prolixity and needless complexity, instead of phrasing the issue before us in this chapter as the issue of whether or not God's permission of such evils is necessary for the possibility or occurrence of certain high-order goods, I shall put it more simply as the issue of whether the *occurrence* of such evils is necessary for the possibility or occurrence of those high-order goods. For more on the point that the distinction between divine permission and occurrence is not void in respect to moral evil, see William Hasker, "Chrzan on Necessary Gratuitous Evil," *Faith and Philosophy* 12, no. 3 (July 1995): 423–25.

7. Hasker, "The Necessity of Gratuitous Evil," 39. Two points are worth making here. First, as neither Hasker's argument nor my counterargument turns upon a distinction between our knowing/not knowing something as opposed to our believing/not believing it, I shall use the verb "to know" as my only epistemic verb here. This is no disservice to Hasker, for, (1) he also mostly uses only that verb as his epistemic verb and (2) when he uses other epistemic terms instead (e.g., "really believe,"), it is clear that the substitution is not done for the purpose of downgrading the intended epistemic claim from knowledge to mere belief. See Hasker, "The

Necessity of Gratuitous Evil," 39. Second, among the moral goods that Hasker thinks we would be robbed of motivation to acquire, if we knew that all the natural evil in PW were OGNE, is knowledge—presumably including the kind of knowledge necessary for moral choice to be possible. But that is false. For, even with no GGNE in PW, there would still be ample evils from experience of which we could acquire the knowledge necessary for moral development, as there would be no less moral evil and OGNE in PW than in the actual world, and there is no shortage of either one in either of those worlds. On this see my "Swinburne on Natural Evil from Natural Processes," *International Journal for Philosophy of Religion* 30, no. 2 (1991): 77–89, and also chapter 5 below.

8. An implication in both (i) and (ii) is that we know God exists. Richard Swinburne has an argument that we would be robbed of moral motivation if we knew for sure that God existed. But it is not the same as the argument of Hasker's we are now considering, for Hasker's does not turn upon our knowing that God exists. See Swinburne, *The Existence of God*, 211–12. For a counterargument, see my "Swinburne on Natural Evil," *Religious Studies* 19, no. 1 (1983): 68–71.

9. I express my point here in the language of moral obligation. Essentially the same point will hold if, instead of confining ourselves to such language, we follow the lead of Judith Jarvis Thomson in using terms like "moral decency," "moral indecency," "moral indifference," "callousness," "good samaritanism," "bad samaritanism," and so on, that is, terms less immediately connotative of requirements and prohibitions than the terminology of obligations. See her much anthologized "A Defense of Abortion," in *The Abortion Controversy*, ed. Louis P. Pojman and Francis J. Beckwith (Boston: Jones & Bartlett, 1994), 140–44.

10. Hasker, "The Necessity of Gratuitous Evil," 36.

11. William K. Frankena, *Ethics*, 2d ed. (Englewood Cliffs, N. J.: Prentice-Hall, 1973), 113.

12. Hasker, "The Necessity of Gratuitous Evil," 28–29.

13. This raises the following question about OT: is OT committed to the proposition that, in a God-made world, there is (and could be) no (genuinely) gratuitous (natural) evil, or only to the weaker claim that, in a God-made world, not all (genuinely) gratuitous (natural) evil is logically inconsistent with God? As I have said from the beginning, it is the latter that I regard as OT's commitment. Perhaps OT is really committed to the former. I don't know. But no harm is done by committing it only to the weaker of the two propositions, for thereby the stronger is not denied or precluded.

14. Hasker, "The Necessity of Gratuitous Evil," 24.

15. Hasker, "The Necessity of Gratuitous Evil," 39.

16. Hasker, "The Necessity of Gratuitous Evil," 39.

17. My harmless assumption here is that the removal of all GGNE from PW3 occurs after human civilization has developed to approximately its present level in

the actual world. This assumption is a harmless one to make here, for it is essentially what Hasker himself is assuming, thus it does no disservice to his position to accept it here. If, contrary to the assumption, God removes (and prevents the recurrence of) all GGNE *before* civilization develops to the stage in question, then we would be dealing with a version of what I will describe in a moment as another possible world, PW4.

18. In part 2 we will have occasion to use a concept of a possible world very similar to PW4 as just now described. For further description of such a world, see section 3 of my "On the Problem of Evil's Still Not Being What It Seems," *The Philosophical Quarterly* 40, no. 158 (January 1990): 76–78, and the second part ("The Suppression Model") of section 3 of my "On Failing to Resolve Theism-versus-Atheism Empirically," *Religious Studies* 26, no. 1 (March 1990): 99–101 for a fuller account of PW4.

Getting back now to my present argument about PW4, two points come up. The first concerns the relationship between PW4 and the actual world. Orthodox theism's view, as I understand it, is that, subject to a qualification to be introduced in section 4, (1) there could be no GGNE in a God-made world and (2) there is no GGNE in the actual world, appearances and arguments to the contrary notwithstanding. The conjunction of (1) and (2), predicated of the actual world, does not make the actual world and PW4 one and the same, even though there is no GGNE in PW4, for, to my knowledge, it is not a standard credendum of orthodox theism that there is no GGNE in the actual world *because* God pre-emptively prevented it. Rather, my understanding of the orthodox theistic view of the matter is that, all things considered, there is no GGNE in the actual world because, in the future, God will responsively prevent all GGNE. However, both are compatible with OT, and, with a slight adjustment, with each other. Thus, the mechanism of prevention of GGNE might be different in PW4 and the actual world, assuming that in the latter it is true that there is no GGNE. Orthodox theism concedes, however, that the actual world contains prima facie GGNE. I make the foregoing claim tentatively. It is denied by the skeptical theistic defenders of OT to be discussed in chapters 10 and 11, and maybe they are right. I do not think that skeptical theism (as we find it in Alston, van Inwagen, or Wykstra) is widely reflective of orthodox theistic thinking, but that could change. And if it did, then the foregoing tentative claim would be false. The second point to address here is this. If there is no GGNE, but we do not know there is no GGNE, and if the nonexistence of GGNE is so clearly a credendum of orthodox theism as I have been saying it is (although see note 13 for a qualification), and as Hasker seems to agree it is (see Hasker, "The Necessity of Gratuitous Evil," 24), why do we not know there is no GGNE? Perhaps the best answer is analogical. Our not *knowing* there is no GGNE is akin to our not knowing the world is God-made, or that human beings are God's creatures. These are central precepts of OT, too, but the theist does not know them to be true, when knowledge is understood as some form of justified, true, belief, justifiably arrived at. Of course, a different conception of knowledge could lead to a different outcome. But that is a topic much too large for discussion here.

19. Hasker, "The Necessity of Gratuitous Evil," 39. This point is also provisional pending the qualification due to van Inwagen that we will discuss in the fourth section.

20. Hasker, "The Necessity of Gratuitous Evil," 38.

21. Richard Swinburne, "Theodicy, Our Well-Being, and God's Rights," 76.

22. Peter van Inwagen, "The Place of Chance in a World Sustained by God," 50.

23. van Inwagen, "The Place of Chance," 60.

24. This passage is a fusion of portions of the passages cited in notes 23 above and 30 below.

25. Peter van Inwagen, "The Magnitude, Duration, and Distribution of Evil: A Theodicy," 103. See also his "Introduction" to part 1 of *God, Knowledge, and Mystery*, 17.

26. van Inwagen, "The Magnitude," 103.

27. van Inwagen, "The Magnitude," 104.

28. van Inwagen, "The Magnitude," 104.

29. On this point see Daniel Howard-Snyder, "The Argument from Inscrutable Evil," in *The Evidential Argument from Evil*, 289. The radical question of whether inscrutable evil gives us any reason at all to believe there is no God is discussed in part 2.

30. Peter van Inwagen, "The Place of Chance," 60.

Chapter 4

1. For instance, see William L. Rowe, "Evil and the Theistic Hypothesis: A Response to Wykstra," *International Journal for Philosophy of Religion* 16 (1984): 95; also William L. Rowe, "The Empirical Argument from Evil," in *Rationality, Religious Belief, and Moral Commitment*, 239, and William L. Rowe, "The Problem of Evil and Some Varieties of Atheism," *American Philosophical Quarterly* 16 (1997): 335. In addition, see Swinburne, *The Existence of God*, 1, and *The Coherence of Theism*, 2. See also McCloskey, "God and Evil," throughout, and Paul Draper, "Pain and Pleasure: An Evidential Problem for Theists," *Nous* 23 (1989): 331. Other citations could be added, but perhaps enough influential works have been cited to make the point. For discussion of versions of theism beyond restricted theism, see Terry Christlieb, "Which Theisms Face an Evidential Problem?" *Faith and Philosophy* 9 (January 1992): 56–62. The philosophers who, for purposes of discussing the problem of evil, proceed on the basis of the ad hoc synonymy between belief in God and the proposition that God exists in all probability do not believe there is no more, or

no more of philosophical significance, to religious belief than affirmation of that proposition. Now a separate, but related, point: as we saw in the first chapter, it is also not uncommon in philosophical defenses of restricted theism to find recourse made to propositions other than "God exists" and its entailments. In effect, it is not uncommon to find a version of expanded theism presupposed in defenses of restricted theism. For instance, the defense offered by Stephen J. Wykstra is cited by Rowe as doing just this. See the first article of Rowe's listed above. In addition, Swinburne's defense of theism in *The Existence of God* draws on a much fuller conception of theism than restricted theism.

2. See, for instance, Louis Dupre, "Theodicy: The Case for a Theologically Inclusive Model of Philosophy," *American Catholic Philosophical Association Proceedings* 64 (1990): 25–27, and 39, and Dupre, "Evil—A Religious Mystery," *Faith and Philosophy* 7 (July 1990): 261–66. For a more extreme version of such a view, see Kenneth Surin, *Theology and the Problem of Evil* (New York: Basil Blackwell, 1986). My substitution of OT for restricted theism as the target of the reformed logical argument either circumnavigates or dilutes Dupre's (and others') complaint about the reductionism in analytical philosophy of religion insofar as the problem of evil is concerned, and in essence involves my entering a plea of "no contest" in the debate over evil and restricted theism.

3. See chapter 3, n.4 for related discussion of William Hasker's and Richard Swinburne's thinking on divine purposes in world making. As I tell it, the divine plan insofar as human moral and spiritual development is concerned is that such development is *possible* in any God-made world that contains human beings. But as we saw, Hasker may be committed to a stronger account of the divine plan, namely, as a plan for a world in which such development actually occurs. However, given that the occurrence of such development is conditional upon various counterfactuals of freedom, it is not clear to me that this could be God's *plan*, although I see no difficulty in its being one of God's desiderata in world actualization. It is worth noting as well that, in his "The Inductive Argument from Evil and the Human Cognitive Condition," *Philosophical Perspectives* 5, 39–43, William P. Alston emphasizes, in his description of conceivable divine purposes in making a world containing evils for whose existence we can discern no God-justifying reason, the possibility, not the actuality, of human persons' developing in the sorts of ways we have been discussing. In that particular section of his paper Alston is drawing upon Hick's concept of soul-making, as do I in formulating propositions 4 and 5 of OT.

4. Presumably it is not an essential credendum of OT that all human persons are, in fact, capable of freely choosing their individual destinies. For, among instances of natural evil resulting just from natural processes, there are human beings born so severely brain damaged that moral choices are not a live option for them. Neither are such choices a logical option for them. The latter point may be contested and so, perhaps, requires argument showing it to be true. However, we do

not need to settle or to even pronounce an opinion on the issue here. Another issue on which no opinion need be expressed here, and indeed on which I have no opinion, is that of *when* after death the final judgment occurs. My understanding of the traditional understanding of the point is that the final judgment occurs at death or very shortly thereafter. But Daniel Howard-Snyder has suggested to me that the traditional understanding may be compatible with a looser schedule than this. Maybe he is right: I do not know. Nothing in this book hinges on answering the question either way.

5. If we die in that sense, and if a soul theory is true, then it will be a soul theory of an Aristotelian sort, although not necessarily Aristotle's own.

6. The Thomistic theory of the soul also provides for divine reconstitution of the person at a point after death, inasmuch as the person, on that theory, is an embodied intellect and not a soul, understood as a purely spiritual substance. For a recent sympathetic discussion of Aquinas's version of the relation of soul and body, see Eleonore Stump, "Non-Cartesian Substance Dualism and Materialism without Reductionism," *Faith and Philosophy* 12, no.4 (October 1995): 505–31. John Hick is the best-known advocate, among contemporary analytical philosophers of religion, of a (non-Platonic, non-Cartesian, and non-Thomistic soul) reconstitution theory of life after death. For a representative account of his position, see, for instance, *Death and Eternal Life* (San Francisco: Harper and Row, 1976).

7. The relationship between theories and their supporting arguments plays an important role in my argument in part 1. In addition to our earlier discussion of it in chapters 1 and 2, I say more on the subject in chapter 8. The present point is that a theory is more than a free-standing set of claims, that of its nature a theory involves the attempt both to establish certain propositions and, if and when necessary, to defend them against attack. That is, a theory is tied in an essential way to supporting arguments, although not necessarily to *all* of its supporting arguments. As we saw in chapter 2, however, this relationship is not reciprocated.

8. Richard Swinburne has argued that, other things being equal, it is moral *knowledge* and practical *knowledge*, not just moral and practical beliefs, that are needed for human beings to be able to develop in the ways reflected in the divine plan (as that is stated in proposition 4 of OT). But that is too strong. Justified true belief is enough, maybe even justified belief alone, provided it is sufficiently universal. See Richard Swinburne, "Knowledge from Experience, and the Problem of Evil," in *The Rationality of Religious Belief*, ed. W.J. Abraham and S.W. Holtzer (New York: Clarendon Press, 1987), 149–52.

9. As these terms are Alvin Plantinga's, let us use his definitions. "Let us say that God *strongly* actualizes a state of affairs S if and only if he causes S to be actual and causes to be actual every contingent state of affairs S* such that S includes S*; and let's say that God *weakly* actualizes a state of affairs S if and only if he strongly actualizes a state of affairs S* that counterfactually implies S" (Alvin Plantinga,

"Self-Profile," in *Alvin Plantinga*, 49). Accordingly, God-made worlds that contain free creatures are weakly, not strongly, actualized worlds.

10. Robert M. Adams, "Must God Create the Best?" in *The Virtue of Faith*, 53.

11. Philip L. Quinn, "God, Moral Perfection, and Possible Worlds," in *The Problem of Evil*, ed. Michael J. Peterson (Notre Dame: University of Notre Dame Press, 1992), 300. Quinn's paper originally appeared in *God: The Contemporary Discussion*, ed. Frederick Sontag and M. Darrol Bryant (New York: Rose of Sharon Press, 1982).

12. William P. Alston, "The Inductive Argument from Evil," 39.

13. For van Inwagen-type reasons, it is possible that W^p would contain some NERNP, including some that seems to be NENP[i]. But such NERNP, if any, would not be needed for provision of NEM, and so could not be (God-)justified that way. Thus, any such amount of NERNP does not tell against the present point.

14. Michael Martin, "Reichenbach on Natural Evil," *Religious Studies* 24 (March 1988): 93–94.

15. Gale, *On the Nature and Existence of God*, 113.

16. If it could be shown that it is impossible for God to actualize a world with no indigenous natural evil (no NERNP), then that would represent the basis of a potentially deadly counterargument to Plantinga's free-will defense against arguments from natural evil. Likewise to my reformed logical argument from natural evil.

17. In chapter 5, we will see Swinburne maintain that NERNP *is* logically necessary for NEM to be possible. See also the final subsection in this chapter.

18. This point is subject to the scope reduction mentioned in note 4 above.

Chapter 5

1. Swinburne, *The Existence of God*, 219–24.

2. Swinburne, "Knowledge from Experience," 165.

3. Swinburne, *Is There a God?* 98. In addition, see Richard Swinburne, "Some Major Strands of Theodicy," in *The Evidential Argument from Evil*, 38. Parenthetically, let us recall from chapter 1 that Swinburne's use of the word "theodicy" does not fully accord with the division of labor between defense and theodicy (in a somewhat different sense of the term) that I took over from Plantinga. See chapter 1, note 1.

4. Swinburne, "Knowledge from Experience," 152, 153, 156, 161, 163, 165.

5. Swinburne, *Is There a God?* 98.

6. Swinburne, *Is There a God?* 101.

7. Swinburne, "Some Major Strands of Theodicy," 37. Also see page 39 of that essay, and Swinburne, *Is There a God?* 101. I believe Swinburne is right about this. See my "A Variation on the Free Will Defense," *Faith and Philosophy* 4, no. 2 (April 1987): 160–67, for a fuller account.

8. Swinburne, "Some Major Strands of Theodicy," 46.

9. Swinburne, *Is There a God?* 98.

10. Alvin Plantinga, *The Nature of Necessity*, 180–84. Also see his "Self-Profile" in *Alvin Plantinga*, 51.

11. Swinburne, "Some Major Strands of Theodicy," 39.

12. The attribution to God of middle knowledge (and of foreknowledge) is part of the Mackie-Plantinga debate on which possible worlds God could and could not actualize, hence I include it here in my description of Mackie's point. But it should be emphasized that Swinburne rejects the idea that God has either middle knowledge or foreknowledge. His most recent statement of the point is in his *Is There a God?* 7–8.

13. Plantinga, *The Nature of Necessity*, 167–90.

14. Swinburne, "Knowledge from Experience," 146.

15. Swinburne, "Knowledge from Experience," 150.

16. Swinburne, "Knowledge from Experience," 150–51. Although I argued in the previous chapter that true practical belief is sufficient for moral decisions to be possible, I do not insist on the point. Instead, I accept for the sake of argument Swinburne's point that practical *knowledge* is required.

17. Swinburne, "Knowledge from Experience," 151–52.

18. Swinburne, "Knowledge from Experience," 150.

19. For an argument against Swinburne's being justified in discounting those possibilities, see Eleonore Stump, "Knowledge, Freedom, and the Problem of Evil," *International Journal for Philosophy of Religion* 14 (1983): 49–58. For additional arguments to the same end, see my "Swinburne on Natural Evil," 65–74, and my "Swinburne on Natural Evil from Natural Processes," 77–88.

20. Swinburne, *The Existence of God*, 211.

21. Swinburne, "Knowledge from Experience," 161.

22. Swinburne, "Knowledge from Experience," 159.

23. Swinburne, "Knowledge from Experience," 163. Two pages later, he puts the point this way: "God cannot give to men the sort of belief needed for a free and responsible choice of destiny without producing natural processes which bring about natural evils, and letting men observe and experience them" (165).

24. This point needs a little modification. For van Inwagen-type reasons, W^P may contain some NERNP although none whose God-justifying reason to exist is that it is a necessary precondition of NEM. Furthermore, the amount of NERNP that W^P might contain for van Inwagen-type reasons would be small, thus insufficient to provide for NEM. Thus, van Inwagen-type reasons do not establish Swinburne's conclusion.

25. Swinburne, "Knowledge from Experience," 155–56. This point represents part of a response to the papers cited in note 19 above.

26. Swinburne, "Knowledge from Experience," 156. This is the other and more important part of Swinburne's response to the papers cited in note 19 above.

27. Swinburne, "Knowledge from Experience," 164.
28. Swinburne, "Knowledge from Experience," 158.
29. Swinburne, "Knowledge from Experience," 165.
30. Swinburne, "Knowledge from Experience," 155–56.
31. Locke, *An Essay Concerning Human Understanding*, bk. 2, chap. 1, no. 2, 77.

Chapter 6

1. Plantinga, *The Nature of Necessity*, 165–66.
2. Plantinga, *The Nature of Necessity*, 171.
3. Swinburne, *Is There a God?* 98.
4. Plantinga's point may be clarified by means of a distinction between it and St. Augustine's position on the applicability to natural evil of the free-will defense. For St. Augustine, in Plantinga's words, "believes that [some] natural evil . . . is *in fact* to be ascribed to the activity of beings that are free and rational but non-human" (*The Nature of Necessity*, 192). Recalling Gale's version of the difference between defense and theodicy, the "in fact" is the key to the difference between Plantinga's and Augustine's positions, making the latter (at least as described by Plantinga) a theodicy, whereas the former is a defense.
5. Nor does such thinking belong only to the past in philosophy. Richard Swinburne, for instance, argues for an unabashed substance dualism. See his *Is There a God?* 69–94—"mental life . . . is the state of an immaterial substance, a soul, which is connected to the body" (73)—and also see both his debate with Sydney Shoemaker in Sydney Shoemaker and Richard Swinburne, *Personal Identity* (Oxford: Basil Blackwell, 1984), especially 22–34, and his *The Evolution of the Soul* (Oxford: Clarendon Press, 1986), chapter 8 and additional note 2, for a fuller account of the view expressed in *Is There a God?* To my knowledge, Swinburne's most recent defenses of his view against some of its critics are his "Dualism Intact," *Faith and Philosophy* 13, no. 1 (January 1996), 68–77, and his "Reply to Stump and Kretzmann," *Faith and Philosophy* 13, no. 3 (July 1996), 413–14. In the former article, Swinburne describes his position as "an improved version [of Descartes's modal argument in Meditation 6]," and the latter is his reply to Eleonore Stump and Norman Kretzmann, "An Objection to Swinburne's Argument for Dualism," *Faith and Philosophy* 13, no. 3 (July 1996): 405–12.
6. Plantinga, *The Nature of Necessity*, 192.
7. Mackie, "Evil and Omnipotence," 25.
8. Aiken, "God and Evil," 48; Flew, "Divine Omnipotence and Human Freedom"; McCloskey, "God and Evil."
9. The references are: first, to Plantinga's "Advice to Christian Philosophers," *Faith and Philosophy* 1 (July 1984): 253–71, and second, to his announcement in *Warrant: The Current Debate*, vi and viii.

10. Hume, *Dialogues*, pt. XI, 69.

11. Plantinga, "Self-Profile," 49.

12. Plantinga, "Self-Profile," 50, 96 n.15.

13. Gale, *On the Nature and Existence of God*, 128. Also see Plantinga, *The Nature of Necessity*, 187–89.

14. For brevity and conciseness, let us mostly omit references to cohorts of good and bad angels in what follows.

15. Plantinga, *The Nature of Necessity*, 185–86; also Alvin Plantinga, *God, Freedom and Evil* (New York: Harper Torchbooks, 1974), 42–43. In his 1985 "Self-Profile," Plantinga speculates about a version of the free-will defense without ascription to God of middle knowledge. Parenthetically, Gale, *On the Nature and Existence of God*, 168–78, argues that, like the original, such a modified version of the free-will defense will fail.

16. Swinburne, *Is There a God?* 101, and Swinburne, "Some Major Strands of Theodicy," 37. See also the opening pages of chapter 5 above.

17. Mackie, "Evil and Omnipotence," 33.

18. Plantinga, "Self-Profile," 52.

19. Plantinga, "Self-Profile," 52.

20. Plantinga, "Self-Profile," 50.

21. David K. Lewis, *Counterfactuals* (Cambridge, Mass: Harvard University Press, 1976), 1.

22. Plantinga, "Self-Profile," 50, 96 n.15.

23. Plantinga, "Self-Profile," 51–52.

24. Plantinga, *The Nature of Necessity*, 189.

25. Plantinga, "Self-Profile," 41.

26. Plantinga, *God and Other Minds* (Ithaca, N. Y.: Cornell University Press, 1967), 132.

27. Plantinga, "Self-Profile," 41. But it is clear that this point has no applicability to W^p, inasmuch as no determinism of free choice obtains in W^p. Furthermore, it has no applicability to Mackie's proposal in "Evil and Omnipotence" either, for the idea there is that God would actualize only those human persons who, from among all possible human persons, would always freely choose only the good.

28. Gale, *On the Nature and Existence of God*, 111, argues that a successful defense must do more than show that, as a contingent matter, there is no gratuitous evil in the actual world. His point is that, to be successful, a defense that aims to provide an alibi—in the sense of the term specified in the first chapter—must show that there could not be such evil.

29. Gale, *On The Nature and Existence of God*, 158, 159.

30. Gale, *On the Nature and Existence of God*, 160.

31. Gale, *On the Nature and Existence of God*, 160.

32. Both Mackie and Adams agree that no wrong would thereby be done to any

merely possible being under the kinds of circumstances just described. Implicit in Mackie's core idea in "Evil and Omnipotence" that, knowing what he knows by virtue of his middle knowledge, God could and would have actualized only those human persons who, freely, never choose evil over good is the idea that in such a world *we* would not exist, and that we would not have been wronged by our not having been actualized. For Adams's concurrence see his "Must God Create the Best?" 53.

33. Ludwig Wittgenstein, *Philosophical Investigations*, ed. G. E. M. Anscombe and R. Rhees, trans. G. E. M. Anscombe, (Oxford: Basil Blackwell, 1968), sections 2–9.

Chapter 7

1. Plantinga, *The Nature of Necessity*, 168–91; Swinburne, *The Existence of God*, 113–14, and also see Swinburne, "Some Major Strands of Theodicy," 48, n.19. George N. Schlesinger, in his *Religion and Scientific Method* (Dordrecht: Reidel, 1977), 77, argues that, in one sense of the term, there is no such thing as the best of all possible worlds, but that, in another sense, there is. Schlesinger's distinction does not require any change in my point in the text, so we need not dwell on it.

2. Bruce Reichenbach, *Evil and a Good God* (New York: Fordham University Press, 1982), 121–91, 128 in particular.

3. van Inwagen, "The Magnitude, Duration, and Distribution of Evil: A Theodicy," 104.

4. This denial of the status of evidence to facts of evil is also the principal defensive tactic of those skeptical theists to be discussed in part 2. While in agreement with Schlesinger on *what* they deny, though, *why* they deny it is quite different. Furthermore, those skeptical defenders of theism do, presumably, agree that *some* facts of gratuitous[p] evil, if they obtained, would be NENP[i], even if we could not know or justifiably believe that those facts *were* NENP[i]. Two further differences between Schlesinger and the skeptical defenders of OT are worth noting as well. They are, first, that Schlesinger is principally interested in the logical, not the empirical, form of the problem of evil, although his argument covers the latter as well, and second, his denial that we are justified in expecting a God-made world to be such-and-such and not so-and-so is not rooted in any deflationary estimate of our capacity for knowing (or justifiably believing) such things, but rather in the radical idea that God is simply not obligated to actualize better rather than worse possible worlds.

5. Schlesinger, *Religion and Scientific Method*, 62–63.

6. Robert Elliot, "Divine Perfection, Axiology and The No Best Possible World Defence," *Religious Studies* 29, no. 4 (December 1993): 536.

7. Schlesinger, *Religion and Scientific Method*, 76.

8. For a good account of this aspect of Schlesinger's defense, see Thomas V. Morris, "A Response to The Problem of Evil," *Philosophia* 14 (August 1984): 177–78. In Morris's words, the essence of Schlesinger's position is that "the existence of any amount of pain, suffering, and unhappiness in the world is perfectly compatible with the existence of an omnipotent, omniscient, and wholly good God as its creator" (178).

9. George N. Schlesinger, *New Perspectives on Old-time Religion* (Oxford: Clarendon Press, 1988), 54

10. Schlesinger, *New Perspectives*, 53–54.

11. Both quotations are from Schlesinger, *New Perspectives*, 54.

12. Schlesinger, *Religion and Scientific Method*, 61.

13. Schlesinger, *Religion and Scientific Method*, 61.

14. Schlesinger, *New Perspectives*, 55.

15. Keith Chrzan, "The Irrelevance of the No Best Possible World Defense," *Philosophia* 17, no. 2 (October 1987): 165-166.

16. Chrzan, "The Irrelevance," 165.

17. This line of argument is a variation on the argument in my "Schlesinger and the Morally Perfect Man," *The Journal of Value Inquiry* 20, no. 3 (1986): 245–49.

18. In their recent article, "How an Unsurpassable Being Can Create a Surpassable World," *Faith and Philosophy* 11, no. 2 (April 1994): 260–68, Daniel and Frances Howard-Snyder argue that, from the fact that an omnipotent, omniscient being actualizes a world inferior to a world another omnipotent, omniscient being could actualize, it does not follow, other things being equal, that the first omnipotent being is morally inferior to the second. Then in their "The Real Problem of No Best World," *Faith and Philosophy* 13, no. 3 (July 1996): 422–25, they defend the idea against an argument of William Rowe's. See Rowe's "The Problem of No Best World," *Faith and Philosophy* 11, no. 2 (April 1994): 269–70. In their first article, the Howard-Snyders describe a randomizing device that both omnipotent beings use to settle upon which worlds to actualize. In those circumstances, if one omnipotent being, say God, randomly actualized the actual world and another omnipotent being, Jove, randomly actualized W^P, their thinking goes, then it would not logically follow from this that Jove morally surpasses God. (As in the main body of our text, W^P surpasses the actual world.) Now arguably, God, being God, could not resort to use of a randomizing device in selecting for actualization a world with free human beings, but would *choose* from among possible worlds the one he wished to actualize, but let us not press the point. Relatedly, Rowe's objection, in essence, turns on the plausible idea of substituting for the Howard-Snyders's notion of random world-actualization the concept of world-actualization in play in this book, namely, deliberately chosen actualization by an essentially free, omnipotent, omniscient, perfectly good being—with middle knowledge included in essential omniscience—of the world he or she intends to actualize. Framed in those terms, God knowingly

settles for the actual world while Jove knowingly settles for a better world instead. The point here is not that Jove himself is morally unsurpassable or beyond reproach for his choice. Rather, the point is that, prima facie, Jove morally surpasses God. In their second article, the Howard-Snyders challenge this ranking of omnipotent beings on the basis used. They challenge Rowe to articulate the principles in use in the omnipotent being's choice (as opposed to using the randomizer) of which world to actualize, and then, having supplied some candidate-principles of their own, challenge the coherence of Rowe's story of one omnipotent being's surpassing the other. They raise some very interesting points relative to my enterprise in this section, which unfortunately, having only recently received their second article, I do not have the time to think through and discuss here. For a very illuminating examination of a set of related issues closely related to those in the Howard-Snyders's discussion with Rowe, see William J. Wainwright, "Jonathan Edwards, William Rowe, and the Necessity of Creation," in *Faith, Freedom, and Rationality*, 128–33. Wainwright is there carrying on his own discussion with Rowe on the question of when an omnipotent being may justifiably not actualize a better world than one he has actualized.

19. A point of Peter van Inwagen's, although made in a different context and with a different purpose, converges on my point here and amplifies it. In van Inwagen's words, "*having* come into existence, we are *now* in God's care and the objects of His love and the instruments of His purpose" ("The Place of Chance in a World Sustained by God," 56. [italics original, but the italicized words are those I would (counterfactually) have italicized to make my point, too.])

20. Chrzan, "The Irrelevance," 163.

Chapter 8

1. As previously observed, my indirect empirical argument belongs to the same family as Michael Martin's. See his *Atheism*, 341–61, also his "Is Evil Evidence against The Existence of God?" The latter work is his original formulation of the argument.

2 Daniel Howard-Snyder, in his "Seeing through CORNEA," *International Journal for Philosophy of Religion* 32, no. 1 (August 1992): 46, brings into sharp focus the following interesting idea that traces to the silence of God in the face of vast amounts of appalling, inscrutable evil: "the justificatory value of inscrutability as a basis for atheism depends on the likelihood that God would make himself or His purposes more evident than He does (if He exists)." To my knowledge, this is the first introduction of the fact of divine silence into the current debate on the empirical problem of evil. For an original and interesting examination of the evidentiary support that the fact of divine hiddenness—which would include divine silence in

NOTES

the face of inscrutable evil—provides to atheism, see Schellenberg, *Divine Hidden-ness and Human Reason.*

Chapter 9

1. Hume, *Dialogues*, pt. X, 61.
2. Hume, *Dialogues*, pt. X, 64.
3. Hume, *Dialogues*, pt. X, 64.
4. Hume, *Dialogues*, pt. X, 64–65.
5. Hume, *Dialogues*, pt. XI, 68.
6. As well as being friendly in Rowe's sense of the term, this version of atheism is "square" in Wykstra's sense of that term. The meanings of these two terms will become clear as this chapter progresses, so for now let us say that by square atheism is meant a firm belief that there is no God, that theism is false, and by friendly atheism is meant square atheism that answers the following question in the affirmative: whether, in this day and age, "some people . . . who are aware of the usual grounds for belief and disbelief and are acquainted to some degree with modern science, are yet rationally justified in accepting theism[?]." The quotation and the term "friendly atheism" are from William L. Rowe, "The Problem of Evil and Some Varieties of Atheism," 136. On square atheism, square agnosticism, and square theism, respectively, see Stephen J. Wykstra, "Rowe's Noseeum Arguments from Evil," 130–31 and following.
7. In large part this is tied to the (earlier noted) emerging consensus that the logical form of the problem of evil is moribund. Among versions of the direct empirical argument from evil, the most discussed, thus arguably the most influential, are Rowe's—first presented in 1979 and modified and refined several times since—and Draper's. See Draper, "Pain and Pleasure: An Evidential Problem for Theists," 331–50, and "Probabilistic Arguments from Evil," *Religious Studies* 28 (1993): 303–17, in particular.
8. Jeff Jordan, "Not In Kansas Anymore," *God and the Philosophers*, 133. In chapter 11 I take up the question of whether the detente between a Rowe-style "friendly" atheism and a correspondingly friendly theism obtains only when friendly atheism is associated with Rowe's version of the direct empirical argument. My answer to that question is that it does not obtain only then.
9. van Inwagen, *Metaphysics*, 16.
10. G. E. Moore, *Some Main Problems of Philosophy* (London: Allen & Unwin, 1969), 119–22.
11. Among Rowe's subsequent formulations of his argument, the following are the most significant: "Evil and the Theistic Hypothesis: A Response to Wykstra," 161–67; "The Empirical Argument from Evil," in *Rationality, Religious Belief, and*

260

Moral Commitment, 227–47; "Evil and Theodicy," in *Philosophical Topics* 16 (1988): 119–32; "Ruminations about Evil," in *Philosophical Perspectives* 5, 69–88; "The Evidential Argument from Evil: A Second Look," in *The Evidential Argument from Evil*, 262–85.

12. By "earlier" in this context I mean before 1988 and by "later" I mean after that date. That was the year of publication in *Philosophical Topics* of Rowe's "Evil and Theodicy." For explanation of 1988 as the pivotal year, see Rowe, "The Evidential Argument from Evil: A Second Look," 262.

13. Arguably, for van Inwagen-type reasons, some such instances are divinely nonculpable gratuitous[p], thus not a basis for an argument from evil. But we have good reason to think that a vast amount of intense suffering that God could have prevented without entailing a loss of a greater good does belong to the class of NENP[i], and as such provides a basis for such an argument. Henceforth, let us take it for granted that the instances of inscrutable evil that Rowe cites belong to that category, prima facie NENP[i].

14. In a recent discussion of John Hick's Irenaean hypothesis, Rowe introduces a variation on point (2), as follows:"it not only seems obvious to us that evil occurs far in excess of what an omnipotent being would have to permit for soul-making; it also seems obvious to us that evil occurs far in excess of what an omnipotent being would have to permit for us to be rational in believing that excess evil occurs" (William L. Rowe, "Paradox and Promise: Hick's Solution to the Problem of Evil," in *Problems in the Philosophy of Religion*, ed. Harold Hewitt, Jr. [New York: St. Martin's Press, 1991], 120). Rowe is here addressing Hick's paradoxical idea that divine provision for the possibility of significant soul-making requires both the existence of large quantities of evil in the world and our rational belief that the quantity of evil in the world is in *excess* of what is needed for soul-making to be possible. The paradox here is not that evils that are not necessary for soul-making to be possible *are* necessary for soul-making (for that would go beyond paradox): rather, in Rowe's words, it is "that rationally *believing* that there are evils not needed for soul-making, is, after all, needed for soul-making" (Rowe, "Paradox and Promise," 120 [italics added]). In a footnote, Rowe gives the following illuminating example of the point at issue: "suppose a marathon runner is such that, if he believes that he will win, he won't train and, therefore, won't win. But, if he has grounds for believing that he will lose, he will train to the utmost so as to come as close to winning as he can. Of such a person it might be correct, although paradoxical, to say, 'rationally believing that he won't win, is, after all, required if he is to win' " (Rowe, "Paradox and Promise," 124, n.18). Rowe then defends his point that there is evil in excess of what would be required as grounds for us rationally to believe there is evil in excess of what is needed for soul-making in "Response to Linda Zagzebski," in *Problems in the Philosophy of Religion*, 130–32.

15. Rowe, "Ruminations about Evil," 69. For an adjustment in Rowe's second

premise, see William P. Alston, "The Inductive Argument from Evil and the Human Cognitive Condition," 33–35. Although Alston's point is a corrective to Rowe's second premise, my argument here is unaffected, so I shall pass over Alston's point.

16. Rowe, "The Empirical Argument from Evil," 235. Although not stated as such, it is clear that the conjunction of these points, even the conjunction of the first two of them, reflects the point that we have experience of much evil for whose existence we are unable to discern any God-justifying reason. In that connection, Rowe himself goes on as follows: "I set forth an example of intense suffering . . . and observed that as far as we can determine it serves no greater good at all, let alone one that is otherwise unobtainable by an omnipotent being" ("The Empirical Argument from Evil," 235).

17. Bruce Russell, "The Persistent Problem of Evil," *Faith and Philosophy* 6, no. 2, (April 1989): 123. See also Bruce Russell and Stephen J. Wykstra, "The 'Inductive' Argument from Evil: A Dialogue," *Philosophical Topics* 16, no. 2 (1988): 133–34.

18. For an illuminating description of Moore's thinking on this point, see Avrum Stroll, *Moore and Wittgenstein on Certainty* (New York: Oxford University Press, 1994), 44.

19. Although we are focusing in this chapter on certain specific instances of inscrutable evil, it is not in their own right that we do so, but, as before, as representative of the class of prima facie NENP[i], for our interest remains in the amount of prima facie NENP[i] in the world, not in the specific instances of it as such.

20. Rowe, "The Problem of Evil and Some Varieties of Atheism," 130; and William L. Rowe, *Philosophy of Religion: An Introduction*, 2nd. ed. (Belmont, Calif.: Wadsworth Publishing Company, 1993), 80.

21. Rowe, "The Empirical Argument from Evil," 234.

22. Rowe, "Ruminations about Evil," 72.

23. Rowe, "Ruminations about Evil," 72.

24. Rowe, "Ruminations about Evil," 72.

25. The quoted lines are from Rowe, "The Evidential Argument from Evil: A Second Look," 263–65, but they do not appear there in as close proximity to one another as I put them here.

26. Moore, *Some Main Problems of Philosophy*, 119–20.

27. Moore, *Some Main Problems of Philosophy*, 121–22.

28. See my *The Metaphysics of G.E. Moore* (Dordrecht: Reidel, 1982), chap. 3.

29. For more on this relativization or contextualization of skepticism and cognitivism respectively see my "Was Moore a Positivist?" *Philosophia* 20, no. 3 (December 1990): 258–60, and for a very good discussion of the same points in Hume's understanding of skepticism and its relationship to its opposite, see Michael Williams, *Unnatural Doubts* (Princeton: Princeton University Press, 1996), 9 and following.

30. Rescher, *A System of Pragmatic Idealism*, xiv.

Chapter 10

1. Stephen J. Wykstra, "The Humean Obstacle to Evidential Arguments from Suffering: On Avoiding the Evils of 'Appearance,' " in *The Problem of Evil*, 139.

2. Stephen J. Wykstra, "Rowe's Noseeum Arguments from Evil," 137, 146, 148 footnote 12.

3. Wykstra, "The Humean Obstacle," 152.

4. Wykstra, "The Humean Obstacle," 148–50.

5. Wykstra, "The Humean Obstacle," 146.

6. Wykstra, "The Humean Obstacle," 155: see also Bruce Russell and Stephen J. Wykstra, "The 'Inductive' Argument from Evil: A Dialogue," 147.

7. Wykstra, "The Humean Obstacle," 156.

8. On this point I am following the 1996 version of his argument, not the original.

9. William P. Alston, "The Inductive Argument from Evil and The Human Cognitive Condition," 30.

10. Alston, "The Inductive Argument," 59–60.

11. William L. Rowe, "Evil and the Theistic Hypothesis: A Response to Wykstra," 164.

12. Rowe, "Evil and the Theistic Hypothesis," 166–67.

13. The existence of a God-justifying reason does not presuppose the existence of God. To be sure, the existence of the former without the latter is, I would judge, extremely unlikely, but its nonexistence is not entailed by the nonexistence of God. For there could be reasons such that God, if God existed, would use to justify God's permission of certain evils. On this point see William L. Rowe, "Ruminations about Evil," 77.

14. Wykstra, "The Humean Obstacle," 156.

15. van Inwagen, "The Problem of Evil, the Problem of Air, and the Problem of Silence," 72.

16. van Inwagen, "The Problem of Evil," 73.

17. Rowe, "Evil and the Theistic Hypothesis," 166.

18. Rowe, "The Evidential Argument from Evil: A Second Look," 276.

19. Daniel Howard-Snyder, "The Argument from Inscrutable Evil," 307.

20. On this see John O'Leary-Howthorne and Daniel Howard-Snyder, "God, Schmod and Gratuitous Evil," *Philosophy and Phenomenological Research* 53, no.4 (December 1993): 869–70. The model of confirmation in play is Clark Glymour's so-called bootstrapping model, as developed in his *Theory and Evidence* (Princeton: Princeton University Press, 1980).

21. Russell and Wykstra, "The 'Inductive' Argument from Evil: A Dialogue," 158.

22. In this regard see Wykstra, "Rowe's Noseeum Arguments from Evil," 145–46.

In addition see Garth L. Hallett, "Evil and Human Understanding," *The Heythrop Journal* 32, no.4 (October 1991): 471–72 for the following, representative, point: "in answer to authors like Mackie and Flew, one might . . . question our ability to argue one way or the other, given our primitive understanding of such matters [as, for instance, what is possible for omnipotence]" (471).

23. Recall that in theism, no less than in atheism, it is widely accepted that the world is not obviously God-made. Among the best theistic articulations of this is John Hick's concept of epistemic distance between humankind and God.

24. To a Popperian this would raise in a very serious way the question whether theism is a philosophical theory at all. We noted in the first chapter that some theistic philosophers are also unconvinced that theism is a theory (or contains a theory within it). But the reason that, in our present context, a Popperian would have to think theism is not a theory is not, I suspect, the same reason those theists would have. The Popperian's reason would be that theism fails a threshold criterion of theoryhood, namely, falsifiability in principle. That being so, to a Popperian, there would be good grounds to ascribe to theism epistemic parity with an absurd view such as old-earth creationism. And surely no theist would welcome the ascription, hence, I suspect theists would be slow to buy theory-free status for theism in the Popperian way.

25. O'Leary-Hawthorne and Howard-Snyder, "God, Schmod," 862.

26. O'Leary-Hawthorne and Howard-Snyder, "God, Schmod," 866.

27. Rescher, *A System of Pragmatic Idealism*, xiv.

28. Rescher, *A System of Pragmatic Idealism*, xiv.

29. Rowe, "The Problem of Evil and Some Varieties of Atheism," 135–36.

30. Hallett, "Evil and Human Understanding," 471.

31. For thoughts in a similar vein, see Paul Draper, "The Skeptical Theist," 188. In his words, "skeptical theism is a double-edged sword. And the sharper edge may be the one threatening the theist." As my remarks in the text indicate, I think Draper is on the right track here. In a related, although not quite similar, vein see Richard Gale on what he calls "modal modesty," "Some Difficulties in Theistic Treatments of Evil," in *The Evidential Argument from Evil*, 212–13. Also see Gale's *On the Nature and Existence of God*, 234–37.

32. Here I place the emphasis differently to how Hallett, for instance, does. See Hallett, "Evil and Human Understanding," 471.

33. Arguably the prime instance of this in contemporary philosophy is Swinburne's undertaking to update the traditional project in natural theology, namely, to make out a disinterestedly persuasive case for theism, thus one taking into account the best theories that science has to offer.

34. The basic point here can be adapted to be a criticism of Schlesinger's reliance, in fleshing out his no-best-possible-world defense, on justice in a hereafter for victims of injustice who die unrequited. See his *Religion and Scientific Method*, 76.

Chapter 11

1. Wykstra, "Rowe's Noseeum Arguments from Evil," 146.

2. To avoid the appearance of conflict between r and my acceptance of van Inwagen's point that some evils can be both gratuitous[p] and not inconsistent with God, the proposition that "r" stands for should be adjusted. I do not make the adjustment in the text, for it would add an unnecessary convolution and possibly deflect us from the line of thought being pursued. But I make the adjustment here. First, though, why is an adjustment needed at all? Because the evils in question in van Inwagen's point are gratuitous[p], they are both not needed for any good nor part of anyone's plan or purpose, and they are preventable by God; thus, how can they have a God-justifying reason to exist? The adjustment is this: those evils are evils for which God is not culpable in any sense that would count as evidence for atheism and against theism. Consistent with this, "r" stands for "no inscrutable evil (individually or collectively) is evil for whose existence God is culpable."

3. One's being justified in believing a proposition p is not the same as one's justifying believing that p, the former being the more basic of the two. As we have seen, the relevant justifier of the theist's belief that $r + \tilde{}d$ is the skeptical defense tied to CORNEA. The *locus classicus* of the distinction between one's being justified in believing that p and one's justifying one's belief that p is William P. Alston, "Concepts of Epistemic Justification," in *Empirical Knowledge*, ed. Paul K. Moser (Lanham, Md: Rowman and Littlefield Publishers, Inc, 1986), 23–24.

4. I use the term "anti-theistic" here to include both atheism and agnosticism.

5. The atheistic argument as it reflects assumption 2[a] is more limited than a version reflecting assumption 2.

6. This point is subject to the same rider as before. See note 2 above.

7. I say here that we *might* then be able to settle matters for, as we saw before, it is logically possible for there to exist a God-justifying reason for prima facie NENP[i] and, at the same time, for there to be no God.

8. Who are *we* here? We are not just square atheists, for, as we saw in previous chapters, it has been an orthodoxy among *all* parties to the standard debate that certain facts of evil in the world constitute a serious case against theism. And the power behind that orthodoxy is reflected in the reasons Rowe gives for thinking there are evils that have no God-justifying reason to exist, a set of reasons that, in turn, reflect the basic assumptions of the standard debate.

9. I include under the designation "Wykstra-like skepticism" the relevant skepticisms of William P. Alston, F. J. Fitzpatrick (see his "The Onus of Proof in Arguments about the Problem of Evil," *Religious Studies* 18 [1981]: 19–38), Garth L. Hallett, Peter van Inwagen, and others whose (previously cited) views on the matter converge.

10. I suggest this kinship with hesitation, for, to the cognoscenti, there will be

connotations of Marcel's use of these terms that I do not intend to apply here. Nonetheless, used roughly, his terms seem apt.

11. T. S. Eliot, "Little Gidding" *Four Quartets* (London: Faber & Faber, 1972), 59, ll. 239–42.

INDEX

Abraham, W. T., 252
Abrahamic theistic tradition, 7, 18, 20, 25, 31, 34, 35, 46, 47, 50, 51, 77–79, 138, 165, 176, 189, 219, 221
actualization of worlds, strong or weak, 83, 88, 97, 118–38, 164, 193, 204, 252–53n9; random, 258
Adams, Marilyn M., 238n3
Adams, Robert M., 83, 238n3, 242n32, 253n10, 256–57n32
agnosticism, xi–xii, 12, 23, 41, 46, 178, 186, 206, 234, 245n12, 265n4; square, 186–8, 191, 211, 224, 234, 236, 260; strong, xii; weak, xii
Aiken, H. D., 12, 116, 240n21, 255n8
akrasia, 78
Alston, William P., xii, 2, 43, 84, 185, 203, 220, 242n26, 249n18, 251n3, 253n12, 262n15, 263nn9–10, 265n3
Angst (Heideggerian), 16
analogy between God and human persons, 50–51, 94, 97, 208–9, 220
Anscombe, G. E. M., 257n33
antitheism, 228, 245n12, 265n4
apologetics, theistic, 1, 21, 32, 209, 237n1; evidentialist, 29
appearance claims, 200
Aquinas, St. Thomas, 252n6
Archangel Michael, 120, 126
argument from evil: ad hominem argument, 25–26; analogical, 32, 33; direct empirical, 14, 175–236, 241n23, 260nn7–8; empirical, 4–7, 13, 14, 175–236, 237–38nn1–3, 241nn23–24, 257n4; indirect empirical, 11, 13,

41, 178–80, 231, 241nn23–24, 259n1; logical, 4–7, 11, 13, 14, 22, 149, 178, 233, 237n1, 238n3, 238n8, 242n24, 257n4, 260n7; reformed logical, 6, 7–13, 14, 17, 38, 41, 70, 76–91, 95, 103–11, 116, 117–38, 161, 165, 172, 173, 175, 177, 179, 226, 231, 233, 239–40n17, 251n4, 253n16; specified, 3–4, 12, 68, 94, 191, 238n4; unspecified, 3–4, 68, 94, 238n4. *See also* problem of evil
Aristotle, 158, 252n5
atheism, 12, 23, 34, 41, 43, 46, 178, 186, 196, 206, 210–36, 244n9, 260n6, 260n8, 265n2, 265n4, 265n8; friendly, xi–xii, 185, 188, 197, 199–226, 227, 235, 236, 260n8; justified belief in, xi, 178, 185, 211, 213; moral, 34, 42, 46, 244n9; square, 186, 188, 191, 192, 197, 202, 213, 229, 230, 236, 260n6, 265n8; theoretical commitments of, 23
Audi, Robert, 17, 19, 240–41n22, 242n32, 243n33
Augustine, St., 255n4

balance of good and evil, 118
Beckwith, Francis J., 248n9
belief: Audi's distinction between qualified and unqualified, 19; in God, 17, 20, 77, 176; latency of "belief that" in "belief in," 18–19, 21, 175, 176, 221, 243n32; moral, 80, 252n8; no latency of "belief in" in "belief that," 20, 176; practical, 80, 90, 99, 104,

267

106, 108, 140, 141, 252n8, 254n16;
and presupposition, 19. *See also*
knowledge, practical
Berkeley, George, 45
brain-in-a-vat, 140, 141
Bryant, M. Darrol, 253n11
Bultmann, Rudolf, 20
burden of proof, 22–26

Cahn, S. M., 246n2
Capaldi, Nicholas, 245n21
Cartesian conception of self, soul, 79,
159 , 160, 169–70
Cartesian version of theism, 114
Catholic philosophy, 219
chance, in a God-made world, 71, 85,
118, 119, 125
Chisholm, Roderick, 200
choice, epistemic precondition of, 80;
moral, 80, 81
Christlieb, Terry, 250n1
Chrzan, Keith, 161, 162, 171, 172,
258n16, 259n20
cognitivism, 197, 262
compatibility, empirical 14, 31, 32, 77,
231; logical, 4–7, 14, 32, 34, 53, 70,
77, 115, 231, 258n8
Condition of Reasonable Epistemic Access (CORNEA), 200–5, 211, 215,
220, 221, 224, 225, 228, 233, 265n3
consistency, logical. *See* compatibility,
logical
counterfactuals of freedom, 121
criteria of divine world-actualization,
83, 95, 110, 119, 136, 156, 165
Cupitt, Don, 20

De Morgan's Theorem, 228, 229
death, life after, 19
DeBello, Louis, xiii
defense, in contrast to theodicy, 1–3, 14,
237nn1–2, 255n4; by disputing the
prosecution's case, 14, 15; maximal
and minimal, 2, 9, 15, 109, 140; skeptical. *See* theism, skeptical; substan-

tive and nonsubstantive, 2, 155,
232–36; succeeding on a technicality, 2; theism's need for, 34–35
depravity, 95, 96, 122; transworld, 122,
126, 128, 135, 136
deism, attenuated, 33, 46, 244n8
Descartes, Rene, 255n5
design, argument for the existence of
God, 31, 32–34, 40, 177, 219, 244n7;
supernatural, 20, 46
desirability, subjective or objective, 158–
63, 166, 170
destiny, choice of, 10, 20, 78, 80, 81, 91,
96, 99, 102–5, 165, 251n4, 254n23
détente, between theism and atheism,
xi–xii, 23, 185, 197, 217, 227–36
determinism, 51, 97, 114, 132, 217,
256n27
diminished person. *See* person-essence
diminished world. *See* world-essence
divine plan for the world, 8, 10, 11, 78,
82, 84, 85, 91, 94, 96, 99, 103, 104,
107–11, 118, 127, 128, 136, 140, 141,
146, 147, 154, 166, 171, 220, 251n3,
252n8
Draper, Paul, 6, 185, 238, 250, 260, 264.
dualism, substance, 159, 255n5
Dupre, Louis, 77, 251n5

Eliot, T. S., 236, 266n11
Elliot, Robert, 154–55, 257n6
Enlightenment, the, 36, 184, 234
epistemic obligation, 192; permissibil-
ity, 192, 202; standing of theism, 10,
13, 21, 22, 25, 29, 30, 31, 35, 43, 51,
176, 177, 234
eschatological theory, 183, 203
Euthyphro, 235
evidence, 18, 25, 29, 30, 222; manque,
200
evidentialism, 29–35, 53, 184; ascendant
in analytical philosophy of religion,
42; negative, 29–35, 36, 52, 53, 205,
233–34; positive, 29–35, 36; shift in
center of gravity within, 31

About the Author

David O'Connor is professor of philosophy and chairman of the philosophy department at Seton Hall University. His articles have appeared in *Faith and Philosophy, International Journal for Philosophy of Religion, Metaphilosophy, Philosophia, Philosophy, The Philosophical Quarterly, Philosophical Studies, Religious Studies,* as well as in other journals. He is the author of *The Metaphysics of G. E. Moore* (1982).

DATE DUE

			Printed in USA